C000184341

The Popular Guide to Norfolk Churches

C.V. Roberts: Literary editor and drama critic of the *Eastern Daily Press* since 1976, he has worked for the paper for 13 years. He came to Norfolk, he recalls, on a six-month stop gap: 'But the place quickly put its spell on me,' he says, 'and I'm now very firmly adopted.' As a schoolboy in his native North Staffordshire one of his absorbing pastimes – in company with a friend who was subsequently ordained – was to cycle around the villages in the area, exploring their churches and writing accounts of them. His later newspaper and magazine work, first at various points in this country and then abroad, enabled that old interest to broaden – with a change to mosques and temples when he lived and worked in the Middle East for 2½ years.

D.P. Mortlock: County Librarian of Norfolk since 1965 and born in Suffolk in 1927. Spent most of his childhood at Mildenhall where he was a choirboy at St Mary's – one of the finest churches in the county. Grammar school was followed by service in the Indian Army. His library career began in 1947 with the old West Suffolk County. By this time 'church bagging' was a compulsive habit and continued in the West Riding and in Derbyshire before he came back to East Anglia in 1960. He started making notes on Norfolk churches at that time, and records 400 of them visited, some many times. Hopes to complete the tally of all 659 medieval churches in Norfolk by the time this series of books is completed.

Front and back cover: Little Snoring St Andrew

D.P. Mortlock and C.V. Roberts

The Popular Guide
to Norfolk Churches

1: North-East Norfolk

With an encylopaedic Glossary

Acknowledgement

The map on pp. viii and ix is reproduced from Nikolaus Pevsner: North-East Norfolk & Norwich (Buildings of England 1962), copyright © Nikolaus Pevsner 1962 by permission of Penguin Books Ltd.

Acorn Editions
Fakenham, Norfolk

First published 1981

© Acorn Editions 1981

ISBN 0 906554 04 7

Designed and produced by Sharp Print Management, Fakenham, Norfolk
Printed in Great Britain by Whitstable Litho Ltd., Whitstable, Kent

Contents

	page
Introduction	vi
Map of North-East Norfolk	viii
Alphabetical Guide to Churches	1
Glossary of Terms	113

Introduction

Another book on Norfolk churches? Yes. But the first one, we believe, which combines a straightforward pocket guide to every 'living' medieval church in the area covered; with a substantial reference back-up in encyclopaedic form to a host of questions and queries which may tease the church visitor. All these are pinpointed in the main body of the text by being printed *in italics*, immediately indicating that they will be found in the glossary.

This book (the first of three volumes planned for the whole county) is moreover written not by specialists, but by enthusiasts, whose declared object is to share as widely as possible their own lively pleasure and fascination with the subject in hand. To us the real appeal is that, once you've broken the code and learned the language, then every church is different; every single one, be it ever so humble, has something of its own to offer.

The essentials of a good building, wrote James I's writer-diplomat Sir Henry Wotton, early in the 17th century, are 'commoditie, firmness and delight'. Lovely! But what he didn't mention were the delights to be found inside these commodious buildings – spelled out, in our churches, in centuries of additions and oddities, glories and disasters, eccentricities and ornamentations, which can turn a simple visit into a voyage of discovery.

At random: Why do so many churches have *north doors* . . . and yet so often have them blocked up? What's so interesting historically about the word 'Hollimus' being substituted for 'Christmas' on a monument? (See Witton-by-Walsham entry). Why does that painted saint hold a *scallop shell*? – or that one have a couple of does skipping round her feet? (See *Saint Withburga*, one of Norfolk's own saints).

At South Walsham the medieval screen reminds us that there was serfdom and slavery in these gentle Norfolk acres. Blakeney Church recalls for us, in its registers, that this little town provided Elizabeth with three ships against the Spanish Armada in 1587. At Great Snoring, a poignant memorial recording the death of three brothers in 1710 who all 'fell to the same shaft from the quiver, namely smallpox', brings home the epidemic horrors of earlier times. And who occupied the three seats in the *three decker pulpit* at Warham St Mary? And the three in the *sedilia* beside innumerable Norfolk altars? So the intriguing questions go on – and we have tried to answer as many of them as we can.

But a church is not just a building, constructed to specific architectural patterns, absorbingly interesting as they often are. It is, much more importantly, a mirror of the community it has served for centuries and a microcosm of the history of England itself. Also, in a wonderful, indefinable way, it is a living thing, an ageless symbol of continuity, the links of its chain formed through the years by the countless good souls who have worshipped here, loved the place, and at last been buried here.

Walk into a church, now neglected, damp, dismal, unloved – and the sadness you feel is much more than regret at seeing a beautiful work of mens' hands being allowed to rot away. Rather the sadness is contained within the building itself, as the very place seems to mourn its desertion. In a county like Norfolk with a depleted rural population, there are numerous churches like that. There would be many more, but for the splendid work of the Norfolk Churches Trust who, led by devoted officers, keep open for worship and for visitors many churches which would otherwise have closed their doors for ever.

Not that the situation is new. In 1562 *The Second Book of Homilies* – a work of religious 'thoughts for the day' – talks of the '. . . sin and shame to see so many churches so ruinous and so foully decayed in almost every corner . . . Suffer them not to be defiled with rain and weather, with dung of doves, owls, choughs . . . and other filthiness.'

It is our good fortune that so much of our heritage still remains to us. Especially so in Norfolk, with its rich profusion of well over 600 medieval churches, of which nearly 240 are viewed in this first volume of *The Popular Guide*. Our policy from the start of this project, it should be said, was to include only medieval churches (with two or three notable and special exceptions, like Gunton and Bawdeswell) which are 'in use', including non-parochial and only occasionally used buildings. Redundant churches were definitely 'out'.

A final point. That so many parish churches are kept locked today is an unhappy sign of the times, when nothing is safe from the attentions of thieves and vandals. While researching this book – for which every church was visited – the matter of obtaining keys occasionally became more than a little trying. Though judging from *Sketches for an Ecclesiology of the Deaneries of*

Sparham, Taverham and Ingworth, written in 1846, this problem is not new either: 'It is very tiresome when one has travelled so far – in our case 12 miles – to see a church, to find that the *parish clerk* lives a mile off: and on reaching his cottage to hear that he has gone out, and has taken the key in his pocket. . .'

Could we make this appeal to today's clergy: That a clear notice should be exhibited in the porch, saying not only who has the key . . . but giving directions as to where the key-keeper may be found. 'Mrs. Brown, The Loke' may not, as experience shows us, be quite enough for strangers.

To all those incumbents, churchwardens, key-keepers and numerous others who have extended to us their help and kindness, we return our warmest thanks.

C.V.R. & D.P.M.
Norwich
May 1981

viii

N.W. & S. Norfolk

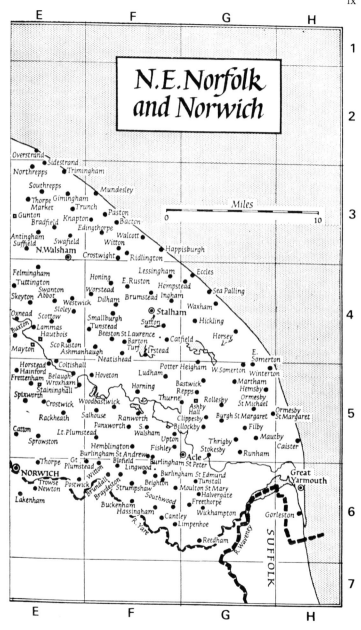

N.E. Norfolk and Norwich

Miles

0 10

Overstrand
Sidestrand
Northrepps — Trimingham
Southrepps
Mundesley
Thorpe — Gimingham
Market — Trunch — Paston
Gunton — Knapton — Bacton
Bradfield — Edingthorpe
Antingham — Swafield — Walcott
Suffield — Witton
N.Walsham — Crostwight — Ridlington
Happisburgh
Felmingham — Lessingham — Eccles
Honing — E.Ruston — Hempstead
Tuttington — Worstead — Ingham
Swanton — Brumstead — Sea Palling
Skeyton — Abbot — Dilham
Westwick — Waxham
Oxnead — Sloley — Smallburgh — Stalham
Scottow — Tunstead — Hickling
Buxton — Lammas — Beeston St Laurence
Hautbois — Barton — Horsey L.
Mayton — Sco Ruston — Turf — Irstead
Ashmanhaugh — Neatishead — Catfield
E. Somerton
Horstead — Coltishall — Potter Heigham — W.Somerton — Winterton
Hainford — Belaugh — Hoveton — Ludham
Frettenham — Wroxham — Bastwick — Martham
Spixworth — Staininghall — Horning — Repps — Hemsby
Crostwick — Woodbastwick — Thurne — Rollesby — Ormesby St Michael
Rackheath — Salhouse — Ranworth — Ashby Hall — Ormesby St Margaret
Catton — Panxworth — S. — Clippesby — Burgh St Margaret
Sprowston — Lt.Plumstead — Walsham — Billockby — Filby
Hemblington — Upton — Thrigby — Mautby
Thorpe — Gt. — Fishley — Stokesby — Runham — Caister
NORWICH — Plumstead — Burlingham St Andrew — Acle — Burlingham St Peter
Trowse — Witton — Blofield — Lingwood
Newton — Postwick — Brundall — Burlingham St Edmund — Great Yarmouth
Lakenham — Braydeston — Strumpshaw — Beighton — Tunstall
Southwood — Moulton St Mary — Gorleston
Buckenham — Halvergate
Hassingham — Freethorpe
Cantley — Wickhampton
R.Yare — Limpenhoe
Reedham — R.Waveney
SUFFOLK

Map references in brackets after church names refer to map on pp. viii and ix
Glossary entries appear in *italic* type

North-East Norfolk
Alphabetical Guide to Churches

Acle, St Edmund (G5): Many Norfolk church towers have a mark showing where an earlier roof has been superceded by one of lower pitch, but here the thatched nave roof partially obscures the *lancet* bell opening in the e. face of the octagonal top and is obviously not original. The round lower stages of the tower probably date from before the Conquest. Entry is by way of the C15 n. porch which has an interesting carving in the left-hand *spandrel*. A couple kneel with their rosaries and may well be the donors. Inside the porch, the e. window sill has 'God Save the King 1616' roughly carved, and one wonders whether the King James' Bible of 1611 had just reached the village to prompt a loyal response. The font is a fine piece, and is one of the few that can be dated accurately. On the top step is incised in Latin 'Pray for the souls of those who gave this font to the glory of God A.D. 1410.' The bowl panels have: e., the Trinity – God the Father crowned and bearded, with a cross between his knees (from which the figure of Christ has been removed) and a (replacement) dove on his shoulder; s., an angel holding a Trinity shield; w., a Pieta (the dead Christ in His Mother's arms) with the head of the Virgin re-cut; n., an angel with a shield depicting the *Instruments of the Passion*; the four *Evangelistic symbols* in the other four panels. The stem has alternating *woodwoses* and lions. A great deal of the original colour survives. The C15 *rood screen* is

said to have come from elsewhere and it enhances the church wonderfully. It was well restored in the 1920s and has two lovely ranges of tracery, one above the other. The panels are dappled with sacred monograms and 'E's for *St Edmund* with crossed arrows as the sign of his martyrdom. The *rood stairs* were in a C16 brick and flint exterior turret, and the base of this has been converted into a sacristy behind a grill. At a glance, this seems to have a fireplace but it is really a collection of fragments from a *Norman* doorway discovered in the nave wall in 1927. On the n. wall of the chancel a board labelled 'Do not remove' covers the fascinating remains of an inscription in Latin which translates:

> O lamentable death – how many dost thou cast into the pit.
> Anon the infants fade away, and of the aged, death makes an end;
> Now these, now those, thou ravishest, O death on every side.
> These that wear horn (headdresses) or veils, fate spareth not.
> Therefore while in the world the brute beast plague rages hour by hour.
> With prayer and with remembrance deplore death's deadliness.

Although *Dr Pevsner* dates it as C15, Dr M.R. James, a leading antiquary of a previous generation, picks out the reference to 'ladies' horned hats' as a pointer to the period of the *Black Death* in 1349. Both wall and inscription are now in poor state and in need of urgent attention. Below it, a brass to Thomas Stones (d.1627). This is an exceptionally late date, and is one of only six known from the reign of Charles I. In beautiful condition, it bears the lines

> 'The Lord has caused this painful (i.e. diligent) shepherd die,
> To live with Him in joy eternally'.

Alby, St Ethelbert (D3): C15 tower, but the nave is earlier and has *clerestory* windows although there is no trace of aisles having been built. There is a coarse unadorned *piscina* in the chancel with two *credence shelves* that might well be original. Another rudimentary piscina for the nave altar is cut in the step below the window on the s. side, and opposite there are stairs to the *rood loft*. One can still see the stub of the *rood beam* and loft floor high on the n. wall. There are four *consecration crosses* incised in the walls on either side of the chancel arch, and the heavily varnished bottom half of the *screen* remains.

Aldborough, St Mary the Virgin (D3): Well away to the s.w. of the village, on the Matlask road and, having lost its tower in the C18, easy to miss. The church was extensively restored in 1847, and the perky bell-turret of 1906 renovated in 1968. *Carstone* quoins (corner stones) at the w. end of the nave and halfway along the s. wall indicate *Norman* origins, but the windows and much of the present building are C14. The n. aisle was probably added in the C13 and the piercing of the nave wall was roughly done. The three good *brasses* in the nave were moved to their present position early this century. Close to the chancel step, the brass to Anne Herward (d.1485) shows the elegant butterfly headdress of the period. West of this is a brass to a civilian c.1490, and further w. still is the brass to Robert Herward (d.1481),

Anne's husband, shown in armour. There is an interesting series of small *corbels* in the porch, nave and aisle, and the exterior modern metal *gargoyles* are an unusual feature. The statues of the Virgin and Child in the sanctuary and in the niche over the s. door are by H. Rogers.

Alderford, St John the Baptist (D5): One of the thin C14 towers with added w. buttresses which are common in the county – made to look taller than it is by having small and narrow bell openings very close to the top. There was a C14 n. aisle but this has gone, leaving the *arcade* embedded in the nave wall. The s. side of the continuous nave/chancel has a nicely varied range of windows – two with flowing (slightly different) tracery, one with a four-centred *Perpendicular* arch, and easternmost (blocked) with three *ogee*-headed lights under a square label. Over the porch door, a wooden sundial (C19?) with 'Redeem the time' in raised letters. The *seven sacrament font* is unusually placed just e. of the n. door and, being on two deep steps, it dominates the little nave. Some of the figures round the shaft are identifiable – *St James the Great* (pilgrim's purse), *St Andrew* (cross saltire), *St John the Evangelist* (chalice), *St Philip* (loaves). There are demi-figures of angels with scrolls in the corona, and the bowl panels are (clockwise from the e.): baptism, ordination, mass, penance (note how the angel all in feathers drives the devil back), confirmation, marriage, extreme unction, Crucifixion. Traces of colour remain. The altar *reredos* is made up of recoloured panels – probably from the former *rood screen*, and the stairs for the *rood loft* are set in the s. wall, marking the division between nave and chancel. As you leave, have a look at the old knocker in the centre of the door – it has been there at least 600 years.

Antingham, St Mary (E3): Two churches in one churchyard and an old wives' tale that they were built by two sisters, virtuous Mary whose church remains, and dissolute Margaret whose church lies ruined and swathed in ivy. St Mary's is mainly mid C14 with a later variation to the top of the tower, and the windows have a common theme of *reticulated* tracery. The wide and high *arch-braced* roof runs right through with no division between nave and chancel, but there are extra struts at the e. end so it may have had a ceiling at one time. The chancel *piscina* is matched by another just e. of the *rood loft* stairs so there was no doubt a nave altar nearby. The two head *corbels* set in the chancel walls are puzzling. *Munro Cautley* suggests that they were used for the *Lenten veil*, but they are awkwardly sited and may have been moved. The s.e. window is good C19 glass – two sisters again, Martha and Mary on either side of the Virgin. Martha endearingly has a saucepan tucked under her arm as well as carrying a spoon and a leather bottle. At the e. end of the nave is a good *brass* to Richard Calthorp (1562), a 17in bearded figure in full armour. His wife's brass is gone, but below a long inscription there is a separate plate with 19 of their progeny grouped in mourning.

Ashmanhaugh, St Swithin (F4): Nicely set at the end of a narrow lane in a neat churchyard. The round tower was rebuilt in 1849 and, with a diameter of only 10ft, it is the smallest in the county. Just inside the door, the back of the nearest bench has an interesting series of shields carved with the Wounds of Christ, and another range below carry initials and the date 1531. The *rood loft* stairs are in the n. wall and the sockets for the front floor beam of the loft itself still remain. The lower doorway has been fitted with neat oak half-doors to form a seemly cupboard for the electrical mains panel. The sanctuary has a large *aumbry* in the n. wall, and in the s.e. corner is the tomb of Honor Bacon who, in 1591 died on the eve or the morning (tradition varies) of

her wedding day. The epitaph is decayed and hard to decipher in full, but plainly,

> 'A better mayden lived not then,
> And now her lyke doth lacke. . .'

Attlebridge, St Andrew (D5): A thin unbuttressed tower with a niche below the *lancet* window on the ground floor. The triple lancets of the early C14 e. window are contained within one arch, and it has particularly good *headstops* outside which turn toward each other. They look unrestored. The 1864 restoration was doubtless responsible for the curious wooden chancel arch which rests on stone *corbels*. In the chancel s. wall, a *low side window* in the bottom third of a lancet, a blocked priest's door, and *dropped sill sedilia*. There is a *squint* in the n. wall of the chancel, cut through from the aisle, but the angle is not acute enough for it to align with the high altar and so its use is doubtful. The bulbous baluster lectern recorded by *Pevsner* has given way to a very plain reading desk-cum-pulpit in Columbian pine, but the priest's desk has ten C17 turned balusters with acanthus leaf carving which must have been taken from something else. There is a little *chalice brass* to George Conyngham (d.1525) by the sanctuary rail.

Aylmerton, St John the Baptist (D3): The upper stage of the *Norman* round tower was rebuilt to the old design in 1912, when a long-blocked doorway was discovered at its base. The two-storey s. porch is tall and shallow, and looks well as one comes up the steep approach path. Its staircase fits snugly in the angle with the nave, and the original entrance door inside is beautifully solid and iron banded. The chancel was rebuilt in the mid-C14 and has a pretty *piscina* and two-bay *sedilia*, with a *cusped* and *crocketted* canopy over it. The little round faces of the *headstops* crop up again at the w. end of the church by the *holy water stoup* which was discovered behind plaster in 1840. Before you leave, note the most unusual capitals of the s. doorway. They are castellated with arrow slits, and are reminiscent of the arms of Castile, in Spain. *John of Gaunt* (a great landowner in this part of Norfolk in the C14) was the patron here, and through marriage he inherited the Crown of Castile in 1371 – which may account for this minor architectural puzzle.

Aylsham, St Michael (D4): At a distance, the C17 spike on the top gives the tower a distinctive silhouette, particularly from the n.e. and the whole exterior of the church is impressive in its size when approached from the nearby marketplace. The s. porch was enlarged to two stories in the late C15, and has rich *flushwork* panelling, the arms of France and England, and a beautiful canopied niche flanked by windows above the arch. The alternating circular and octagonal pillars of the early C14 *arcade* are very effective, and the later transepts and chancel chapels are on a generous scale. The font is early C15, and has *Symbols of the Evangelists, Instruments of the Passion*, and the Crucifixion around the bowl. The shaft carries four shields, one of which is *John of Gaunt's*, who is credited with the building of the church. The base of the *rood screen* survives, and has been beautifully restored recently by Miss Pauline Plummer. The sixteen painted figures in the panels include the donor Thomas Wymer, who died in 1507 and whose *brass* is on the n. side of the sanctuary. The little *gesso* figures on the screen buttresses are very similar to those at Cawston. Bishop Jegon, a chaplain to Queen Elizabeth and successively Dean and Bishop of Norwich died in Aylsham in 1617, and his monument is on the n. wall of the chancel. The eccentric *reredos* was put together by John Adey Repton in 1833; besides incorporating pieces of the top of the rood screen, it has some *misericords* built in. *Humphrey Repton*, the renowned landscape gardener, has his

memorial outside the church against the s. wall of the chancel. Composed by himself, his epitaph reads:

'Not like Egyptian tyrants consecrate, Unmixed with others shall my dust remain;
But mold'ring, blending, melting into Earth,
Mine shall give form and colour to the Rose,
And while its vivid blossoms cheer Mankind,
Its perfumed odours shall ascend to Heaven'.

Baconsthorpe, St Mary (D3): A restrained, yet elegant little church. The tower was rebuilt in 1740, having fallen down the previous year – a neat reproduction, in the *Perpendicular* style. Body of the church is mainly of the *Decorated* period, with Perpendicular windows. The chancel is older, pre-1300, but fairly heavily restored. There are some appealing things inside: a little *screen* at the end of the n. aisle (one authority says it used to be in Bessingham Church, a few miles away) is beautifully simple and unaffected, and Perpendicular in date; another under the tower arch looks as if it was made up from old bench backs. The angled double *piscina* in the chancel is lovely, simple and rural, and like its adjoining *sedilia* is C13. Opposite, a C14 *Easter Sepulchre* – a bit of pomp in miniature, all crockets and arches. Crammed into the s. aisle is a huge monument to Sir William Heydon and his wife, 1592 (the Heydons were great folk hereabouts for around a century – one of them rebuilt Salthouse Church). The monument is a typical example of a commission carried out in a London workshop, and just too big when it arrived . . . nothing changes, it seems. Note in the s. aisle window the remnants of heraldic stained glass – they are bits rescued after the rectory next door received a direct hit from a stray German bomb in 1941, and the blast blew out the church windows. See also the charming little brass to Anne Heydon, 1561, set in the wall to the left of the big Heydon monument.

Bacton, St Andrew (F3): Approached from the s., an avenue of trees, grazing black sheep and a donkey provided a fitting foreground for this pretty church ... though beyond the scene changes drastically, to the hard-edged sprawl of the great gas terminal complex. The church tower is neat Perpendicular, with contrasting battlements, and sound holes with shields set in tracery; and large carved figure niches set low down in the angle buttresses. Nave and chancel are a Decorated/Perpendicular mix. Indeed, the early Perpendicular windows of the nave have more than a hint of Decorated nostalgia in their tracery. The e. window has been renewed in Decorated style. An agreeable, meticulously cared for interior, with the blue-roofed chancel, richly-coloured e. window glass, the particularly lovely Decalogues painted on the e. wall like ancient illuminated manuscripts; and at the time of our deep-winter visit, masses of fresh flowers everywhere, all contribute colour and buoyancy. The 'vulgar tiled reredos' noted by Charles Cox in 1911 is discreetly obscured by curtains, and the altar brought forward. There is a C15 piscina with handsome cusped arch, and shields in the spandrels with a lot of original colour remaining, adjoining a very small triple sedilia, also C15, all plain, under flattened arches. Placed here is a dumpy stone angel with a scroll, said to have come from one of the tower buttress niches. In the nave, a few old poppyheads remain at the w. end. Very good and unusual font, the finely carved rectangular bowl having angels with shields alternating with the Symbols of the Evangelists; immediately under the bowl and flowing down to the base are more angels and garland-like canopies; and around the base, indeterminate animal heads ... though the n.e. one surely suggests a calf.

Bale, All Saints (C3): A magnificent group of 18 ilexes – evergreen small-leafed oaks – provide a noble entrance to this attractive church. The grove, which since 1919 has been in the care of the National Trust, replaces the huge and famous Bale Oak which, 36ft in circumference, had to be removed in 1869 when it became unsafe. The C14, late Decorated tower has below its west window, with its pretty Decorated tracery, a figure niche – a feature to be found in several towers hereabouts. The nave dates from the late C14, but the superb glass assembled in the s.e. window in 1938 is mostly C15 Norwich work. Gabriel, Mary, and a fine old bearded saint dominate a splended Annunciation scene. Above Mary, a delightful feathered Angel. Below her, two apostles against dark red backgrounds – high quality and possibly C14. Note the tiny black-and-white heraldic shields right at the bottom of the window – they bear the arms of Thomas Wilby, lord of the manor here in the reign of Henry IV (d.1413), who probably built the present church. A wonderful window, deserving of your time. Don't miss the candle beam pulley-block high up at the east end of the nave roof – a very rare survival, it was used to raise and lower the candle beam which lit the rood. Handsome font, dated 1470, showing the Instruments of the Passion etc. The Royal Arms are a nice example of patch-and-make-do – they were originally Stuart arms, but dated 1698, which is William & Mary ... but initialled for King George, who came still later. In the nave and in the pretty n. transept (with its well preserved rood stair entrance) are remnants of wall paintings, the consecration crosses on the e. walls of nave and transept being the best. Lovely chancel of about 1300, with possibly original rafter roof; splendid e. window with very distinctive, generous tracery; and simple and most appealing side windows, deeply recessed and standing out beautifully against the white painted walls. Simple but beautfiul angle piscina. Deep, flat and oblong recess, low in wall to left of altar, is puzzling.

Banningham, St Botolph (E4): The C15 tower is beautifully proportioned with more than the usual number of *drip courses*, and the detailing of the parapet and sound holes is particularly good. The inside, with its C14 *arcades*, has a spacious feeling mainly because there are no choir stalls in the chancel which opens to the Lady chapel on the s. side. The *spandrels* of the nave *hammer beam* roof have varied tracery and the two at the e. end have lovely carvings of angels swinging incense censers, one standing in a boat set in a choppy sea. The beam of the *rood* is still there above the chancel arch and is an unusual survival. There are two wall paintings above the nave n. arcade and one is a St George (minus his head) and the Dragon. The other was apparently a *St Christopher* but is now hard to make out. The font cover is rather good late C17 in pine, with slim classical columns supporting an *ogee* shaped top. The medieval glass collected in one of the s. aisle windows is interesting. Top l. is part of the *Nine Orders of Angels* – the Seraphim is labelled and has purple feathers, and next to him a Cherub whose feathers are covered with eyes (reference to Ezekiel 10:12)

> 'Their entire bodies, including their backs, their hands and their wings, were completely full of eyes. . .'

For its date, the monument on the n. chancel wall to Samuel Wanley (d.1723) is surprisingly naive. His coat of arms rests against stacked books and at the bottom a fearsome skull clutches a bone in its teeth. He was rector for 38 years and gave his 'commodious and pleasant dwelling with its appurtenances for the parsonage house'. Below in the centre lies his wife Mary (d.1709)

> '. . .none at ye door would She let craveing stay,
> Or ever goe without an almes away'.

Barney, St Mary (B3): A most appealing church, full of interest, though much restored. A very simple, early C16 *Perpendicular* tower. Beside the (unattractive) s. porch, note outline of roundheaded doorway, probably *Saxon* and as early as C10, with typical tile *jambs*. In the angle of s. transept and chancel (behind large tomb slab) is more Saxon work – tiles and a hunk of dark brown stone – built into fabric. Note too the windows of the late C13 chancel: contemporary *Early English* double *lancets*. The e. window is very pretty C15 *Decorated*. On n. side of church there is another filled-in doorway, C13 Early English – and a diminutive 27in wide. Back now to the s. porch, with its pleasingly rustic inner doorway, dated about 1200. Inside, a really charming little church, rural and fascinating. The age-mellowed roof of the nave, decorated with angels and *bosses* with *Tudor* roses, is simple *arch-braced* and mainly C15. Alas the roof – also arch-braced – in the pretty s. transept is in a desperate state of decay. Excellent C15 font, richly carved on its eight faces with sacred emblems: clockwise from the e. face – Agnus Dei; the *'ihs' motif* for Jesus; Our Lady; Holy Trinity; St. Peter; *Pelican*; St Andrew; arms of Lords of the Manor. There is a *Jacobean* pulpit, delightfully carved. Fine *rood stairs* with immediately above and opposite, enchantingly carved roof *corbels* – pussy cats? All the nave corbels are worth a careful look – portraits, Tudor roses (very good) and a grotesque. In chancel, attractively solid, stolid angle *piscina*, with a tiny niche to left (*credence shelf*?), all of a C13 piece with the lancet windows in their deep recesses, and the *dropped sill sedilia*. As you leave, notice the high, carved *Jacobean* bench-back by the door and, right, the homely hat pegs from the C18.

Barningham Winter (or Town), St Mary the Virgin (D3): A little difficult to find, as the church is set in the centre of Barningham Park, next door to the fine hall which was built in 1612 for Sir Edward Paston (see glossary, *The Pastons*). Once found, the effort is worth it for the pleasure of the setting and the generally picturesque impression of a curiously shaped building approached through ruins. You go in through the remains of the s. porch, nave and tower which have been ruinous since the early C17. The original C14 chancel of the *Decorated* period, with its elegantly traceried windows, now serves as the church: onto it the Victorians built a small west-end addition, vestries below, a gallery above, with an outside entrance and stairway (for the servants and estate workers?) and incorporating the original chancel arch. Most attractive inside, light and airy and meticulously looked after. A fine *Royal Arms* (with initials 'CR', but not clear whether Charles I or II) in mellow colours is the only stained glass in the e. window (save for some older fragments in the tracery above) and so presents a fine central feature. Two C18 *hatchments* dominate on the e. wall to l. and r. of the window: Paston impaling Barney, another old Norfolk family; r. Mott impaling Partridge (the Motts bought rningham from the Pastons in 1785; the present squire, Sir Charles Mott-adclyffe, is great-great-grandson of e Partridges). Attractive *piscina* and raduated *sedilia*, all under continuous ches; fine remounted and lovingly paired *brass* to John Wynter, about 10, in full armour. No font – a portle one is used these days. But there is a old one under the ruined tower, which was used a few years ago for the baptism of the Barningham game-keeper's child – a nice continuance of tradition.

Burton Turf, St Michael and All Angels (F4): The C15 tower is handsomely proportioned, and entry to the church is through a two-storied n. porch which is quite elaborate. It has three niches above the arch, *flushwork* panelling, a base *course* of shields, and a

vaulted ceiling. The church is renowned for its *screens*. The head of the chancel screen is coved (hollowed) with a graceful *crocketted* centre arch, and there are twelve painted panels of exceptional merit. From l. to r. they represent *St Apollonia*, St Citha (or *Zita*), Powers (Raphael fighting a devil), Virtues, Dominions, Seraphim, Cherubim, Principalities, Thrones, Archangels, Angels, and *St Barbara*. Those of the Virgin Saints are lovely, with a naive and sweet demureness characteristic of English work of this period at its best. The Angel Hierarchy is a rare subject, (see glossary, *Nine Orders of Angels*) and there is no other screen example in Norfolk, although part of a series can be seen in the e. window at Salle. Here, details of the armour dates the work as 1480-90. The s. aisle screen has four kings: Henry VI, Edmund, Edward the Confessor, and St Olaf (or Holofius) King of Norway. He is distinguished by the punning emblem of a 'whole loaf' of bread. There are two more panels of *St Edmund* and *St Stephen* above the n. aisle altar which came from Rackheath church. In the s. aisle chapel is a fine wall monument to Anthony Norris (d.1786), one of Norfolk's earliest antiquaries, and by some happy chance, the copy of Rubens' 'Descent from the Cross' in the chancel once belonged to Dawson Turner, the C19 local historian. A walk round the outside will disclose a monument on the e. wall of the s. porch to the four young sons of Mr and Mrs Doyley. They were all drowned in Barton Broad on Boxing Day 1781, and one reflects on 'the changes and chances of this fleeting world'.

Bawdeswell, All Saints (C4): A delightful reversion to the C18. The little brick and flint Victorian church which replaced a 'pseudo classical building' was itself destroyed by an aircraft crash in 1944. In 1950, J. Fletcher Watson used local flint pebbles and brick as primary materials for the new church which, with its little shingled lantern topped by

a weathercock, would not look out of place in colonial Virginia. The interior is charming. It has a w. gallery with balustrade and classical columns for the organ, matching columns flank the apse, and a suite of solid comfortable panelled pews is complemented by what is surely the only modern *three-decker pulpit* in the country. It needs only an *hour-glass* to complete the illusion. Small roundels of Flemish glass have been inserted effectively in the nave windows, and a fine melon-legged table is in use as a side altar. It may be unfashionable to imitate but Bawdeswell needs no justification. Go and see.

Beeston, St Lawrence (F4): There was still a small village here in the C18 but now there are only a few houses within sight of the church. The lower part of the tower and the n. wall have a lot of *carstone* work and probably pre-date the Conquest. The nave, with a porch added, was rebuilt in the early C14. The chancel followed a little later in rather more lavish style; the buttresses have decorative gables, the corners have battlements, and there is a wide band of *flushwork* under the e. window. The inside was transformed in 1803 when the church was 'new roof't and repair'd'. The ceiling is gently coved (hollowed) with widely spaced gothick ribs, and the alternating shields and ornament on the cornice have now been picked out in bright colours – with all the white-ness, this gives the effect of a birthday cake inside-out. The chancel has a fine collection of Preston family monuments, of which the earliest is the tomb chest of Jacob (d. 1673). Coloured shields set in curly *cartouches* flank the in-scription on the front. Sir Isaac Preston not only has a *ledger stone* in the sanctuary with curly italic script, but also a big architectural tablet in white marble on the wall above. Opposite, the monument to Alicia Preston (d. 1743) is quite grand. A sarcophagus

Bawdeswell All Saints: interior.

topped by a small urn in an arched recess, with curtains drawn back to reappear again outside the frame and drop in folds. A long Latin inscription is cut on marble drapery below the plinth.

Beeston Regis, All Saints (D2): Lovely position, alone on rising land above the sea (if one can ignore the unfeeling sprawl of caravans which disfigure the meadow to the n. w.). The tower, unlike most of its C11 and C12 Norfolk con-temporaries, is square, and has quoins (corner stones) formed of large flints. The nave *arcades* are of the same date as the e. window, with its pretty *Decorated* tracery. But the *sedilia* is *Perpendicular*, and its awkward in-sertion into a window embrasure suggests that it originally belonged to nearby Beeston Priory. The C15 *rood screen* is beautiful, and alone makes the church well worth a visit. Carefully restored after many misfortunes, its twelve panels of Apostles still have their original colour, and not one has been defaced. The saints' names have been discreetly added recently above the middle rail to help the visitor. Nice plain set of *Laudian* altar rails and a super Elizabethan 'melon legged' com-munion table in the s. aisle. Thoughtful reminder inside s. door of the last of a dynasty of vergers who died in 1975.

Beighton, All Saints (F6): The C14 tower has a renewed top stage and the battlements, with their prominent corner figures, are dated 1890. The thatched roof of the nave forms attractive hoods over the *clerestory* windows, and inside the reeds show through the pattern of *scissors-braced* beams. In the chancel the early C14 stepped *sedilia* and *piscina* are grouped under a range of handsome *ogee* arches, but only one of the *headstops* survives. With the exception of the middle rail, the *screen* is mainly restored work and the modern *rood* has four attendant figures instead of the more usual two. There are two medieval stall ends in the chancel but the rest look like good C19 work and so does the excellent sow with suckling litter on a bench end at the w. end of the n. aisle. The fine yew chest which was a feature of the church is no longer there, and there are ominous signs of structural decay.

Belaugh, St Peter (E5): The church stands on a rise, and the land falls steeply away w. of the tower down to the river, as it does at nearby Wroxham. There are signs of Norman work in carstone at the n.e. corner of the chancel, and there are blocked round-headed arches to be seen on the outside of the s. wall which may be earlier still. The font is a heavy Norman bowl, which has large shallow arches linking the four supporting columns. The tall screen has traces of gilding on the upper tracery, and the base panels have painted saints which are of good quality, although their faces have been obliterated. From l. to r. they are: St James the Less, Philip, Thomas, Bartholomew, St John Baptist, Peter, Paul, St John the Evangelist, Andrew (with a rustic cross), St James the Great, Simon, Jude. The rood stair remains in the angle of the chancel and the n. aisle.

Bessingham, St Mary (D3): A delightful little church, perched up on its mound in a neat and well-kept churchyard. The venerable, time-grained round tower is one of the earliest in the county and certainly pre-Conquest. Built of carstone rather than flint (gingerbread stone, they call it where it comes from in West Norfolk) it has splendid, rough-built bell openings with triangular heads, the classic Saxon outline; equally typical of that period is the interior tower opening high up and looking into the nave. Little of interest inside – largely Perpendicular, but heavily restored last century. Pulpit is about 1500.

Billockby, All Saints (G5): All alone in

the fields shielded by tall trees, this late C14 church must have been exceptionally fine. Already in decay, it was struck by lightning in a great gale of 1762, leaving the tower, porch and nave all in ruins. The chancel remained to serve as the present church and is 'clean and decent'. It is worth looking at the ruins to appreciate the obvious quality of the original work. There is a good n. doorway, the rood loft stairs are virtually complete, and on the s. side of the nave, note the curious 'ragged staff' set at an angle in the flushwork by the side of each window.

Binham, St Mary (B3): Approached across the rolling landscape from the direction of the great pilgrimage centre of Walsingham, this must in its prime have been a glorious and inspiring sight, when the church was the centrepiece of a vast Benedictine house. Our visit for this book coincided, quite by chance, with the 1500th birthday (July 11th) of St Benedict – which we took for a good omen. Even now the great west front of what remains of the majestic priory church – the nave only – is a fine spectacle, despite its battered details and its huge west window bricked in. This magnificent example of Early English work can be accurately dated, since it was built during the time of Prior Richard de Parco, 1226-44. This gives it an added interest and importance, for the west window has 'bar tracery' (see 'Early English', under Styles of Architecture) which indicates that this could be the very earliest tracery of its kind in England. Inside, the scene is superb: soaring Norman strength, massive yet not weighty – most of the great rounded arches are plain, but those either side of the altar have fine billet and zig-zag moulding. The arches were bricked in soon after Henry VIII's Dissolution of the Priory, leaving the aisles beyond, and the transepts, to decay – and Tudor windows, with their typical depressed arches,

Binham St Mary: w. front.

inserted into the new brickwork. Note that not all the interior is Norman – at the west end it is early English work of the C13, like the west front, either an extension or a rebuilding. Very interesting in the sanctuary is a triple *sedilia* and blocked priest's door, under one continuous Early English moulding. The nail-studded frame set into the wall, above right of the altar, is a puzzle. The lovely early *Stuart* altar table is exposed to view; and now serving as sanctuary chairs are two exceedingly ill used *misericords*, rescued from the troublous past. There are some fine original benches; and excellent *poppyhead* bench ends carved with figures – look for the little lion, the only individual here not to lose his head at the *Reformation* ... perhaps his Royalty saved him. Which leads us on to the *Royal Arms* at the back of the church, originally set up in 1815, that great Waterloo year for Britain, painted by William Archer of Foulsham, whose name appears on the back (his tombstone is at Foulsham church). The Arms were for long left to decay in a dark corner, but in 1969 were restored to their former glory and placed in a gothicky wooden frame. Just below the arms, a mutilated *holy water stoup.* The C15 *seven sacrament font* is fine, though much defaced. Remnants of an old *screen*, painted over with 'goodly texts', now serves as a bench back to the rear pew.

Bintree, St Swithin (C4): One of four churches in the county dedicated to the saint of Winchester. There is a modern statue of him in the niche over the s. porch entrance. The tower is early C14 with simple Y-tracery in the w. window. The same style is found in the transept e. windows, but the s. window is much more ambitious with fine *reticulated* tracery enclosing smaller designs. The transept was restored in 1928 and now forms an attractive Lady chapel. The C14 font has unusually fine panels of shallow tracery in a variety of forms. The greater part of the

chancel collapsed in 1806 and was rebuilt to half its original length. There is a tablet outside over the e. window 'I.A. Rector 1761', but this must have been re-set. Having been rediscovered in 1903, the C12 pillar *piscina* has survived at least two rebuildings, and a short column of the same date or a little later has been let into the *jamb* of the chancel s. window. A bell was sold in 1864 to provide the present pulpit – a monstrous cube on four elephantine legs. Near the font there is a *chalice brass* to a C16 rector, Thomas Hoont, and an epitaph to another incumbent in the C17, Ralph Outlaw:

> 'Reader pray stay, death's trophies view and see. . .
> In them what thou thyself ere long must be'.

The processional cross is a reminder of an almost forgotten facet of Anglican history. It belonged to Fr. William Enracht, rector 1895-8, who was the last priest to be imprisoned for introducing Roman ritual into his services. The indictment was brought under the Public Worship Regulation Act – a piece of legislation which was soon withdrawn following a public outcry.

Blakeney, St Nicholas (C2): A large, powerful *Perpendicular* building of the first half of the C15, with a great lofty tower (104ft high), and enormous four-light aisle windows and three-light *clerestory* windows, presenting an impressive pattern of mathematical order. The odd little tower at the n.e. angle of the chancel – again C15 Perpendicular – was probably a lighthouse of sorts, containing a beacon light to guide mariners in the days when Blakeney was a bustling port. A large-scale restoration of the church in the 1880s took place when the tower and complete outer walls of the church were given a new 'skin' – thus its well preserved appearance now. Base of the tower is richly panelled, and the but-

Blakeney St Nicholas: C13 chancel.

tresses decorated with *flushwork* and, at the n. and s. corners, with shields representing the arms (inaccurately?) of the bishoprics of Thetford and Norwich. The n.w. buttress of the n. aisle has a shield bearing the *Instruments of the Passion*. At the e. end of the church, note the small window high over the *Early English* chancel window – this lights a vault above the *groined* chancel roof. The church inside is impressive, albeit a trifle gloomy. A lofty nave of six great bays, its handsome *hammer beam* roof carved with figures on the beam angles and with decorative fretted work in the *spandrels*. Up above the chancel arch is the original *rood beam*, carved with fleur-de-lys. Despite the mutilated faces of its carved figures – the four *Evangelists* with their symbols – the C15 font is fine. Other shields carry the *Instruments of the Passion* and the *Five Wounds of Christ*. Under the tower, note the little recess (n. side) with holes in its base – probably a rare 'cresset stone' (wicks floating in oil made primitive candles). Both aisles have some original C15 open-work benches and *poppyheads* (the nave pews are Victorian), and their window sills are let down to form seats in some churches locally. In n. aisle, some good C15 glass in window adjacent to pulpit; in s.e. corner, stairs to former *rood loft* (present great *rood screen* and loft date from 1910, with the exception of two small original panels); over entrance door, *Royal Arms* of George III, dated 1818 – though the Arms shown were not by then in use in that form. Immediately opposite, on wall of s. aisle, handsome painted *Decalogue Boards*, with Lord's Prayer and Creed, with a framing of cherubs' heads. Set into the pavement in front of the screen is a tiny *brass* with shield to John Calthorp, 1508, one of the benefactors of the Carmelite Friary whose church this originally was ... Calthorp was precise in his Will – his 'Synfull body' was to be buried 'in the myddys of the chancell'. And what a chancel this is – a feast of subdued C13, *Early English*

beauty, with its groined and vaulted roof with boldly-leafed *bosses*, its fine e. window of seven *lancets*, an *Easter Sepulchre* (with a Victorian canopy), an attractive triple *sedilia* on s. side; and a few original *misericords* among the otherwise modern reproductions. Both inside and outside this church, several memorials testify to Blakeney's sea-going past ... and the price so many paid for it. Like John Easter, whose stone is in the churchyard, dated Feburary 9th 1861. . .

> 'I with seven others went
> Our fellow men to save
> A heavy wave upset our boat
> We met a watery grave'.

Blickling, St Andrew (D4): Conveniently placed, by the entrance to Blickling Hall. The tower, porch, and much of the exterior is Victorian, although the s. door is C13, and the arcades C15. A massive iron-banded chest with five locks stands just inside the door, and is inscribed:

> 'Mayster Adam Ilee mad ys chest
> and Robert Filipis payed yer for God
> have mercy on yar soules'.

Beyond it is a font in the conventional E. Anglian style, but a profusion of remarkably smug lions, and traces of colour give it a highly satisfactory feeling. Still at the w. end, within the n. arcade, is the large monument to the eighth Marquis of Lothian by G.F. Watts (1878). Considering that he was buried elsewhere it is a somewhat overstated reminder. Two life-size angels strike attitudes of concern at head and foot of the recumbent figure which, swathed in a generous shroud, sports a beard of Old Testament proportions. His widow's memorial by the door, by A.G. Walker, is comparatively tame. There are many *brasses*, and a series of replicas grouped in the n. aisle for the convenience of rubbers is a very sensible idea. The original to Sir Nicholas Dagworth (d.1401) lies before the tomb-chest at the e. end of the s. aisle. He built the first Blickling Hall, and is shown in full armour, with a massive helm behind his head and with a lion at his feet. Nearby, the brass to Anne Astley (d.1512) shows her with two babes in arms, and the Latin inscription describes her death after the birth of twins. In front of the pulpit, the brass to Roger and Cecily Felthorp (1454) portrays their sixteen children as well, and in the chancel, Isabelle Cheyne's effigy depicts the fleeting style of the butterfly headdress of the 1480s. The chancel has a nice *angle piscina*, with a tiny eagle and young in a wicker nest serving as a stop to the arches. In the s. wall is the alcove monument to Elizabeth Gurdon, who died at seventeen on a visit to Blickling, just before the Armada. Rigid in cap and ruff, and with sadly mutilated stumps for hands, she half turns her head; a wide-eyed girl wearing a faint smile. Sir Edward Clere provided her memorial, and his own is the large alabaster tomb-chest at the e. end of the s. aisle. Now lacking its effigy, it carries an armorially illustrated pedigree around the sides which stretches fancifully back to the Conquest. Outside the church, on a stone n.w. of the tower, there is a salutory corrective to all the temporalities inside. It concerns James Howard, parish clerk for fifty years, who died aged 88 in 1829:

'Praises on tombs is oft times vainly spent
Mans good deeds is his best Monument'.

Blofield, St Andrew (F6): An impressive church with a fine, soaring *Perpendicular* tower, beautifully panelled with flushwork around the base and on the faces of the buttresses; modern shield carvings handsomely adorn the battlements; there are enormous three-light belfry windows; rectangular openings with unusual honeycomb tracery in the third stage; and a great west window with an imposing doorway below it (the cross of *St Andrew* and keys of *St Peter* carved in the *spandrels*) in stylish harmony. The n. porch used to have an upper room, now gone, which for many years housed the village school. We pass through it to a grand interior, with lofty *arcade* (with *quatrefoil* grouped pillars) of five bays, of the late C14. Note that the easternmost bay on the s. side has 'slipped' badly – and a massive transverse arch in the aisle been put in to take the strain. The *clerestory* is Perpendicular, around 1400, though somehow its two-light windows have a hint about their tracery of *Decorated* nostalgia! The roof above, supported on deep *wall posts* and battlemented *corbels*, is modern. Raised up at the back of the nave are some old C18 *box pews*; a lot of old benches and *poppyheads* here, some with carved figures, those on the arms of the front benches being particularly worthy of note. The lovely chancel arch is enormous, yet has a look of lightness and fragility; and is complemented by an equally lofty tower arch, framing the splendid w. window. The aisle windows are all replacements, as is the e. window, but are Perpendicular in style and carefully in sympathy with all. At one time the chancel must have been a grand sight – but three of its great side windows have been blocked in. One of these is dropped to form a plain *sedilia*, adjoining a Perpendicular and most attractive *angle piscina*, with good pierced tracery. The stone *reredos* is – forcefully – Victorian Gothic! On the n. wall is an appealingly formalised marble monument to Edward Paston, 1630, who was attached to the court of Henry VIII (see glossary, *The Pastons*): it has mother and father, with children two deep, five sons and four daughters; a lugubrious skull tops all. Hanging above it, a Conquistador-ish helmet of about 1530. Nearby, up in the chancel n.w. corner, is the blocked-off entrance to the *rood loft*, its stair entrance being in the n. aisle. The remains of the *rood screen* has restored paintings of the apostles – and on top, modern carvings of St Andrew (cross) and St Peter (keys).

Note, under centre window in n. aisle, the faded remains of a painted *consecration cross*. The roof here, with its plain, solid beams, looks original. Finally – the medieval font: it is extremely interesting in that the carvings set into the eight panels round its bowl represent incidents in the life of Christ, from Nativity to Crucifixion, most unusual subjects for a font.

Bodham, All Saints (D3): Recently rescued from neglect, this plain but pleasant little church is now as neat and well-kept, inside and out, as loving care can make it. It is mostly simple *Perpendicular* in style, with a neat, earlier tower. The unfortunate red-brick buttresses on the n. side are Victorian restoration. In the porch, with its attractive *Decorated* outer arch, is a *holy water stoup* interestingly lined with old, rough-glazed tiles. How old, and from where, are intriguing questions? There's another stoup on the inside wall. A bright, light uncomplicated village church inside, whose timeless character is enhanced by highly ornamental, but also very practical, hanging oil lanterns – there being no electricity here. The furnishings, including the splendidly solid, 'Town Hall Victorian' pulpit, are said to have come from Beckham Workhouse chapel. A plain figure niche above, a nice *piscina* to the r. of, the nave altar – no doubt it was originally a *guild altar* belonging to one of the three guilds who *Blomefield* says had their 'lights' in this church in medieval times. Entrance to *rood stair* may be seen at left of the early C14 chancel arch. Two of the pleasant, square headed Perpendicular windows on the north side of the nave interestingly have wooden frames, carved and coloured to match the surrounding stonework. *Royal Arms* of Queen Anne above indentation of old n. doorway (which is clearly defined outside).

Booton, St Michael and All Angels (D4): Some readers will blench at the inclusion of Booton, others would never forgive us if it were ignored – you must judge for yourself. The Reverend Whitwell Elwin was not only Rector for fifty years, he was also editor of the prestigious 'Quarterly Review', and entirely dissatisfied with the parish church. It was unprepossessing, in poor state, and he began to improve it. In the end, he rebuilt the whole thing, keeping only the walls of nave and chancel encased in new work. Lack of training as architect or draughtsman was no impediment, and he gaily filched designs from here, there, everywhere and nowhere – nave windows from Temple Balsall, w. window from St Stephen's chapel, Westminster, n. porch from Burgh, the diagonally placed twin towers from a fertile imagination. The outside is a riot – pinnacles of all shapes and sizes, some with *crocketting* so lush it verges on the fungoid. The priest's door has a porch like part of Peterborough w. front seen through the wrong end of a telescope, and from a distance, the fairytale outline of the towers looks like an errant fragment of Milan cathedral peeping over the trees. The interior keeps it up. Enormous angels with upswept wings jut from the *hammer beams*, and there is an extraordinary rounded triangle of a window above the chancel arch lighting nothing and giving no light. The chancel side windows are deeply recessed (to mask the old walls), and the glass is a series of angel themes from the Old and New Testaments. The glass in the nave windows is really very pleasing, full of muted greens and blues with, here and there, a flash of brighter colour. A procession of musicians on the s. side is matched on the n. by female saints and attendant angels, all wending their way dreamily eastward. Elwin has a simple memorial in his far from simple chancel. Below, one of the few survivals from the old church – a small *brass* with lettering of real quality:

Booton: Priest's door.

'Here Lyeth The Bodi of Master Edward Fentone preacher of ye worde in Boton 46 yeares buried in the yeare of our Lord 1610'.

In the n. porch another remnant – what must have been a beautiful statue of the Virgin and Child, but when found in a blocked doorway during the rebuilding, the heads had already been hacked away. Sir Edwin Lutyens, architect of New Delhi and Liverpool's Catholic cathedral, called Booton 'very naughty, but in the right spirit'. Who shall say he was wrong?

Braydeston, St Michael (F6): Only about a quarter mile as the crow flies, southward from Brundall's great church, but a trek through winding lanes actually to reach its remote site. A neat little place, as interesting as it looks. The tower – *Decorated* originally, and with a nice *Tudor* w. window – is so over-restored that it looks like a rebuild. The nave has large and rather fine *Perpendicular* windows, with elegant tracery. The chancel is originally C13 *Early English* – the *lancet* in the n. wall looks contemporary. Beautiful C14 Decorated e. window with 'net' tracery (*reticulated*). In the porch, with its attractive hooded outer arch, note on the old wooden benches, among assorted graffiti, the *nine men's morris* boards, one at centre each side. Interior is small – but full of interest: under the tower, a rare *wafer oven*. Old font with coarsely carved six-sided bowl (w. panel – rough copy of the e. window tracery? e. panel – one of the 'wheels with eyes' of the *Nine Orders of Angels*?). Behind the font, a tiny inscription *brass*, restored to the church in recent years after unknown wanderings, to Henry Love of Norwich, 1518. A remnant of a pillar in the nave s. wall indicates an earlier, C13 Early English *arcade*, as does the triple pillar of the arch framing the organ. Note vestiges of colour on a *jamb* of one of the fine n. windows of the nave. On both sides, indications of the *rood* and stairs, with the entrance

behind the sturdy little pulpit – the latter, like the rest of the furnishings, is modern, but it has on top an older and curious *hour-glass stand*. The *screen* is modern too –though the silvery-aged tracery in five of the six lower panels is evidently ancient, C15 by the form of it, with its leaves, flowers and cusps, and very good. Note especially, s. side, the lovely *pelican* feeding its young with its own blood. In the chancel pretty Early English C13 *piscina* with beside it a great rarity, a little corner shelf supported on large, coarse mouldings. Below sanctuary steps, extreme right, a small inscription in Latin is all that remains of a brass to Osbert, son of John Barney of Reedham, killed in 1469 by an arrow during the siege of Caister Castle. Note the *ledger slab* poignantly reminding us of the rate of child mortality in the past:

'Here lyeth the body of Ann, daughter of John & Eliz. Cotton, who died Aug 13, 1727, aged 2 years and 6 months, adjacent lie nine more of their children'.

Nearby also are the graves of yet two more sons, who both died before reaching the age of 20. In the w. window – striking modern stained glass, with bold Faith, Hope & Charity, in memory of first world war fallen.

Bradfield, St Giles (E3): All alone up a narrow lane, with its fine four-stage *Perpendicular* tower dominating its surroundings – even though it is rather blunt on top, as it was never finished! Most attractive are the buttresses at the e. end of the chancel, with their sprightly carved pinnacles. Nave and chancel are basically mid-C14, but the church was much knocked-about in an early C18 'rebuilding' – which meant demolishing the nave aisle and walling in the *arcades*, as can be clearly seen inside. As you go in, you seem to step back a century and more – a slightly mouldering air, old hanging oil lamps and a little pedal organ in a beautiful mellow walnut case; time here has stood still.

There is a C14 font. Brass memorial inscriptions let into the nave pavement are, w. to e., John Tebald and his wife Agnes, 1490; Margaret, wife of Thomas Heins, 1534; and John Tebald, 1506. Over chancel arch remains of the medieval painting about which the experts disagree: like a crude Trinity, says one; Christ on a rainbow displaying his wounds, says a second. The second, we think, wins on points. Now the chancel: C14, very fine, with super five-light e. window. In s. wall, a nice *piscina* of the *Decorated* period with *cinquefoil* (five-leaf) head; opposite, a big recess where there was probably an *Easter Sepulchre*.

Brampton, St Peter (E4): The round *Norman* tower has a C15 brick octagonal top, and a single roof now covers what was nave and s. aisle. The *arcade* has disappeared and also the chapel that opened from it into the chancel. The s. door looks to be C19, but has fine C15 tracery with *crocketted* arches applied to it. By the door on the s. wall a very big and very curly *cartouche* to Margaret Beevor (1716) sprouts acanthus leaves with two cherub heads below. The chancel has a fine array of *brasses*. On the s. side of the sanctuary are the delicately engraved figures of Edward Brampton and his wife Joan (1622). They turn towards each other and have most expressive faces. East of them, two shrouded figures, Robert Brampton and his wife, with a little Virgin and child inset above them. On the n. wall are the figures of John Brampton (d. 1535) in armour and chain-mail with his two wives Thomaseyne and Anne wearing kennel headdresses. As a mild eccentricity, a Roman urn dug up in a nearby field has found a resting place on a bracket above the pulpit.

Briningham, St Maurice (C3): A remarkable four-light window in the s. side of the nave, with beautiful, intricate flowing tracery, is one of the features of this church – it is of C14

date, probably about 1360, which makes it an interesting survivor of the *Black Death*, the catastrophe of 1349-50 which so abruptly curtailed the glories of the *Decorated* period. Inside, the *jambs* of this window have most curious little C12 *Norman* columns attached, less than three feet high: what their purpose originally was, one can only guess at. The purple Victorian glass in this window alas does no credit to a magnificent piece of medieval craftsmanship. The base of the C14 tower serves as a porch, leading into the earlier nave. This part of the church is in a sad state of repair, and divided off from the chancel – which in contrast is beautifully maintained – by a crude hardboard partition. But still, note the pretty fluted columns of the chancel arch as you go into the Decorated chancel. Attractive *arch-braced* (modern?) roof, and a super communion rail, about 1700, with plump *pillasters* like those round a gentleman's formal garden of the period. Finely traceried and deeply recessed e. window, flanked by huge *ogee*-headed niches now containing forbidding – and dare one suggest it, even slightly sinister? – large wooden figures of the Virgin on one side, and the church's dedicatory soldier-saint, *Maurice*, on the other. Nice *piscina* and interesting remains of a *sedilia*. Equally interesting (and most odd seen from the outside) a blocked-up, square *low-side window* in the traditional place near the chancel arch. Also blocked, a plain, lop-sided little priest's door. Note the 1930 Brereton memorial on the n. wall, recalling through its names, continued in the family through the years, their descent from the ill-fated Norfolk born admiral, *Sir Clowdisley Shovel*. Outside, at e. end, a massive pyramid obelisque to the Breretons, topped by a haltered bear, their family crest.

Brinton, St Andrew (C3): Lovely setting in a pretty village. Church has lost its chancel, but has a fine *arch-braced roof*, restored (with the n. transept roof) in 1964, when the angels were re-coloured. Contemporary with the roof are the solid benches, which have good figures. Two of these are in the form of a rebus on the village name – Brinton = BRYNING A TUN (barrel), and BRIN (burnt) TUN. See the date and initials, '1544 R.P.', on the westernmost bench end. Fine and rare example of Elizabethan 'fruitful and profitable sentences' on n. wall, restored in 1869 when the gallery was removed. Fireplace in base of tower was still in use in the 1890s. Excellent *Jacobean* chest.

Briston, All Saints (C3): There was a round tower here but it was pronounced unsafe in 1785 and removed; a n. aisle has also disappeared, leaving the *arcade* set in the nave wall. There are marks too of a porch over the blocked s. door. The early C14 chancel is handsome. The priest's door has deep mouldings with good *headstops*, and a well defined *dripstone* runs below the windows. The e. window has a tight design (technically, *reticulated*) in the head which is very effective outside. Less so inside, but there the slender columns in the *jambs* are enhanced by battlemented rings halfway up – unusual and attractive. The C14 *sedilia* has clustered columns with *cinquefoils* and *ogee* arches. The elaborate double *piscina* has a pierced *quatrefoil* in the head and a stone *credence shelf* crossing it halfway up like a window division. Holes in both jambs look like hinge placements, so perhaps it doubled as an *aumbry* at some stage. The early C18 communion rails are very sturdy – plump turning and broad mouldings. The parish chest in the sanctuary is huge (5ft 6in x 2ft 6in x 2ft 6in) and completely swathed in iron. It has four locks, and lugs for a long bar to cover them all. Briston has its own unique curiosity – a metal cello made by Mr. Clithero the village blacksmith in 1700 and apparently played by him for many years . . . authority is silent as to its tone. Now the church also has one of the ugliest bell-cotes in Christendom – two brick pillars, late C20.

Brumstead, St Peter (F4): Surprisingly fine, lofty tower to an otherwise unpretentious church; it is of early *Perpendicular* character, as is the porch – that is, very soon after the *Black Death* of 1349-50. The body of the church is early C14 *Decorated*, with three-light windows of simple intersecting tracery on each side – the tracery of those on the s. side has *cusping*, but on the n. side is totally plain. The large e. window is a Victorian replacement of 1875. The signs of neglect evident outside the church are accentuated in the bleak, bare interior – a barnlike 'hall' with no separate chancel, under a plain boarded roof of 1834. There is a pretty traceried *piscina*, next to the bricked-in doorway to the old *rood stair*. Did the stone *corbel* (a carved lion's head) immediately above the doorway, and that on the opposite wall (a helmeted head, face obliterated) formerly support a low *rood beam*? Perhaps the square headed small windows (same date as tower?) placed just above this point on each side were put there to light the rood? Simple C14 font carved with *quatrefoils*. A first world war memorial on the n. wall is carved like an open book – most effective and tasteful.

Brundall, St Lawrence (F6): Set in a most beautiful garden-like churchyard, this is a charming little church, even though it is most heavily restored and modernised (a n. aisle and vestry were added in 1900). A particular feature is its pretty double bellcote, which just could be a happy survivor from the late C13 – the tiny entrance door arch (entered through a sweet little porch) suggests that period too. Inside, almost everything is modern but in apple-pie order, including a handsome *screen*. In the vestry, a bland window by *Charles Eames Kempe*, one of the foremost stained glass artists of his time. In centre window of the n. aisle a small roundel – about 10in across, delicately coloured, and thought to be C16 – showing the church's dedicatory saint, *Lawrence*, with his grill. Finally, the church's treasure – a round, C13 font, lead-covered (the only one in Norfolk) and bearing tiny crucifixes punctuated by ornamental strips . . . plus a lot of scratched on graffiti from several centuries.

Buckenham, St Nicholas (F6): Out of use for some years and now in the care of the Redundant Churches Fund. The octagonal tower has an *Early English* belfry stage with tall *lancets* in each face, giving it a very distinctive look. Vandalism has been rampant here and, despite the considerable amount of money spent by the Fund on urgent repairs during the statutory 'waiting period', the scene inside is depressing. There is no glass in the e. window and much has gone elsewhere; filth overlays everything. Apart from the block of C19 pews, only the font remains. This is a fine piece and has very well preserved figures of saints and apostles under flattened *ogee* arches in the panels. There are four civilians at the angles of the stem. A gilt crucifix and an alabaster panel of the martyrdom of St Erasmus were found under the chancel floor in 1840, and *Cautley* regretted that they had been presented to Norwich Museum instead of being preserved as objects of interest here. It is just as well that they were not.

Burgh, St Margaret (C3): The whole church has been virtually rebuilt, but entry is by a *Norman* s. doorway, with zig-zag and *billet* decoration in the arch. Remains of a second Norman doorway are still visible outside on the north. The C19 *gallery* is lit by a cottage like dormer window in the thatched roof. There is a little *brass* to John Burton (d.1608) on the wall of the chancel, and the e. window has modern glass depicting *St Margaret of Antioch, St Luke* and the Virgin. The C19 Creed and *Decalogue Boards* in the chancel rest on re-used *corbels*, carved with foliage and animals, which are *Early English* in date.

Burgh-next-Aylsham, St Mary the Virgin (E4): Prettily placed with a path through the churchyard to a footbridge over the river Bure. The C15 tower has attractive sound-holes and a decorative series of Maria Regina monograms in the *flushwork* of the battlements. Inside this small church there is a delightful surprise for the newcomer. The chancel, lower than the nave, provides a lovely little vista of tall *lancets* and matching *arcading* below. Original work of about 1220 was extended eastwards two bays by R.M. Phipson in 1876, and it was done well. The n. chapel is also Victorian, but the splendid arch is original; the three shafts on either side have stiffleaf capitals, and birds peck at the foliage on the e. side. It is intriguing to find such strong echoes of the work at Lincoln in this small Norfolk parish. The *Seven Sacrament font* is not as perfect as that at Sloley, but has the same *Evangelistic signs* at its base. As at Salle, the sacramental emblems are held by angels. The bowl panels are: (clockwise from the e.) Mass, Mass of *St Gregory* (the saint had visions of Christ while saying mass), Extreme Unction, Matrimony, Penance, Baptism, Confirmation (at an early age as was usual), Ordination. This font has the distinction of being signed – the mason's mark can be seen incised below the Penance panel. Under the tower is a set of George I arms in stone inscribed 'Matt Burr Gent Churchwarden 1721'. They are very weathered and must have been outside originally. Above them, a monument to Lt. John Woolsey, who served under Maj. Gen. Wolfe in the victorious expedition against Quebec in 1759 – and returned to live to a ripe old age in the peace of Burgh.

Burlingham, St Andrew (F5): Neatly compact in its *Perpendicular* lines, in a well-groomed churchyard, backed by lofty trees – an agreeable picture. Nice tower, built about 1466, well panelled base (*flushwork*) and battlements, the latter inset with lozenge-shapes bearing shields carved with the cross of St Andrew. The bell openings have attractive tracery which is Perpendicular – but seems in its flow to want to be *Decorated*! On each side of the tower is a small square sound-hole, each set with different and most individual tracery – charming. Nave, chancel and aisle windows (all neatly set off by slim pink bricks over the heads) are Perpendicular, though the fabric is earlier, as the lovely flowing Decorated tracery of the e. window, and the bricked-in n. doorway, indicate; moreover, on the s. side of the chancel is a *low side window* which appears to be *Early English*. The entrance porch is Perpendicular, but note, over outer arch, a *hood-mould* which is re-used *Norman* material, studded with star moulding – tiny petal-like stars set in circles. Inside the church are rewarding surprises. A striking nave roof (a bequest dates it at 1487) with *arch braces* plus *hammer beams*, the first with fine *bosses* at the intersections, the second with lovely winged angels at the angles . . . and all in the faded beauty of their original colouring; then there are rich, generously carved *wall plates;* and deep *wall posts* sitting on *corbels* carved with delightfully funny faces . . . save for a very disturbing hollow-eyed creature at left above the *rood screen*. The nave's Perpendicular five-bay n. *arcade* is coarse, but appealing. The screen is very interesting, dated 1536, the last addition to the church before the *Reformation* – and thus possibly the latest dated screen in Norfolk (Horsham's is 1528). The saints, painted on *gesso* with gilt decoration, are badly mutilated but still discernible: l. to r., Norfolk's own *Withburga*, with her does – and Dereham church in her hand, *Benedict, Edward the Confessor, Thomas of Canterbury, John the Baptist, Cecilia, Walston of Bawburgh, Catherine*, unidentifiable figure, and *Etheldreda*. At the modern top of the screen a medieval angel – he fell from the roof some years ago. The chancel has a plain (probably C18) plaster ceiling, a *dropped sill sedilia* and severely simple *piscina*.

Opposite, a fine memorial tablet (which came from the now ruinous Burlingham St Peter's) to Gregory Mileham, 1615, flanked by two *putti* (cherubs) – unusual in that one carries a spade, the other an extinguished torch. Below, a tiny, endearing inscription to one William Gilman:

'Wil Gilman heere lies buried in dust
Who thirty two yeares was a servant just
To masters twoe, the second whereof came
First in his armes to church to get a name
And least his name should with his bodye die
His master heere hath placed his memorye'.

On nave wall by s. door, and in pavement of n. aisle, two *palimpsest* (ie, re-used) brass inscriptions, one to Elizabeth Framlingham (1559), on the underside, part of a lady (about 1375); the other to John Randes and his wife (1503), on the reverse an inscription to Nicholas Man, Clerk (1441). Across the tower arch, a beautiful medieval screen (again, salvaged from St Peter's): it has two athletically lean and handsomely featured angels holding shields carved with the keys of *St Peter*; while the cusps of the elegant arches are carved with tiny floral motifs – and with miniature grotesques and animals, and one powerful human face. In the tower, an octagonal Decorated font; and on the walls a fine collection of tablets and *cartouches* to the Burroughes family, notably one to a gentleman who was evidently a paragon of all the virtues.

Burlingham, St Edmund (F6): A lovely church full of character, with only the farm opposite to keep it company in the open fields. Nave and chancel are all under one continuous thatched roof and the porch is thatched too. There is a blocked *Norman* n. doorway which was evidently intended to have beakhead ornament in the arch, but the carving was never completed. The s. doorway is also Norman with a head above the arch. Both nave and chancel have Y-traceried windows of about 1300 – one in the s. nave wall has a dropped sill to form a seat, and on that side the outline of the *rood stairs* can be seen cut into the wall. The church's treasure catches the eye immediately – a pulpit which is the finest C15 example in Norfolk, beautifully restored with the help of the Pilgrim Trust in 1964. It has eight narrow panels, with a tall *crocketted* arch and canopy set in each; painted panels run below, and in the bottom third there is more rich tracery. An inscription is set midway like a band:

> 'Inter Natos Mulierum Non Surrexit Major Johanne Baptista' (Among them that are born of women there hath not arisen a greater than John the Baptist. Matt. XI, 11.)

The upper stage of each buttress is ornamented with *gesso* and the whole piece glows with colour. Both the castellated rim and the base are carved from a single piece of timber – an eccentricity even for the period. Later additions are the *Jacobean* backboard and *tester*, and the *hour-glass stand*. The *screen* is a fitting companion to the pulpit, with fine open tracery, *ogee* arches and good cresting. Below the rail there are remains of a gilt diaper (surface decoration) pattern, but most of it was lost when the *box pews* (since removed) were built on to the screen. The nave benches have lovely solid ends with charming figures on the arms. An unlikely looking elephant has more of a proboscis than a trunk and a miniature castle on his back; there is a fox with a goose over its shoulder, and three figures seated in chairs. Some of the *poppyheads* in the chancel incorporate faces – a bishop and a king. The communion rails are sturdy and unpretentious C17. The really interesting thing in the chancel is the big painting on the s. wall. Although virtually all the colouring has gone, it is instantly recognisable as the martyrdom of *St Thomas Becket,* and is the only one on this scale to survive in Norfolk. Dis-covered in 1856, it shows St Thomas kneeling and being attacked by the four knights – one can be identified as Reginald Fitze Urse by the bear on his shield. The other painting in the church is a faint *St Christopher* on the n. wall of the nave. This delightful and most interesting church faces the problems of isolation and a tiny congregation – long may it survive.

Buxton, St Andrew (E4): The tower and some of the rest of the church was entirely rebuilt in 1881, and the s. porch of similar date was set at an angle to the nave – rather oddly. There are quatrefoil *clerestory* windows above the tall and graceful C14 *arcades.* The base of the C16 *screen* now stands between the chancel and the s. aisle chapel, and has been built up to full height with new work. There is a C13 *piscina* and *sedilia,* with plain arches and a single headstop at one end. On the chancel n. wall an alabaster monument to Margaret Robinson (d.1638) has black marble *Corinthian* columns, with a broken pediment above; cherubs peep out above the tablet. opposite is a tablet to Mary Ann Kent (d.1773 aged 4); she

> 'died under Inoculation . . . her fond parents deluded by prevalent Custom suffered the rough officious hand of Art to wound the flourishing root of Nature & rob the little Innocent of the gracious gift of life'.

Caister on Sea, Holy Trinity (H5): A church that is splendidly cared for. Slim C14 tower with buttresses to the w. only, and mid-C15 bell openings with transoms (horizontal bars). The steep line of an old thatched roof shows clearly on the e. face, but since then the covering has been lead, then slate and now good looking pantiles. The nave still has a C13 *lancet* in the n. wall and in the C14 s. aisle the Lady chapel retains the original lower floor level. The *sedilia* and *piscina* in the chancel are nicely grouped under a range of *cinquefoil, ogee* arches with detached shafts. The church has what may be the biggest font in the county, and by chance rather than by design. There was originally a C13 Purbeck font but this was swapped in 1830 for a modern one, and then in 1902 the present C14 monster was discovered in a cottage garden at Eye, Suffolk and bought for £5. Even without steps it is 5ft high and measures 3ft 4in across the bowl. The stem has shafts at the angles, highly individual tracery in four of the bowl panels and a castellated rim. It could look even better if the surface were relieved of its thick coating of staring whitewash. The *Royal Arms* hanging on the *arcade* pillar are dated 1786 for George III, but look at the initials and you will see that they have been altered; the shield is correctly painted for its date, 1786, but the motto – Exurgat Deus Dissipentur Inimic – strongly suggests that it was originally painted for James I. The arms are set in a square frame, but diamond-wise so that they look just like a *hatchment* from a distance. Also at the w. end, commandment or *Decalogue* boards of well above average quality; on two panels 8ft x 6ft (Caister goes in for the ecclesiastical 'outsize'!) the figures of Moses and Aaron stand, each with their half of the decalogue. The paintings are well restored and good, and date from the late C17. The view into the chancel is narrowed by the twin organ cases on the walls, but their curves effectively frame the e. window which is filled with a study of Christ and his fishermen disciples. It is a memorial to the nine Caister men who died when the lifeboat 'Beauchamp' was lost in 1901 trying to reach a stricken vessel. To the question 'Why?', came the reply 'Caister men never turn back' – simple statement of a great tradition. Also in the chancel, a memorial to Sir William Crowe (d.1668); a fine bust with shoulder-length hair and head half turned. In the churchyard w. of the tower you will find the grave of Sarah Martin (d.1843) She worked as a dressmaker, but found time to visit Yarmouth Jail each week to

teach, hold services, and help the prisoners. Though not as well known as Elizabeth Fry, hers was and is a potent example.

Calthorpe, Our Lady and St Margaret (D3): Apart from the e. window of 1822, the chancel is C13 and in all probability so is the tower, although it looks as though it was updated when the nave was rebuilt in the C15. Inside, the tower arch is low and deeply moulded brick with no capitals. There was a s. porch originally and the recess above the n. door inside may have contained a *St Christopher* in the usual position opposite the main entrance. The C15 font is very robust and has four amiable and well fed lions at the angles of the stem, with varied tracery between them and in the panels of the bowl. It has a bright new cover in the style of the period. The *Laudian* altar rails have been carefully restored and the balusters (supporting pillars) are set diagonally – a thoughtful variation. The *consecration crosses* have been repainted and a fine new *rood* with its attendant figures has been placed on the original stone *corbels* above the chancel arch. This church is cherished and it shows.

Cantley, St Margaret (F6): There is a remnant of a *Norman* arch over the priest's door which gives a clue to an earlier building, but the bell openings in the tower and most of the chancel windows point to the early C14. The s. door is C14 too, and has good clusters of oak leaves with acorns as stops to the arch, and the finely traceried *spandrels* contain arms of the Philips and Bardolph families. There is a short s. transept chapel, with a flat panelled ceiling and a *piscina*, which is now stuffed with pews. Some good memorials: that to the brothers Jonathan and Charles Layton of Reedham and Clippesby Halls (d.1801 & 1791) is striking – a gilded sheaf of wheat tied with a band stands against the obelisk, and there is a bull in bas relief on a roundel below.

In the chancel Simon Kidball (d.1735) – florid lettering with the names in Gothic, and a monogram in the *cartouche* above. On the chancel floor opposite, a lively epitaph to a local Jorrocks, Robert Gilbert (d.1714)

> '. . .That subtile FOX DEATH,
> Earth'd him here at last,
> And left a Fragrant Scent, so sweet behind,
> That ought to be persu'd by all Mankind'.

Is he, I wonder, pursued across Eternity by the shades of all those foxes?

Catfield, All Saints (F4): Most of the building is C14 and the aisle windows have a pleasing alternation of tracery patterns. There is no *clerestory*, but at one time the walls above the *arcades* and elsewhere were covered with paintings. Now, about all that can be discerned is the Stoning of *Stephen*, above the second pillar of the s. arcade. The *rood screen* has sixteen paintings of Kings, somewhat mutilated. *St Edmund* can be seen with his arrow emblem to the r. of the opening. In the embrasures of both easternmost aisle windows there are steps which evidently led up to the *rood loft*. It would appear that this originally stretched right across the church, some 10ft w. of where the screen is now. Behind the ponderous pitchpine pulpit is an C18 echo – an *hour-glass* stand high on the wall. On the n. wall of the sanctuary is a tablet by the sculptor *William Groves*, with a *peepul tree* (see glossary – *William Groves*) at the top, and a sheathed sword below, to Lt. Thomas Cubitt (d.1848) who 'met a soldier's death in his country's cause before Moultan'. (Moultan is a town in the Indian Punjab).

Catton, St Margaret (E5): Circular *Norman* tower with handsome later octagonal belfry. Rest of church, early C14 *Decorated* and C15 *Perpendicular*. Very nice C15 porch with priest's chamber above, crow-stepped gables, niche containing figure of *Saint Margaret* (probably of Antioch); above her, an C18 sundial. The chancel – which is pebble dashed and, surprisingly, looks very acceptable – has a *priest's door* with Norman hood and *head-stops*: above it, a *consecration cross*. Inside, there's an C18 gothicky w. gallery; an interesting *Tudor* pulpit, dated 1537, bearing Arms of the Guilds of Norwich came from St George's in Colegate, Norwich in mid C19. In n. transept (originally in chancel, from where it was moved in 1852 when the church was enlarged and restored) is a good monument, with two sad *'putti'* – little naked angelic boys – wringing their hands, to Bussy Green and family, 1745, by *Robert Page* of Norwich. Also a delicate and chaste memorial to Jeremiah Ives, Mayor of Norwich in 1820.

Cawston, St Agnes (D4): A big and impressive church which has, like many in Norfolk, a small village clustered round it. Apart from the chancel and s. transept which are earlier, the building dates from the early C15. The tower is tall and gaunt with a decidedly unfinished look at the top, but the rich combination of great w. window and deeply moulded doorway, with attendant wild man and dragon, more than compensates for this. The fine *base course* can be seen inside the church as well, and suggests that the tower was completed ahead of the rest of the work. The interior tower arch is very tall and is spanned by a C15 ringers' gallery resting on massive corner posts. Across its front runs an inscription which can be read more easily from the replica in the n. aisle:

> 'God spede the plow and send us ale corn enow our purpose for to make at crow of cok of ye plowlete of Sygate, be mery and glade wat good ale yis work mad'.

Whether or no the last line is a reference to the profit from church ales or a pun on Walter Goodale's name, the connection of the plough guild with the church is maintained by the sign of the Plough Inn. It was hung above the n. door when the inn (formerly the guildhall) was closed in 1950. The *hammerbeam* roof of the nave is superb with each post backed by tracery, and supporting a standing angel with outspread wings. More angels line the cornice and the apex. Binoculars are a help here in appreciating the detail. At the e. end, the outline of the *rood* (uncovered in 1911) can be seen above the chancel arch. Below is an unusually tall early C16 *screen*, complete with doors to their full height. It was well restored in 1952, and the finely painted figures, some with most expressive faces, are ascribed to Flemish artists. From n. to s. the saints are: *St Agnes, St Helena, St Thomas, St John the Evangelist, St James the Great, St Andrew, St Paul, St Peter,* the *Four Latin Doctors, St James the less, St Bartholomew, St Philip, St Simon, St Jude, St Matthew, St Matthias,* and *Sir John Schorne.* The buttresses still carry traces of the tiny figures within canopies worked in *gesso,* a rich embellishment that can also be seen on the screens at nearby Aylsham and Marsham. The C15 pulpit is very well preserved and the treatment of the panels is reminiscent of the canopies seen on *brasses* of the period. The s. transept has a good roof with *bosses,* and traces of a painting on the e. wall, possibly of the Virgin. The *piscina* is extraordinary, and has a wild man and dragon with huge heads in the *spandrels.*

Cley-next-the-sea, St Margaret (C2): A marvellous, vital building, resplendent with carving and *crocketting,* niches and pinnacles – and a ruined s. transept paradoxically adding to its visual impact; crowning all, a thoroughly individual *clerestory.* This is all from the s., from the delightful green which fronts the churchyard.

The n. side is sober but nonetheless rewarding with, above the clerestory, a magnificent range of battlements in richly fretted stonework, beautifully inlaid with *flushwork.* The n. porch is a poor thing contrasted with its opposite number, but just around the corner is the splendid w. front with its huge dominant window. But then, the s.w. angle was intended to impress. Look across the serene meadows to Wiveton church on its own hill – 500 years ago that expanse between was a harbour, alive with the shipping and commerce of a prosperous port. Towards the mid C14 the church took its present shape, on the back of a flourishing trade, virtually replacing its predecessor apart from the tall, slightly severe mid-C13 tower. This was the age of *Decorated* architecture, reaching in the ruined s. transept's beautiful window tracery, a peak of artistic opulence. Then came the *Black Death* in 1349 – and work stopped. When it resumed some years later, the consummate craftsmen were no longer available, and the *Perpendicular* style began to emerge. We have it grandly here in the aisle windows and the great w. window. Slowly from this time the sea withdrew, the river shrank – and with it went Cley's fat years, leaving a small coastal community with a huge church on its hands. Unable to maintain it all, they bricked off the transepts – already ruinous by the end of the C16. The s. porch is C15, of remarkably rich design, its upper chamber with handsome little windows, and a sundial between them. Above, battlements of beautiful filigree work, flanking buttresses highly ornamented with canopied niches; the outer arch and *jambs* carved with heraldic emblems, and inside, a *groined* roof with badly eroded *bosses* – though one has great vitality, with a fox making off with a chicken, pursued by a furious old woman. Inside, the church is a blaze of light, pouring in from the clerestory with its great *cinquefoil* windows alternating with a two-light

Cley St Margaret: s. transept.

design, from the soaring w. window, and from the aisles – where the dropped window sills all form seats. The C15 *arch braced* aisle roofs have flower and foliage bosses and delicate tracery in the *spandrels*. In the nave and s. aisle are echoes of the exuberance outside – for between the arches of the elegant C14 *arcade* are some highly individual ornaments richly canopied. From e. to w. they represent an imp with a glass eye, a distinctly apprehensive St George wrestling with a very angry dragon, an enchantingly happy lion gnawing a bone, an angel with cymbals, a contortionist musician with pipe and tabor, and tucked away in the s.w. corner, a very sulky little man. On the other side of the arcade, acting as *hood mould* stops in the s. aisle, are more figures cavorting joyously, with one very naughty fellow showing his bare bottom. Below is a fine *brass* for John Symondes (d.1511) and his wife Agnes (d.1508), shown in their shrouds, with their eight children lined up below them, each with a 'name plate'. Other interesting brass remnants will be found westward in this aisle near the door, and in the n. aisle a splendid priest brass. Note in the n.w. corner of the nave the battered *Royal Arms,* crudely altered for Anne, from Charles II. The *seven sacrament font* is much defaced but still very fine, and there are some good bench ends – touched with the same buoyant humour which infects the arcade carvings. In the chancel, the *piscina, dropped sill sedilia* and the window above it are simple C14 Decorated, marrying happily with the earlier Y-traceried windows in the n. and s. walls. The large, five-light e. window is Perpendicular, but this too, with its uncluttered lines, remains in cool harmony with the rest. The altar stands on the medieval *mensa,* and there are six *misericords* carved with shields. The *rood stairs* are unusual – two entrances, one in the chancel, the other in the n. aisle. Outside, under the s. transept window seek out the tomb slab with interesting inscription to a loyal officer of the ill-fated Norfolk admiral,

Sir Clowdisley Shovel. The whole churchyard is worth exploring for the magnificent range of C18 headstones.

Clippesby, St. Peter (G5): Buried in trees away from the road and easily missed. A typical round tower, this time with a C19 octagonal top. There is a *Norman* n. doorway, with remains of another in what is now the main s. entrance porch. There is a little *Mass dial* here on the outer jamb. Early C13 *lancets* in the nave are about the same date as the *piscina,* which has supporting shafts and simple spiralled capitals. In the same s.e. corner of the sanctuary is a good *brass* to the family of John Clippesby (1594) – two adults and three little maids with a *chrysom child.* Another brass in the nave also has two good figures, one with a man in a fur-lined gown with a purse at his belt. The inscription for this is probably the one fixed to the n. door (Thomas Pallyng, 1503).

Cockthorpe, All Saints (B2): A most pleasing and welcoming little place. The tower, enhanced by a fine bit of restoration repointing work, is older than it looks on first glance: about 1300 in fact, as indicated by those nice Y-traceried (albeit bricked up) windows high up. Inside the church, the condition may be far from ideal – yet it was rescued from far worse decay and neglect through the excellent and invaluable work of the Norfolk Churches Trust, in whose care All Saints is now placed. The nave has a rather rustic *arch-braced* C15 roof, with surprisingly opulent carved *wall plates* on the n. side, and very long and carved wooden *wall posts.* The *clerestory* of the same C15 date, on the s. side only, was altered to fit the pitch of the roof. Below, an unsophisticated, agreeable *arcade* of about 1300, very much at one with the sedate and dignified tower arch and the neat chancel arch. There is a lovely old knobbly bench end dated 1647, and a couple of earlier *poppy heads.* Overhead, adding to the character and the lovely atmosphere of this little place, are real candelabra . . . there being no electricity here. The poor chancel has had a bad time of it – a lot of alterations, door and window now blocked and the upper tracery gone from the e. window. The s. aisle has a larger window partly filled in and replaced by a charming smaller one of two lights, seemingly to make way for the large *Jacobean* tomb chest below it to Sir James Calthorpe, 1615, which also shoves rudely into the simple little *angle piscina* (contemporary around 1300 with the aisle, the entrance door and the arcade) in the s.e. corner. At the time of writing, Cockthorpe's other and famous Calthorpe monument is removed from its place at the e. end of the aisle, having been vandalised before the NCT took the church under its wing. However, it is being repaired and restored, and will be back, so we quote in full the fascinating content of this alabaster and marble remembrance of Sir James and his dame:

'In assured hope resteth here the bodies of Sir James Calthorpe, Knight and Dame Barbara his wife, daughter of John Bacon Esq. of Hesset. By her he had 8 sons and 6 daughters, in whose severel marriages and issues the ancient glory of the name of the family (resting then chiefly and almost solely in himself), did reflourish and is dilated into many of the best houses in the country. He was buried the 16th day of June A.D. 1615 and of his age 57. The said Barbara, surviving him, and much comforted with the sight of 193 of their children and their offspring, at the age of 86 years exchanged this life for a better, upon the 3rd of November A.D. 1639'.

Worthy of historical note is that two of Norfolk's famous admirals were born in Cockthorpe and baptised here, *Sir John Narbrough* and the sadly fated *Sir Clowdisley Shovel.*

Colby, St Giles(E3): Apart from the old rectory, quite alone in the fields. A thin mainly C14 tower and a lovely C15 porch. Surrounded by *flushwork*, the doorway has *St George* and the Angel Gabriel in the *spandrels* and a niche between two windows above. The upper room has an open arch to the nave and was used as a Sunday school in the C19. There was a n. aisle but this was demolished in 1749 and a new wall of brick with arched windows replaced the *arcade*; the chancel arch was remodelled to match. The C15 font is interesting – the bowl panels have the *Evangelistic symbols* interspersed with *St Giles* and his attendant hind, the Virgin on a settle with the Child standing on her knee, and the donors kneeling. The restrained architectural cover of 1848 is good – classical columns carrying a moulded flat canopy. Also at the w. end on the n. wall in a glass frame hangs a beautiful C19 velvet altar frontal, richly embroidered and incorporating an earlier border. The chancel C14 *sedilia* and *piscina* are very shapely, with slender shafts carrying *ogee* arches, and the C17 *reredos* has painted panels of Moses and Aaron. The C15 glass in the e. window was arranged there by a C19 rector. The figures in the tracery are some of the Apostles, and in the main panels one sees in the centre *St Peter*, l. and r. at the bottom *St James the Great* and *St John*. The two angels standing on wheels refer to Ezekiel 10. . .

'Go in among the wheels beneath the cherubim'.

Coltishall, St John the Evangelist(E5): The C15 tower has a very nice w. front, with a small but tall w. window flanked by niches, with a frieze of alternating shields and chalices below. The chalice emblem of the Evangelist also figures in the *base course*. Two small round *Saxon* windows have survived, high under the eaves of the thatched roof on the n. side, but it is a pity that somebody in 1865 set a large and inappropriate circular window below them. The C13 square font of Purbeck marble stands on a central drum, with four supporting shafts, a type found in many churches in the county. On the n. wall of the nave is a monument to Sophia St John (d.1827); a female leans pensively against a tomb, posy basket in hand. On the s. aisle wall, James Perkins (d.1711/12) has a *cartouche* around which fat pink and gilt cherub heads are nicely arranged. The monument to John Hapman (d.1719) in the chancel has seated *putti*, one wiping his eye, and the candlesticks above, complete with candles, are rather an odd embellishment. A very fine tablet to Henry Smith (d.1743) and his wife states endearingly:

'they were happy in each other and their children in them'.

Cromer, St Peter and St Paul (E2): The 160ft tower is by far the highest in Norfolk and dominates the town, both from land and sea. Its impressive combination of strength and elegance is enhanced by the fine detail of soundholes, double-opening belfry windows, and intricate parapet. The rest of the building is of the same C15 date, except the 1880s chancel. The church has three large porches, and the western one is lavish. It has a *groined* roof over a fine inner doorway enriched with a large moulding in which shields and angels alternate. The porch abounds with canopied niches, and is topped by traceried battlements and pinnacles. The interior of the church is outstandingly spacious, with very tall *arcades* and arches. Light floods through the great *transomed* windows. There is a good deal of C19 and C20 glass, and the *Pre-Raphaelite* figures in the e. window of the s. aisle are excellent. The modern Rudland and Clark memorial windows in the s. aisle pick up a number of points of local interest, particularly those connected with the sea. The memorial to one of Cromer's most famous sons, Coxwain Henry Blogg,

can be found beneath the tower where there is also a replica of the C15 century font at Yaxham, near East Dereham. During the C18 and C19, Cromer church went through some bad times of neglect – it is recorded, in early Victorian times, that the churchwardens had to buy hedgehogs, at 4d each, to keep down vermin in the churchyard. It had some characterful vicars, however. There was George Glover, appointed about 1800, known as the 'Cardinal of Cromer' because of his strong whig, controversialist views. His successor, William Sharp, was a very small man who required a hassock placed in the pulpit to give him a little more height. The story has it that one Sunday morning he was preaching on the text 'A little while and ye shall see me no more'. Alas, he slipped on his hassock, and to the dismay of his congregation, promptly disappeared from view.

Crostwick, St Peter (E5): Approached across the common from the road, and then up a short avenue of tall limes to the n. porch. The C15 tower is handsome, particularly the parapet, which has pierced tracery alternating with *quatrefoils* below the battlements. This, and the corner pinnacles are now very worn. The C16 porch is of brick, and so are the remains of the *rood loft stair* outside on the s. wall. Inside, there is a beautiful C15 font which has standing figures in niches round the shaft, and seated figures set in recesses round the bowl. On the s. wall opposite the door is the remains of a large *St Christopher painting*.

Crostwight, All Saints (F3): Set deep in fields, a church which has evidently gone through hard times – but is now assured, as is evident at once in its general condition and the neat order of its churchyard. The squat tower was once lofty, but its top had become so dangerous by 1910 that it was removed and capped in red tile. All the window tracery here seems to have been renewed, though the e. window has been done in an attractive *Decorated* style. The porch is very appealing, with its rough rural outer arch and 'battlemented' capitals, tiny figure niches above and a heavy, square pediment roofing it over. A *holy water stoup* has had a *piscina* drain put into it – for a porch altar? Inside, the church is most attractive and rural, with creamwashed walls and sympathetic modern furnishings. The much-restored C13 font is of the common design of double-arcading carved on its eight panels. Then there is a fine range of wall paintings on the n. side – and a really lovely C15 *screen* with carving which is intricate yet restrained: all its colour has gone, though traces of colour remain on the sturdy, Decorated chancel arch. In the simple chancel, there are heavy C13 coffin slabs either side of the altar; an unadorned piscina; and near the screen, two brass inscriptions, one dated 1447. To return to the C14 wall paintings, which were discovered originally in 1846: at the w. end is represented the *Seven Deadly Sins* in the form of a tree; a morality play sequence?; and a huge *St. Christopher*. Between the two windows are numerous small scenes, among them, at top left, Christ with bound hands before Pilate; in the centre, very faintly, the Last Supper; below centre, what looks like a *consecration cross*; top right, Crucifixion; immediately below, the Crown of Thorns being placed on Christ's head; very good in the window splay is Christ's agony in the Garden of Gethsemene. Set into the opposite splay of the window is the old *rood stair* entrance, now filled in.

Dilham, St Nicholas (F4): As long ago as 1700 the churchwardens reported that the church was 'much dilapidated, its buttresses much decayed, and the porch fallen down.' In 1775 it was meanly rebuilt in red brick with wooden windows, but in 1931 all this was pulled down and a new start made. The result is a simple, well finished, but unexciting

building. The only things of interest are the base of the original round tower, the C15 font, and the arms of George III.

Drayton, St Margaret (D5): Architecturally over-restored, much interior 'beautifications' (also exterior 'homes & gardens' *lych-gate*) – and evidently all looked after with loving care. The old tower fell in December 1850, rebuilt the following year using the old materials. Chancel and porch rebuilt, nave restored 1866, n. aisle added 1908. Old portions of church, C13 and C14. Good C12 font and attractive C13 *piscina* in chancel. Good Norwich glass of about 1450 in a n. window, probably originally placed in e. window of s. aisle. Don't miss the poignant headstone to John Eke, 1856, on the church path.

East Barsham, All Saints (B3): A church of ancient foundation, much buffeted over the years, but having a great charm of its own. The 'porch' is the first stage of what is left of the C13 tower, with its C17 top, and leads into the nave. Chancel and s. transept (more probably, a *chantry chapel*) long since gone, but foundations are still visible, with brick *groining* below ground level. The nave is a charming hotchpotch, bits of *Norman* (a blocked-up s. doorway), C14 and C15; most windows *Perpendicular*. Among lovely fragments of C15 Norwich glass, two delicious feathered angels, playing pipe and harp, in head of n. window. Of interest, an alabaster sculpture, probably from an altar, of *St Anne* teaching the Virgin to read – there were three pieces of it recovered from a C15 barn nearby when it was demolished: two have since been stolen! A very impressive wall monument to Mrs. Mary Calthorpe, 1640, full of detail and activity, and with a splendidly lofty inscription. Harrod & Linnell's lovely comment in their 'Shell Guide to Norfolk' (Faber, 1957) deserves repetition:

'Lady Calthorpe's shrouded figure

rises from the grave with such vigour and movement that one feels impelled to rush to the roof of the church to applaud her arrival'.

This delightful church, and the breathtaking *Tudor* manor house nearby, make a trip to East Barsham a 'must' for tourers in Norfolk.

Edgefield, St Peter and St Paul (C3): Except that the tower is placed very oddly at the n.e. corner, this church looks like an average medieval building in remarkably good condition. But appearances are deceptive. What we see is the result of virtually one man's vision, enthusiasm, and sheer hard work over many years. That man was Canon Walter Marcon. He was born in the rectory in 1850, came back on the death of his father to follow him as rector in 1876, and died in the same room in which he was born in 1936 – a record scarcely to be equalled and unlikely to be surpassed. At first it seemed to him 'a moral wilderness', and he found the absence of music particularly hard to bear, 'a sort of slow starvation'. Nonetheless, he drew the village to him, and among many other things, determined to do something about the church. It had been isolated since the *Black Death*, far from the present centre of the village, and was in a sorry state of decay, and so – he moved it! It took ten years to raise the £2000 needed and a further two years to complete the building. Apart from the tall octagonal tower still to be found along the road to Hunworth, and the s. porch, the church was dismantled stone by stone and moved to the new site. Some re-arrangements were made, so that the old e. window is now at the w. end, there is no chancel arch, and the chancel is all new work. Consecrated in 1885, the church was completed by having its tower added in 1908. The main *screen* combines C15 painted and gilded sections with new work very effectively, and the small *parclose* screen to the s. aisle chapel is dated 1526. It has two wide

painted panels, with group portraits of the donors, William Harstrong, his wife and family. Defaced though they are, it is good that they too moved with the living church and keep company with the man behind it all – Walter Hubert Marcon.

Edingthorpe, All Saints (F3): An enchanting little church, as picturesque inside as out. Round *Norman* tower, distinctly narrowing to its octagonal top of about 1400 with bell openings filled with agreeable *Decorated* tracery. Attractive porch, with a pretty figure niche over its outer arch; and a late C12 inner doorway of beautifully simple lines, with one kingly head remaining as a *corbel*. The nave and chancel windows are a real pleasure of diverse Decorated designs, from Y-tracery to geometrical (see glossary, *Styles of Architecture*): all different on s. side, a lovely e. window (*reticulated*) and, on n. side, three with splendidly *cusped* tracery. On n. side also, an ancient doorway, late C12, with rough-hewn *jambs* and arch stones. Inside, the church is a delight of rural character, whiteness and colour. A modern, white painted match-boarding roof to the nave looks charmingly in keeping. On the n. there are some fine remnants of wall paintings, with a very good *St Christopher* (against which is a figure niche) and towards the chancel a splendidly carved and painted statue niche with traceried head over the old *rood stair* entrance. Upon an endearingly battered reading desk, facing the stair, is carved the date 1587. The nave has some very apprentice-like bench ends, flat cut-outs rather than carved; a restrained octagonal *Perpendicular* font; a C17 pulpit and, beside its steps, a little *brass* inscription in Latin, no date, invoking prayers for one Raffe Spor. The chancel arch is richly appealing in its roughness, with the slots still evident which once supported *rood beam* and loft. Below it is the church's treasure, a

East Barsham: Calthorpe monument.

lovely old *rood screen*, with an upper part (clearly C14, says *Pevsner* firmly) having two carved wheels with intricate tracery. The panels below have six painted saints, with symbols: *Bartholomew*, knife; *Paul*, bible and sword; *Catherine* (?), bible and palm frond; *James the Great*, staff and scallop shell; *Andrew*, cross; *Peter*, keys. There is a popular local belief that the numerous small holes in the screen are Roundhead bullet holes from the Civil War – a final romantic touch to a memorable little church.

Erpingham, St Mary (D3): Standing away from the village in a big churchyard, mainly late C14 with a fine C15 tower. This has ERPINGHAM picked out round the battlements, the letters interspersed with crowned 'M's for the dedication. The w. door has been well restored and has unusual brackets for figures in the centre panels. There are little figures too in niches on either side of the door as part of the *base course*. Note the *sanctus bell* turret on the gable of the nave. The interior has a spacious feel about it emphasised by the sparkling white walls, plain brick floor, and general air of cleanliness and care. By the door is the font which came from the bombed Norwich church of St Benedict. The figures round the bowl have been recut and given new heads in some cases. Still at the door, look for the large *squint* to the r. of the chancel arch. Through it one can see the *aumbry* (where the Sacrament is reserved) which is offset to the left so that it is in line with the door. At the e. end of the s. aisle is a big *brass* of Sir John de Erpingham who died in 1370, although the brass dates from 1415. He was the father of Shakespeare's 'Old Sir Thomas' of Agincourt fame, who may well have built the tower and aisle here. The e. window contains a beautiful assembly of German and French C16 glass from Steinfeld monastery in Germany (more from the same source is in the Victoria and Albert Museum). The Adoration with the shepherds in

the bottom l. panel is particularly fine. Much of the statuary in the church is good modern work as is the charming head of the Virgin in the window by the font.

Felbrigg, St. Margaret (E3): Now that the estate has passed to the National Trust, Felbrigg is much more accessible and the church, lying some distance across the park from the house, should not be missed. It has a magnificent series of *brasses*, and of them, the one commemorating Sir Simon de Felbrigg and his wife is one of the finest in England. It is in the aisle between the foremost pews, and is over 9ft long and 4ft wide, with two figures under an elaborate and graceful double canopy. Sir Simon was standard-bearer to Richard II, and his wife Margaret was the Queen's cousin and her maid of honour. This is one of only five old brasses remaining in the country to Knights of the Garter. The chancel has a fine e. window and an early C15 *piscina* – ruined by having the sculptor *Joseph Nollekens*' monument to William Windham, of Felbrigg Hall (d.1813) jammed into it. Other windows in the chancel were blocked up to house an astonishing array of Windham monuments, and one to another William (1686) is by *Grinling Gibbons*, having typical swags of flowers and fruit. The two convex tablets close by are beautiful examples of C17 lettering and design. *Box pews* and a series of *hatchments* add to the delights of this church.

Felmingham, St Andrew (E4): The bulky C15 tower has a distinctive look from a distance because there is no parapet and it seems to bulge. There is quite elaborate *flushwork* around the w. door and the sound-holes are traceried. When the remainder of the church was rebuilt in brick in 1742 the good windows on the s. side with *reticulated* tracery were re-used. The roof is mean matchboarding on stark braces and there is no chancel arch. The C19 pulpit has some old tracery incorporated in it which may have come from the *rood screen;* a *griffin, woodwose,* hawk, and dragon can be seen carved in the little *spandrels.* The local style of C14 font shaft with eight attached columns supports the familiar type of C13 Purbeck marble bowl.

Felthorpe, St Margaret(D5): Attractive churchyard with Scots pines standing above pond. Peculiar, oblong tower with large buttresses. Church almost entirely rebuilt in 1846, and a cramped narrow s. aisle added. Variety of windows, C14 to C15. Inside, a curiosity is a glass frame of photos of World War One servicemen – number roughly tallies with the Roll of Honour. A good *Jacobean* chest, nicely carved with *scallop* frieze, inscribed I.T.F. The C19 stained glass is a matter of taste.

Field Dalling, St Andrew (C3): A handsome church, the outside beautifully cared for, the fine C14 *Decorated* tower (which boasts excellent bell-opening tracery) having only recently, in 1977, been restored and repointed. The windows here are a graphic object lesson of the leap from ambitious late Decorated to noble *Perpendicular.* The first is seen in the fine chancel, all of a piece, including its lofty arch, and said to be dated about 1370 (the *hammer beam* roof is modern). Secondly, the large and imposing Perpendicular nave windows on the s. side, in the tracery of which are some good remnants of C15 glass. The trim nave *arcade,* with its slender columns, is C15, like the excellent *arch-braced* roof with elegant *bosses* at the main beam intersections, carved with *Tudor* flowers. In the s.e. corner is the old *rood stair* entrance (outside the spiral stair juts out, with its tiled cap). Earlier this century, *Charles Cox* recorded that 'a piece of the old rood screen, richly painted, blocks up the stairway'. Not now – just a plain little door. What happened to it? Good

C15 octagonal font, carved with the *Instruments of the Passion.* In the chancel, a funny little *angle piscina,* very sweet, with a rather 'Arabian Nights' arch; *dropped sill sedilia* adjoining. The spacious filled-in arch opposite led to a chapel whose remains can be seen outside. The blocked-in priest's door looks *Tudor.* In n. aisle, an unusual lozenge-shaped (ie, like a *hatchment*) *Royal Arms* for the Hanoverian Georges; undated, but pre-1801. There are some old C18 *box pews* here, now serving the charming purpose of 'play squares' for the children. Nearby, the odd little wall niche was probably for a statue. In this aisle, and in the nave, a lot of medieval *poppyheads,* very simple, complete with their C15 benches. On leaving, note the *corbels* supporting the outer arch of the porch, carved with shields showing the Cross of Christ on one side, and that of *St Andrew* – an 'X' – the church's patron saint, on the other. By the gate is the stump of the ancient preaching cross.

Filby, All Saints (G5): Tall tower with prominent stepped and panelled battlements, with figures of the *Four Latin Doctors* of the Church at the corners. All the windows have been re-worked in the course of restoration except the diminutive *clerestory* circles and *quatrefoils.* The font is C13 Purbeck marble, made to look like new. Near it, the tower stairs door is most odd – heavily banded with iron and with a profusion of locks, it is probably a re-used medieval chest top. The recently restored base of the *rood screen* is very good. Virtually no defacement mars the painted figures, and much of the minor decoration survives. l to r. *St Cecilia, St George, St Catherine of Alexandria, St Peter, St Paul, St Margaret of Antioch, St Michael, St Barbara.* In the chancel, the 'Lucas Angel' monument is a fine piece by Hermann of Dresden. Three *ledger stones* witness 140 years of continuous ministry by successive rectors, 1681-1820.

Fishley, St Mary (F5): This little church is so closely guarded by a thick grove of pines, oaks, and limes, that were it not for the tower one would take it for a copse in the middle of open fields. Less than a mile from the w. outskirts of Acle, its isolation seems absolute. Even after the narrow byroad, there is a long path between high hedges before one reaches the churchyard, and from the e. end the open country drops away to the marshes and the river. The round *Norman* tower has a later top of narrow red bricks with early C14 bell openings. The s. door is also simple Norman work with a *billet* frieze, but drastically re-cut in the 1861 restoration. Everything was rebuilt then and calls for little comment. There is a pretty little C18 chamber organ at the w. end.

Foulsham, The Holy Innocents (C4): The late C15 tower is very handsome. It has *flushwork* around the door and in the *base course*, and the shields in the doorway *spandrels* have the arms of England and Lord Morely. The sound-holes have a honeycomb pattern of lozenges and the stepped battlements are a rich mixture of *cusped* panels and 'M's. To the n.w. of the tower is a table tomb with decorative panels and groups of crowned letters. They spell 'Robert Colles, Cecily his wife' – Foulsham people in 1500. Apart from the mainly Victorian e. window with its strident glass and the roof, the chancel is C14 and this is the date of the lavish *sedilia* and *piscina*, although C19 restoration has overlaid them heavily. The priest's door is tucked away behind the chancel arch on the n. side and its position is curiously improbable. It lies at an angle within the corner formed by the chancel and the n. aisle, and the internal arch shows that this was intentional. There seems no reason why a conventional placing should not have been chosen further along the wall, and there must have been a reason for the extra cost and obvious inconvenience. What was it? The nave still retains three circular piers on the n. side from the earlier C13

building, but the most noticeable thing here is the plaster ceiling – it looks sadly out of place, and its incongruity is emphasised by its immensity. The village was devastated by fire in 1770 and this ceiling is the most permanent reminder. So much of the church was damaged by the fire that few of the original fittings remain, but one might assume that the font did – until the eye lights on an account written in 1846:

'The font consists of a circular mar-ble basin placed on a modern stone pedestal. . .'

The present one is a very good C19 reproduction of what one would have expected to find here. One of the survivors of the fire is a fine wall monu-ment in the chancel to Sir Thomas Hunt (d.1616). He kneels in company with his three wives (he always mar-ried widows, it seems) under triple arches, his coloured coat of arms above: behind him, resting against the wall, is his sword – not in alabaster, but the real thing. A *brass* which also survived is by the lectern . . . a cautionary example of 'you can't take it with you':

Of all I had this only now I have
Nyne akers, wch unto ye poore I gave
Richard Fenn who died March 6 1565

Foxley, St Thomas (C4): Some of the quoins (cornerstones) and the coursed flintwork below the windows on the s. side point to an early original, but the present chancel dates from the late C13 and the tower followed about a century later. The late C15 porch has a nice outer arch with a niche, a shield in one *spandrel* and a ragged staff in the other, a possible reference to the builder's coat of arms? The inner door is older and may be C14. The plain C14 font has a pleasing C18 candle-snuffer cover topped by a gilded dove, and over it is a Regency gallery. The bench ends have *poppyheads* of varying naive designs, with a mask on one and the initials

designed by Robert *Adam* and it is well worth the trek along the rough road through the 1000 acre park to see it. Sir William Harbord commissioned it in 1769 to complement his new house rather as a garden temple would. Although close to the house, it was intended to be almost hidden by trees and when one comes across it suddenly the effect of the classical portico on six great Grecian columns is dramatic. It is severely simple in grey brick, with high windows in the side walls only. Inside, calm simplicity is the keynote again but with richness added. The original plaster ceiling fell in 1976 but has been faithfully restored – a large oval design with centre-piece of feathers and acanthus leaves. Both the *reredos* and the w. gallery are in dark oak with *Corinthian* columns, and on either side of the tall entrance doors the family pews are raised above the others. They have brass candle sconces and a fine set of 1764 Cambridge prayer books. The beautifully tooled bindings have centre labels 'Gunton Chapel 1769' and are faded, but if you turn them over the brilliance of the green and crimson inlays shines again. The church is now in the care of the Redundant Churches Fund and is still used for occasional services. Long may it be so.

Halvergate, St Peter and St Paul (G6): From the s.w. the lovely C15 tower has a perfect setting, with its stepped battlements rising among the trees. It has deep *arcading* in *flushwork* as a *base course*, and a most unusual double range of sound-holes. They are exceptionally small for a tower of this size, and the upper ones have a pretty wheel design. There were figures of the *Four Latin Doctors* on the corner pinnacles until the C19, but they were replaced by others which Dr *Pevsner* describes as 'rustic C19 folk-art', and three of them now stand rather disconsolately around the s. porch, as though craving admittance or pondering upon a summary ejection. The s. door is the best individual feature here, and its *crocketted*,

ogee arch flanked by shafts is excellent. The church was heavily restored in 1874 when the exterior of the chancel was completely refaced and the windows renewed. An early C14 *St Christopher* in the head of a nave n. window was being restored in 1980, but is scheduled for return and should not be overlooked. There are rubbings of an interesting *palimpsest brass* in the chancel – the head of a Yarmouth Franciscan monk (c.1440) on one side, and the bust of Robert Swanes' wife (c.1540) on the other. The brass itself is kept safely in the vestry.

Hanworth, St Bartholomew (D3): Driving through Hanworth village, with its protected Common Land, and on through the park-like landscape to the church on its knoll, is a pleasing excursion into old England. Especially when you enter a churchyard elegant as a gentleman's garden – then turn to get a fine view of the splendid *William & Mary* hall (late C17) across the fields. First appearances are against the church at close view – a 'blind' n. wall (traces of two windows – Saxon?) and nave and porch faced with crumbling plasterwork. But this is a place which repays a little time and attention. The tall, flint *Perpendicular* tower is fine, topped by very odd little red-brick Tudor-like pinnacles, with nice angle buttresses and a hefty tower stair. On the s. side of the church, between modern vestry and end of s. aisle, interesting case of an 'adapted' window, with *Decorated* tracery most coarsely filled in. The s. aisle has very simple Perpendicular windows, with a nice arch to a small door. High on side of chancel, note a curious little *trefoil* opening, blocked in to make way for window below. The e. window has lovely, uncluttered and flowing tracery – a very good example of pre-*Black Death* (1349) workmanship. Inside, the charm of the little *clerestory* windows, with rather flattened arches, at once impresses – and unusually, there are double the number of windows as arches in the rather rustic Perpendicular *arcade* below. So many details of interest in this church, that they must be listed succinctly: the apparently crude and battered chancel arch in fact shows, most fascinatingly, the shapes and indentations of the fittings of the *rood loft*, torn out at the *Reformation*; the heavy pew now at the back of the s. aisle was the old hall pew in more hierarchical days; the *Royal Arms* hanging over the chancel arch are those of Queen Anne, 1702-14; hanging either side of the arch are two Elizabethan helmets – they were found in the lake in the grounds of the nearby hall some years ago; the charming little organ is an original by *'Father' Willis* himself, founder of the famous London organ firm, built in 1865 for £70. The Barclays at the hall seem good at finding things. Apart from those helmets, a great find in the 1890s (by the grandfather of the present squire) was the massive *mensa* slab, discovered buried in the churchyard, which in pre-Reformation times had formed the High Altar. It was put back in its place, and encased in the present wooden altar.

Happisburgh, St Mary (F3): It stands gauntly sentinel, between village and sea, the great 110ft *Perpendicular* tower being truly striking on approach from Walcott. It is of four stages, supported by powerful buttresses which extend right up to the *flushwork* and panelled battlements; there are great three-light bell openings, large square sound-holes in the third stage with delightfully lacy tracery, an enormous and noble Perpendicular w. window and below it, all of a piece, a fine doorway decorated with shields. The tower has a particularly fine *base course* with deep *arcading*. From the s. the prospect is equally grand, the *clerestory*, aisle and two-storey porch, all Perpendicular, having identical panelled battlements with the tower. There is a square headed window high at the nave e. end, over the chancel arch, which is infrequent enough to deserve note. The C14 *Decorated* chancel is part of the earlier church, largely replaced in the C15 rebuilding; its n. side facing the sea is much restored, all the windows, including what must have been a delightful little clerestory, being filled in. The e. window is good Perpendicular with two kingly *corbel* heads to its *dripstone*. The s. chancel windows have beautiful Decorated tracery, but look like replacements. At this point also can be seen the outline of a two-bay chapel, said to have been demolished during the C15 rebuilding. What is less easy to understand is the roof-ridge outline at the w. end of the s. aisle: if it was a chapel, it was in a very unusual position. Entering through the handsome two-storey Perpendicular porch, we come to a grand and spacious interior. What takes the eye at once is the magnificent font, its superb carvings in an astonishingly fine state of preservation; this C15 treasure has the *Symbols of the Evangelists* around the bowl, alternating with angels playing musical instruments; with round the stem alternating lions and *woodwoses* (wild men) . . . all looking wonderfully benign. Modern pews and *arch-braced* roof; a basically C15 *screen*, but much restored and altered; handsome C15 five-bay *arcade* (note at e. end, on n. side, there is a cut-away pillar, indicating a lower arcade in the earlier church). In the s. aisle there is a *piscina* niche, and nearby a big oblong niche with the remnants of what must have been a splendid stone canopy: no doubt these served a *Guild Altar* in pre-Reformation times. The chancel has a piscina, contemporary with the C14 fabric, with a rich, *crocketted* arch; the arcade outline on the s. wall of the disappeared chapel; some good re-used medieval *poppyheads*; and – an intriguing feature – high up on each wall a single, very small stone corbel, whose original use is unclear.

Hassingham, St Mary (F6): This small church stands beautifully on a hillock above a quiet lane that leads through a grove of sallows to the marshes. The round *Norman* tower has a later octagonal battlemented top, and the chancel roof is higher than the nave, imparting a most individual profile to the building. Entry is by way of a simple Norman doorway, and once inside, the whole impression is one of clean austerity. White walls, glazed brick floors in grey and russet; beech interlocking chairs, beech reading desk and altar, all upholstery in black fabric. A gift for a flower arranger. Much of this came about because of a fire in 1971 which gutted the building – although the nice C17 chest escaped damage. Altogether a good example of sensible and sympathetic restoration. Note that the new floor level in the chancel has left the *piscina* high and dry, and also the very narrow *banner stave locker* in the n. wall of the nave. By the gate there is that lovely admonition which ends:

> 'O gently, gently shoulds't thou speak,
> And softly, softly tread,
> Where in the church's peaceful shade,
> With solemn words the dead are laid
> In their last lowly bed'.

Haveringland, St Peter (D4): One of Norfolk's many wartime airfields transformed this parish for a while with runways and buildings breaking up the old pattern of lanes and hedges. Now, a turkey farm and open fields have changed the scene again, leaving St Peter's in a sort of no man's land, approached by one of the wartime concrete tracks. The round *Norman* tower has a C14 square headed window at ground floor level which matches one at the w. end of the n. aisle. Apart from that and the C15 font, virtually everything else was rebuilt in 1858. All good solid stuff but not too interesting.

Hemblington, All Saints (F5): Remote in the deep countryside and interesting

in outline. It has a round Norman tower with very basic bell openings and, atop the tower, an odd little 'cap'. Nave predominantly early C14, most windows having attractive flowing tracery of the *Decorated* period, and one being simple *Perpendicular*. The chancel windows are simply Y-tracery of about 1300; but the e. window is a poor modern replacement. The little entrance porch has a charming brick outer arch and *hood mould* (early C16) with simple crosses in *knapped flint* set flush into the walls on both sides and above. The inner arch is attractive C14 Decorated. Inside, a feast of curiosities awaits. One is arrested at once by the enormous *St Christopher* mural on the facing wall, which was discovered in 1937 under layers of plaster. Enough to say here that it shows a huge St Christopher at centre – he having been in legend a heathen giant – astride a rushing stream with the Christ-child on his shoulder. On the left bank were representations of incidents in his life before his conversion, but most of these are gone; on the right however are no less than ten episodes after his conversion, all of which are clearly recognisable. A wonderful treasure! To right of the mural, a precarious open staircase, set into the window embrasure, led to the old *rood loft*. Just to its right there is a tall canopied niche in the nave e. wall, with some original colouring; on the opposite side, in like position, a most odd, coarsely constructed double recess, again with colour; adjacent, in n. wall behind the pulpit, a plain, deep niche connected by a tiny passage to a crude *piscina*; and built onto the sill of the immediately adjoining window, a square plain pedestal . . . all these things are run together so as to suggest that all served to hold saints' statues. Very likely there were *guild altars* in these two corners of the nave, as it is definitely recorded that in pre-*Reformation* times 'lights' were maintained in this church to three saints. The pulpit just mentioned is C18, neatly panelled, with backboard and *tester*. Several good old benches with *poppyheads* here, some with attractive animal carvings. To left of s. entrance door, an incised C14 stone coffin-lid is placed against the wall. Some seven brass inscriptions, from 1480 to 1630, are set into the nave pavements. Look up now – the roof has its original C15 *arch-brace* beams and simply carved *wall posts*. No chancel arch as such, but a massive cross-beam with 'Tudor cottage' vertical timbers and plaster above. The simple, white-painted chancel has a modern barrel roof, very agreeable; one window is let down to form a *dropped sill sedilia*; beside it, a large, plain angle piscina. Finally, this super little church's beautiful medieval octagonal font, whose carvings (with most subtle modern colouring) are very unusual. It has seated figures set into each face of the bowl, and eight standing figures in niches around the stem. Above, starting from w., God as Holy Trinity, Saints *Augustine of Hippo, Edmund the Confessor, Barbara, Agatha* and an apostle. Around stem: Saints *Leonard, Catherine, Stephen, Citha, Lawrence* and *Margaret of Antioch*; a monk, and a gowned figure.

Hempstead (near Holt), All Saints (D3): A pretty little church, set well back from the village street in a well-kept churchyard. As you approach, the tiny little rounded chancel catches the eye, in neat flint and with a fussily detailed thatched roof as whimsical as a ginger-bread house from 'Hansel and Gretel'. This part was built only in 1925. At the opposite end of the church, there's a solid, stumpy little red brick tower – rebuilt, in 1744, more for form than appearances! Inside, the church is charmingly simple and rural – and lovingly looked after. It has little to show of its ancient past: a severely simple round-headed archway into the vestry, wholly without ornament, is 'reputed to be pre-*Norman*', it's said locally; a w. window with simple *plate tracery* of the early geometrical form from the middle years of the C13; and

a much-battered bench end, on the nave n. side, with mutilated *poppy-heads*. The nave windows are probably C17, the stained glass Victorian. The little west gallery, complete with tiny organ and choir-boy graffiti on the book rests, is delightful. Don't miss the brass memorial wall tablet (like everything else in this appealing place, polished until it gleams) in the n.e. corner of the nave to one 'Edmund Hunt of the gentry' – that he was descended from Thos. Hunt, soap boiler, of London, is tactfully overlooked – who, 'having lived long in service of his King and country', finally 'climbed to the stars of the sky' in February 1610.

Hempstead (near Stalham), St Andrew (G4): A pretty, quiet church in quiet countryside, its plain C15 tower having a very good w. window with agreeable tracery and 'battlemented' transoms (cross pieces), all recently most skilfully restored. The big *Perpendicular* windows to n. and s. of the nave have the same curious *corbels* to their *dripstones* as seen at Swafield, not far away. As conjectured then – Seahorses? At the w. end of the nave, each side of the tower, are (*Decorated*) windows, one filled in – indicating former aisles, which were taken in to make the present unusually wide nave. Look for the C13 *lancets* on n. and s. of chancel, and on s. a super little *Early English* priest's door. Possibly original Y-traceried window to right (about 1300), as might be the e. window with three stepped lancets under one arch. The neat C15 porch, with flush-panelled battlements, formerly had an upper room lit by a delightfully worked two light window separated by a figure niche; but these are now filled in and the porch open to its roof. Inside, a plain modern *arch-braced* roof spans the spacious nave and frames a rather coarse chancel arch – below which is an immensely pleasing C15 *screen*, battered but beautiful, with a fine display of painted saints. There were 16 originally but not all are intact. Recognisable (from l.) are *Juliana*, with the devil haltered on a rope; *Theobald* as a bishop; likewise represented, but wrongly, a rare *John of Bridlington*; *Dionysius (Denys)* with crozier . . . and his own severed head; a martial *George*; *Stephen* with an armful of stones; *Lawrence* with his grid; and a rare *Eligius*, patron of farriers, with hammer . . . and severed horse's leg (for all these, see glossary under *Saints*). A quartet of old *poppyheads* adorns the front pews; there is a gorgeous *Jacobean* pulpit on legs; behind it, the *rood stair*; opposite, a *piscina* with handsome Perpendicular canopy and inside it, on the right, an inner recess for the cruets used in the Eucharist. The plain chancel has a nicely arched (C14?) *piscina* with a flower drain; and a charming little *dropped sill sedilia*. The windows, already described, add great character, including a *low side window* on n. side opposite which is a splendid Jacobean reading desk. Note, as you leave, the C15 font in honey-coloured stone, with roses and plain shields around the bowl, and funny woolly lions on sentry duty round the stem.

Hemsby, St Mary (G5): Large and spacious interior with nave and chancel under one roof. The s. porch has an upper room and is vaulted with a series of *bosses* – unusual in a village church. They depict: God the Father, the Resurrection, Assumption, Ascension, *Annunciation* and Nativity. Close by the *screen* in the s. wall of the nave is a *piscina* which has a surprise inside – the drain is set within a lion's mask. In the chancel s. wall, a 1908 window has good glass by W. Aikman; showing *St George*, and a woman knitting. Further along, armorial glass of the Ferrier family. The church has been heavily restored and most of the fittings are modern, but a print of 1840 shows it with *Jacobean* screen, *three-decker pulpit* and *box pews*. The base of an ancient *sanctuary cross* is by the

churchyard gate, and around are many good C18 and C19 headstones.

Hevingham, St Mary the Virgin and St Botolph (D4): Stands well away from the centre of the village on the road to Aylsham. It is a big church, and even from a distance the lacy tracery in the s. transept window, the *Decorated* butterfly motifs in the s. nave windows, and the massive s. porch catch the eye. The great chestnut tree in front was planted in 1610, and you might like to check to see if it really does measure 19ft round. There was a thorough-going restoration here in the late C19 which introduced a lot of new work, but the *angle piscina* shows that the chancel must have been built around 1300. The C15 porch has an elaborate window for the upper room – two canopied niches one above the other, flanked by traceried windows – but the room itself has lost its floor, so that its little staircase leads nowhere now. Nearly all Norfolk fonts are octagonal but here we have a hexagon, and quite unlike its brethren in design. The traceried top panels are largely C19 restoration but the bottom half is C14, and has clustered columns at the angles. The figures in the deep niches are very worn and mutilated although the Crucifixion at the w. is easily recognisable. The most memorable thing in the church is the set of four benches in the chancel. They are low, with broad tops and were patently designed for school use. The fronts and end have blank arcading – *cusped* arches between half-round columns with varied carving in the *spandrels*; and all in oak which has gone silvery with age in a way no restorer can imitate (compare the two original tops with the two replacements). These marvellously solid pieces are said to have been used in the porch chamber when it was a schoolroom, but their length makes this questionable if you look at the access stair. Still, they predate the porch and could conceivably have been put in during building, and then lowered when the floor was taken out. The chancel has another choice item. When St George's at Gt. Yarmouth was restored in 1882, the superb 20-branch candelabrum, given to the church by its Warden Thomas Grimston in 1741, was sold. Hevingham's rector bought it for £4 and here it still is, in a setting worthy of its quality. High up on either side of the chancel arch, note the four stone brackets which carried the *rood*, showing that it spanned the whole church here and not just the arch. The big blank arch on the n. side is all that remains of a n. transept, and a big village *tithe* map of 1838 now hangs there. The s. transept arch has been filled with a glazed screen to form a self-contained Lady chapel. Furnished and carpeted in simple style, it is a sensible arrangement for a country parish with a small population and huge church.

Heydon, St Peter and St Paul (D4): A blissfully peaceful place, and one of Norfolk's most attractive villages, but particularly in summer when sheep crop the grass in the churchyard and loll against the gravestones like super-annuated clubmen after a good lunch. The C15 tower has bold *string courses*, a staircase turret that reaches the battlements, and sound-holes with inset shields. The dressed flints are packed round with little shards of the same stone – a feature known as 'galletting' often used on Norfolk churches and a marvellous defence against frost and damp. The w. doors are original, with excellent tracery – a trail of *quatrefoils* round the edge and two stools for images like the ones at Erpingham. The tower was part of a great modernisation in the C15, when the walls of the nave were raised, the aisles rebuilt, and the porches added. The s. porch has a vault with a 'Lord in Glory' centre *boss*, and the upper room doorway to the church is high in the wall, which means that it was probably used as a treasury. The late C14 *arcades* and the windows at the w. end of the aisle were kept, but

the *clerestory* of alternating two-light and quatrefoil windows may be either all C15, or a mixture of old and new. Surviving from an even earlier church is the C13 font – a big rounded tub with smooth roll mouldings, looking itself as chubby as a well nourished baby. Repairs in 1970 brought to light a most remarkable series of C14 paintings. On the n. aisle we can now see part of a '*three living and three dead*' sequence – one of the ways that the church in the middle ages used to point out the transience of earthly things. The 'dead' are three skeletons (the skulls are visible), and the 'living' are three kings. The 8ft figures of two of them are beautifully clear, one with a hawk at his wrist and one with a sceptre. The n.e. chapel was dedicated to *St John the Baptist*, and fragments of a series of illustrating his life and death have been uncovered. In the s. aisle Lady chapel, two other sequences have come to light. High in the s.e. corner there is an exquisite head and shoulders of a crowned woman (as yet unidentified) which really merits study through binoculars. On the n. side of the altar, a sequence dating from the late C14 has two kings in ermine robes bearing gifts; they stand behind a kneeling figure and may have been part of a nativity scene. Another survivor from the earlier church is the C13 sacristy door in the n. wall of the chancel – look at the bottom and you can see where the original floor level was. There is a very plain *Easter Sepulchre* recess beside it which has just a trace of colour. The fittings in the church are more than usually interesting because a number of them can be dated. The tall *rood screen* was given by John Dynne in 1480 according to the inscription on the rail, and the panels still have coloured diaper decoration. The 1930s restoration was a bit cavalier and there is no coving or *loft*. The pulpit, a lovely solid piece on a wine glass stem, was given in 1470. The C17 backboard has an inset Flemish carving of the Last Supper dating from the

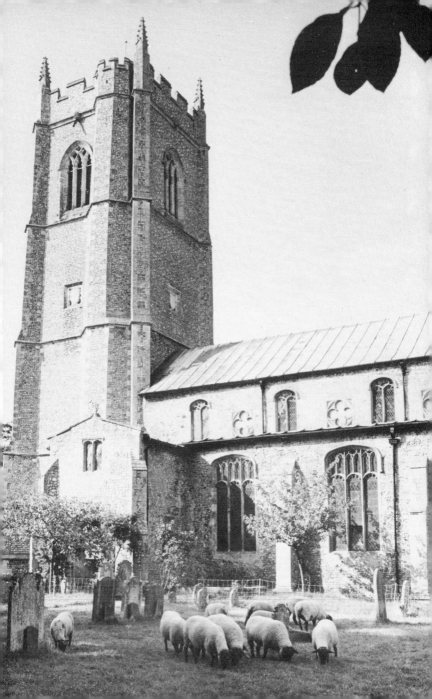

1640s, and the C19 stairs incorporated balusters from the old communion rails. The big manorial box pew built on to the w. side of the chancel screen is very good joinery of 1696, and has its own bible box on the wall. All monuments in the church pale before the majesty of a 12ft x 6ft black slab at the e. end of the n. aisle. They say it broke three bridges on the way to Heydon and the back of one of the men who laid it. It is guarded by a tall and very spiky wrought iron screen, and under it lies Erasmus Earle – M.P. in the Long Paliament from 1640 and Sergeant at Law to Cromwell, who doubtless worshipped here when he stayed at the Hall. Earle passed Christmas Day 1648 sentencing to death the men who raided the Norwich powder magazine which blew up and left St Peter Mancroft windowless. The family of Heydon left the village to settle in Baconsthorpe in 1447, but a unique reminder of their presence hangs on a pillar at the w. end by the font. It is a green painted wooden shield, with the cross of St George and the family name crowned at the top. It may well have been carried in procession – perhaps once only at the funeral of a Heydon returned from the Crusades, in the way that hatchments were used in a later age. This church is not only full of interest, it is full of information. The captions and displays for the benefit of visitors are first class.

Hickling, St Mary (G4): One of the best w. tower elevations in the area, with door, window, niche and sound-hole, all melded into one harmonious composition: a pity that the buttresses stop short at the bell stage and spoil the total effect. Rigorous and repeated C19 restoration has left the church interior rather harsh. Good wall monument in chancel to John Calthrop (d.1688). The tomb chest in the n.e. corner of the n. aisle is covered with C17 graffiti, including Nine Men's Morris frames and 'Roundeheade 1645'. Nearby is a very rich C13 coffin lid, with a floriated cross and a border inscription in Lom-

bardic capitals. The 'melon-legged' communion table is Jacobean.

Hindringham, St Martin (B3): To find so large and fine a church in this tiny village comes as something of a surprise: approaching from the e. end, the visitor's pleasure is redoubled at sight of the magnificent Decorated e. window (though the chancel itself was partly rebuilt in 1870). Move round to the s. and the impression becomes still grander – the tall, slim, beautifully proportioned Decorated tower, with lovely detailed tracery in the bell openings; and the stately Perpendicular aisle windows, finely balanced by the later Perpendicular clerestory windows. The interior proportions are splendid, with the chancel weeping heavily to the s. The five-bay arcades of the nave are C14 Decorated, as is the chancel arch and the two-bay chancel arcade; though the tower arch and the good w. window are later, and Perpendicular. The splendid font deserves close attention – octagonal, C15, richly carved with the Crucifixion, the Arms of England quartering France, the Emblems of the Trinity and the Instruments of the Passion. In the s.e. corner of the nave is Hindringham's greatest treasure: a remarkable chest which is probably the earliest of its kind in England. In the authoritative 'History of Oak Furniture' (The Connoisseur, 1920) Fred Roe says: 'It can hardly have emanated from a later period than the last quarter of the C12', and he places it at about 1175. By the chest is a huge former squint, and an angle piscina – indicating the presence in medieval times of an altar here (see glossary, chantry chapels/guild altars). Note either side of the n. pier of the chancel arch the remains of the rood stairs. Restoration lies heavily upon the chancel itself, including the massively reconstructed triple sedilia, and a blocked-in priest's door.

Holt, St Andrew (C3): Heavy-handed

restorations in the last century have left rather a dull building. Without its spire, the tower sits heavily and the southern vestry extension is quite nasty. Still a nice little *sanctus bell cote* however. Interior *arcades* and chancel arch all of the early C14 and so is the s. aisle *piscina*, which has a large *consecration cross* within. The double piscina and *sedilia* in the chancel are *Decorated* with large headstops. Monument to Edmund Hobart (d.1666) in the chancel by *Linton of Norwich* records that he

> '. . . escaped the malice of the Usurper who . . . sought after his life . . . but his Loyalty carried him steadfast through Ye storms of that Unnatural Rebellion & here at last he found rest'.

Honing, St Peter & St Paul (F4): Sitting handsomely on raised ground above the village, the church has a fine, slim and lofty *Perpendicular* tower, with a good w. window divided by a central transom (cross piece); below the window was a fine doorway, now filled in by a window with woefully out-of-place intersecting tracery and with red brick. This 'addition' presumably dates from the 1795 reconstruction which provided the church with its highly individual body. The chancel was cut down to form a mere alcove inside, and the aisle walls rebuilt and given the same drear tracery as in the tower insertion. Inside one finds that the aisles are no more than passage-ways, and it has been generally assumed that they were narrowed down to this width when the walls were rebuilt. But as *Pevsner* has logically pointed out, the C15 Perpendicular porch is intact, and unless it was rebuilt stone by stone – a most unlikely possibility in the artistic climate of the late C18 – it must therefore indicate the original building line. Rather gaunt inside, with those passage-way aisles, the coarse, heavy *arcade* pillars and arches (of about 1500), the earlier, graceful chancel arch and the 'indent' chancel, oddly combining. But at least, it is different – especially with

the C18 roof, a sensible, solid, barn-like construction, sitting right across the nave, arcades and aisles in one span. *Rood stair* and loft entrance in the tiny chancel interestingly give a better idea than most of how the *rood loft* would have 'sat'. Between the choir stalls is an attractive little *brass* to Nicholas Parker, 1496, he in armour and his hair flowing full and free. The time-weathered C13 octagonal font bowl, of the common variety, carved with shallow arcading, stands on a later and more richly carved Perpendicular stem. Two *hatchments* hang on the n. wall.

Horning, St Benedict (F5): Before going in, note the C13 priest's doorway on the s. side of the chancel, which has *dogtooth* decoration round the arch. There was formerly a n. aisle of the same date, but only the *arcade* remains, embodied in the nave wall. The tower, which has figures rather than pinnacles, the s. arcade, and the w. window of the s. aisle are all C14. In the s. porch is a very decayed C13 chest still held together by fine ironwork. A tiny *squint* in the n. wall of the chancel is a reminder that there was once a chapel where the vestry now is (see glossary, *chantry chapels/guild chapels*). The benchends in the chancel have panels of crude carving below the *poppyheads*, and pierced buttresses on which sit grotesques. One panel on the n. side shows the earliest version of the arms of St Benet's Abbey (whose ruins are a few miles away near Ludham, on the bank of the River Bure). The church has a pottery alms dish, with a *wherry boat* design in the centre – a nice idea.

Horsey, All Saints (G4): The round *Norman* tower has a C15 octagonal top, the haunt of owls and harriers, and the whole church is thatched. The interior, with its simple roof exposing the under-side of the reeds, imparts the homely feeling of a *tithe barn*. There is a simple square-headed *screen* with *ogee arches*, and the sanctuary boasts three little *aumbries* all in a row. A window in the chancel to Miss Catherine Ursula Rising (d.1890) is a good period portrait of the lady herself, posed as an artist before an easel.

Horsford, All Saints (D5): A pleasant thatched church, with a C15 tower (about 1456, says *Blomefield*). *Early English* chancel, with original triple-*lancet* e. window; *Decorated* period nave with square-headed windows; n. aisle built in 1869 when the first of two heavy restorations took place, which manage to make the whole church look Victorian. Square font of Purbeck marble of late *Norman* date. There's a nice plain C16 *screen* with good tracery (the brown paint which not many years ago obscured it has now been removed); also a *Stuart* table and a *low-side window* in the chancel containing note-worthy armorial glass to the ancient Barrett-Lennard family, who held the manor and estate of Horsford by direct family descent from the time of the Conqueror until 1973 when the 35th Lord of the Manor, Sir Richard, sold up to Norwich Corporation to make way for improvements to Norwich aiport. . . The pews in the church came from St Mary's, Tunstead. The altar rails were made from balusters of the staircase at Didlington Hall, deep in the Brecklands of south Norfolk, now demolished. Note two poignant commentaries on their times: a stained glass memorial to three consumptive sisters who died, 1891-93, in Davos and Cairo; and out-side, a headstone near the path to eleven years old John Pirsins, who died serving on a man o' war in the battle of Camperdown, Oct. 11th, 1797 (in which the Dutch were defeated by a British fleet under Admiral Lord Duncan).

Horsham St Faith, Blessed Virgin & St Andrew (E5): An imposing church with a *Decorated* tower, the rest *Perpendicular*, as in the arch between tower and nave, but excepting the original *Early English* e. wall of the

chancel, with distinctive *lancet* win-dows. Exterior wall has fine flint and stone chequer pattern. The two-storied s. porch has a *groined* roof with – most unusual – a figure of St Andrew bound to the cross. Inside, well carved octagonal font of about 1450, with fine *Jacobean* cover; C15 nave *arcades*; a *rood screen* with painted panels, dated 1528 and with names of the donors; C14 oak lectern; a set of medieval stalls, three each side, with *misericords* (from elsewhere?) with good small heads; a few old *poppyhead* benches in n. aisle. Most interesting pulpit, dated 1480, with painted panels, recently restored, of unusual saints, *St Faith* with saw, and *St Wandregisil* (see glossary, *Saints*). In chancel, there is a head bracket on one wall from which was suspended the *Lenten veil*. On n. wall, *brass* to Geoffrey Langeley, 1437, Prior of Hor-sham St Faith (remains of the priory, whose monks are said to have built this church, are now part of nearby Abbey Farm).

Horstead, All Saints (E5): Apart from the C13 tower and the pleasing C14 doorway, the whole church is a re-building of 1879. There is some good stained glass. In the s. aisle, a *William Morris* window has two brilliant figures, Courage and Humility, designed by *Sir Edward Burne-Jones* (d.1898). The chancel e. window is rather overpowering – separate wreaths for all the virtues hang in heavy foliage in the top. Below, however, are four large figures of some interest: Bishop Herbert de Losinga with Norwich Cathedral – the building which he began in 1096; The Virgin Crowned; *St Nicholas of Myra* (otherwise known as Santa Claus!) with the three little boys in a pickling tub whom he miraculously restored to life (see glossary, *Saints*, for another exciting episode!); and also, with her church, *Mother Julian of Norwich* – the celebrated anchoress and mystic who in the late C14 wrote 'Revelations of Divine Love'. The nave monument to John Langley Watts (d.1774) is a very nicely balanced composition in various marbles. The *Royal Arms* of Anne are decidedly murky.

Houghton, St Giles (B3): Rebuilt in the 1870s, but a lot of the original materials re-used. The C15 *screen* is back in place and although, as so often, the faces of the saints are mutilated, much of their original colour remains. From l. to r. they are: *Emeria, Mary Salome* with her sons, *Elizabeth* with her son, *Anne, Gregory, Jerome, Ambrose, Augustine* of Hippo, *Silvester* and *Clement*. The stencil decoration on the back of the screen can still be seen. The *Stuart* altar rails have simple, homely turning.

Hoveton, St John (F5): A *Norman* or earlier church stood here, witness the *carstone* corner *quoins* of the n.e. corner of the nave, visible from the path. The tower is rustic red brick of 1765. There has been much restoration inside, and the modest C15 *screen* is painted brown. In the heads of the plumply *Perpendicular* n. windows there are fragments of good medieval glass, including a figure of *St John* with the devil peeping from his chalice. A tablet on the chancel s. wall, with an urn fronting crossed sword and musket, records that John Spencer Blofeld of the 5th Madras Infantry 'fell a Victim to his Exertions in camp near Hyderabad' in 1803. Above are five *hatchments*. Outside, below the e. window it is recorded that George Brown died at 73 in 1757, having been 'an useful, honest and faithful servant to Thomas Blofeld' for 37 years. The sequence of adjectives is revealing. An oddity by the path to the gate – an oaken memorial slab set upright in a wrought iron decorative frame, to Amos Thrower (d.1882), which is just legible after 100 years.

Hoveton, St Peter (F5): This small church is down a lane off to the w. of the Wroxham-Stalham road, about a mile n. of Hoveton St John. A simple, neat building of red brick, with a thatched roof, little *bell cote*, and crow-stepped gables, it carries its date of 1624 above the arch of the porch. Behind it, open fields stretch away to Hoveton Hall. The set of *Stuart* arms above the w. window are nicely carved in relief against a painted background, and have been re-gilded. The pulpit is of the same period as the building, and there is a series of seven *hatchments* hung around the walls. On the monument to Mrs Aufrere (d.1750) and her daughter, the lettering is cleverly cut over the folds of marble drapery held by a *putto*.

Hunworth, St Lawrence (C3): One of the starkest of interiors in the county, but not uncomfortably so. In fact, the church has an almost Scandinavian simplicity about it. Tall whitewashed walls reach up to *arch-braced* roofs, with no memorial tablets to distract the eye save one – the record of the six men of Hunworth who did not return in 1918. The one spot of colour in the nave comes from a diminutive modern statue of *St Lawrence*. Holding his gridiron like a shield at rest, he stands in a pretty little 12in niche cut on the angle of the C14 window embrasure on the n. side. A Lady chapel opens off the nave to the s. and has fine, big C15 windows and a *piscina* in the corner. A pity that the main fuse box overshadows it, and that this little transept is crammed with pews. The chancel is an 1850s rebuild which fits the church well, and in it hangs a Turkish sanctuary lamp in bronze filigree, said to have belonged to Florence Nightingale (a story there perhaps!). Clues to the real age of the building are outside. A little *Saxon* window was revealed on the s. side during a restoration in 1960, and the tower dates from the C12, although it's disguised a little by western buttresses. These had decorative panels under the *set-offs* and one remains on the s.w. – a *cusped* Star of David, set in a circle of shallow carving. St Lawrence has the last word – look down as you leave the porch and you will see his initial and his gridiron picked out in flushwork at the base.

Ingham, Holy Trinity (F4): A grand church, with a noble four-stage tower with stepped, pinnacled and panelled buttresses, large bell openings (though tracery and mouldings have gone), a magnificent w. window with composite door below, richly ornamented in spandrels and above with shields and coats-of-arms; and a fine flush-panelled base course. There are two n. doors, one (Decorated) in the usual w. end position; another (Perpendicular) in the centre – for this led to the priory whose conventual church (ie, belonging to an Order) this church was. In 1355 Sir Miles Stapleton obtained a licence from the Pope to rebuild the existing parish church and to establish a priory of Trinitarian Canons, dedicated to ransoming captives of war. Just a few ruins of the priory may be seen beyond this door, including the rood stair and, in a dark corner, what was presumably a holy water stoup for the monks on entering the church. Moving on, the n. chancel window is Decorated, in a lovely reticulated style, and the e. window a complex and beautiful pattern of late Decorated craftsmanship; above it is a curious little outline, bricked in, with a trefoil head – was it window or figure niche? The large three-light s. chancel windows are Perpendicular, two with very rich tracery; likewise the aisle windows, in two of which the tracery is still strongly of Decorated character. The clerestory is unusual – round windows with complex flower-like tracery. The Perpendicular C15 porch is splendid and very rare in having three storeys. In the upper two, the story has it, lived the parish priest who was also sacrist of the priory. The entrance has a fine, unadorned groined roof. A spacious and fine interior to the church, with a handsome modern nave roof which combines arch braces with hammer beams, and cross beams with king posts (see glossary, Roofs), and is

adorned with colourful shields. The five-bay C14 arcade is beautiful, with its clustered columns and elegant capitals, and is complemented by the later, soaring tower arch. The nave and n. aisle have numerous old poppyhead bench ends. The font is C13, octagonal, with the simple double-arcading round its bowl excellently preserved; it stands on unfortunate modern stem and shafts of coloured marble. At the e. end of the s. aisle is a fine table-tomb on which lie effigies of Sir Roger de Bois and his wife Margaret, late C14, she, wedding ring slim and wearing a demure headdress, he bluff and armoured with his feet on a dog. Nearby is a brass to a knight and his lady which, until as recently as the 1930s, included a named brass to their dog Jakke – but this has since disappeared, leaving one at Deerhurst in Gloucestershire as the only 'dog brass' in England. In the chancel (beyond the remains of the stone screen, or pulpitum, which divided the monks from the laity) are the sad remnants of two once great brasses, one on the s. side to Sir Miles Stapleton (founder of the priory), 1364, and his wife Joan, and on the n. to a knight, 1410. Then there is the tomb to Sir Oliver de Ingham, 1344, who lies in acutely uncomfortable posture on a bed of cobbles (see also, Reepham Church), under the remnants of what must have been a most opulent canopy. Opposite, there is a lovely graduated piscina and sedilia – C15, though Victorian restored – arched, pinnacled and canopied. There are attractive old choir stalls with back panelling.

Ingworth, St Lawrence (D4): A delicious little church perched prettily on a mound above the village street and thatched throughout. Its round Norman tower fell in 1822 and the remains have been skilfully recapped with a thatched half-cone to provide a small raised vestry within. The nave was of the same period but was rebuilt in the late C14 when the s. porch was added. This has an attractive crowstepped gable in red brick and there is a big mass dial high on the wall. The interior has a 'busy' feeling, as though everything has been fitted in – just. A diminutive organ, for example, is cleverly housed in a gallery tucked into the n.w. corner. The C15 font looks as though it once had the Seven Sacrament scenes round the bowl, but they have been completely chiselled away. The base of the screen is C15, with a lanky Jacobean top said to have come from Aylsham – all painted brown and quite unattractive. The cut-down pulpit portion of a three-decker has an hour-glass stand complete with glass, and it fronts a range of C18 pine box pews on the n. side. Opposite, extraordinarily coarse deal pews have been fitted on to the old oak sills and cut-down ends of the originals. At the w. end above the tower arch is a very fine example of the Royal Arms of William III. The arms are in carved and gilded wood and mounted in a frame on a deep red background. Quite different, but just as nice in its way is the floor of plain salmon pink bricks.

Irstead, St Michael (F4): To be found in a most picturesque setting at the end of a tree-lined, narrow lane, close to the River Ant. The C14 church is thatched, and this shows through between the rafters in a diagonal pattern. There are remains of Norman work in the heads of both the n. and s. doorways, and the C15 s. aisle is separated from the nave by a very rudimentary arcade. The C14 font is unusual in having the Head of Christ in two of the panels, and the Hand of God in another. The pulpit has unremarkable C16 linen-fold panelling, but has part of a C13 stall attached to it as a handrail. With a small carved head and stiffleaf foliage it is a most interesting survival and, like many oddments in this area, it is said to have come from St Benet's Abbey, whose ruins are not far away near Ludham, on the bank of the River Bure. The base of the rood screen has large panels with paintings of the Apostles, three to each panel, apparently painted over earlier

work. There is a tiny rood loft staircase set in the n. wall. The oak chancel rails of 1852 have varied tracery roundels and are rather good. They were a memorial to Lady Palgrave, whose husband Sir Francis, of 'Golden Treasury' fame lies buried at the e. end of the churchyard. There is a modern statue of the church's dedicatory saint, St Michael, wrestling with a very sinuous serpent in the niche above the s. door.

Itteringham, St Mary (D3): Plain unbuttressed tower, simple nave and chancel, dating principally from the C14. The e. end shows clearly that there was a larger window before the C19 restoration when the present one was put in. Entering by the s. porch it is a pleasant surprise to find that a new n. door has been fitted with leaded lights in the top half so that you have a view across the churchyard as a bonus to the additional light inside. The chest by the door looks late C16 or early C17, but is dated 1716 – a good example of time-lag in country craft styles. The box pews have poppyhead bench ends that seem to be of the same vintage, which is rather an odd mixture. The sanctuary has big C17 panels of some quality. They have perspective arches, and are set in later woodwork to form a seemly reredos. Interesting also to see in the chancel a large engraving of Goetze's painting 'Despised and rejected of men' – an Edwardian allegory that spells everything out.

Kelling, St. Mary (C2): Mainly Perpendicular in style, although there are two blocked windows above the n. door which look Norman. There is a n. transept and the ruins of its opposite number to the s. The diminutive C15 porch is charming, with a well-proportioned arch outside and sheltering the C14 doorway. Two things invite attention here: the font, handsome C15 with an inscription round its rim seeking prayers for the De Kelling donor and his wife Beatrice: and the *Easter Sepulchre*, which as usual is in the n.e. corner of the chancel: although the later raising of the floor obscures its base, it is a well-nigh perfect example. *Royal Arms* over the door illustrate the way these are often re-used: the initials are G.R. but the motto ('Semper Eadem') is Queen Anne's.

Kettlestone, All Saints (B3): A late C13 or early C14 octagonal tower (there are only six like it in the county) which has a curious succession of openings. The middle stage has a little door on the s. side, above it the belfry windows, and above them small *quatrefoil* openings. Before the Victorian restoration it was even higher, and some suggest that it may have been used by Lord of the Manor Sir Thomas de Hauville, Keeper of the King's hawks, to watch his charges at work. The s. porch and the chancel are C19 and they blend in well. There are fragments of *Norman* stonework above the porch doorway and the stump of a churchyard cross stands by. The e. window is original C14, and in the top, the excellent tracery forms the shape of a butterfly with outspread wings. A good heraldic C15 font under the tower, with the *Royal Arms* (i.e. England quartering France), arms of the Diocese (with a sprightly crozier added), and emblems of *St Paul, St Peter, St George,* and the Trinity. All are in high relief and set in panels round the octagonal bowl. By the chancel steps is a Lilliputian organ. Although C19, its pipes are all exposed in the modern fashion, and it measures a mere 5ft x 2ft 4in. (The Positive Organ Co. who made it obviously knew when to stop!) In the chancel there is a big *ledger slab* to a vicar, William (Gulielmus) Young (d.1667) with italic lettering of very high quality, and by the s. door a wall tablet to a local boy who did not forget his native village: William Newman was reared by the Parish, and the Wardens apprenticed him to a tailor in 1738. He went on to make his fortune in London, and when he died in 1787 'He

gave by his will the interest of five hundred pounds in the four per cent to the poor of the parish of Kettlestone for ever'. The spacious churchyard is a pleasant place in which to stroll, and it is worth looking round the corner at the e. end just to see the two enormous headstones to James Cory, Rector, and his family (1793). 5ft high and 3ft 6in wide, they have at the head a charming *Adam style* decoration of shell and acanthus leaves. James and his son (also James) had the living for almost a hundred years from 1766 onwards, and their descendants gave the *lych-gate* in 1907. Damaged by enemy action during the war, it was restored in 1955.

Knapton, St Peter and St Paul (F3): A handsome, mostly C14 church, up on its mound, its largely early C14 tower with its shoulder to our 'lazy' east coast winds ('They don't go round – but through you') – note that it's slightly offset from the nave. On top is a weather-vane (cockerel and flag-piece) made from a drawing by the famous artist of the *Norwich School of Painting, John Sell Cotman,* early last century – it is said he did it while giving a drawing lesson at Knapton House. A fine porch, with a treble niche above the entrance arch – but filled-in in ugly cement. The chancel has a pretty *Perpendicular* porch, with trim pillars, over the priest's door. A local feature this – don't miss the one nearby at Trunch, where a buttress actually goes up from the top of the porch. Enter the church now – and stop in your tracks to gasp with wonder and delight. For we have here one of the best roofs in Norfolk, possibly in the kingdom, a glorious double *hammer-beam* carpenter's masterpiece, an amazing 70ft x 30ft 6in wide, thronging with 138 angels – not all original, the lower ones definitely modern . . . but what matter, we feel here, like St Paul to the Hebrews, 'compassed about with so great a Cloud of Witnesses'. This won-

Knapton: Angel roof detail

derful roof can be definitely dated to 1504, when it was given by John Smithe, rector here 1471-1518. Also fine are the font and its cover: the first, C13, in Purbeck marble, resting on shafts, and the whole on three confident steps. The cover, dated 1704, is a jolly piece – like a miniature seaside bandstand. The inscription upon it, in Greek, translates: 'Wash my sins and not my face only'. It's a palindrome – ie, it reads the same backwards as forwards; this one is said to have been composed originally by the Greek Emperor Leo (880-911). Victorian pulpit; a good C15 *screen; rood stair* entrance in s.e. corner of nave; the *corbels* which supported the *rood loft* can still be seen on either side of the chancel arch; in n.e. corner of nave, a double niche, which no doubt once had statues of the church's two dedicatory saints; behind organ, an odd little arch, built into the window, and a rough *piscina* (which probably served a *guild altar* of one of the numerous medieval guilds known to have been connected with this church). In chancel, a reader's desk made up of medieval and *Jacobean* bits and pieces – a happy botched-up job of charm and character; a very attractive C14 piscina; opposite, a recess which probably once contained an *Easter Sepulchre*.

Lammas, St Andrew (E4): A most attractive setting in a broad meadow on the banks of the river Bure. Apart from the slim tower dating from about the beginning of the C15, most of what you see is the product of C19 rebuilding using old materials in some places. The chancel was entirely replaced, but on the old foundations, so that it still '*weeps*' about 6ft to the n. Despite the fanciful theory that such misalignments symbolise the drooping head of Christ on the cross, it was undoubtedly the result of rebuilding the tower on firmer ground, and then extending the nave to meet the chancel (of about 1300) where it would. There is a big scratch or *mass dial* on the easternmost buttress of the

nave, and on the s. chancel wall outside there is a 1741 memorial to the young sons of Henry and Alice Utting. It is worth studying for the charm of the unsophisticated lettering. There is an early C16 font with big fat *Tudor* roses and shields in the panels, and beyond it, behind the organ is a *consecration cross* uncovered in the 1887 restoration. The lid of the parish chest was cut from a solid trunk and probably dates from the C14, although the ends and base are later replacements. *Walter Rye*, that most prolific of Norfolk antiquaries, lived for a time in Lammas, and gave the heraldic roundels in the n. window which display the arms of various Lords of the manor. The 'Sable a turnip proper' of the Damant family in the r. hand corner is good C18 Norfolk eccentricity, and Rye's own memorial below has a touch of it too. Described as 'an antiquary and athlete', he linked his own arms with those of the Thames Hare and Hounds Club.

Langham, St Andrew & St Mary (C2): With its turret staircase thrusting up above the battlements of the high, handsome tower, the church provides a distinctive feature in the landscape. On closer acquaintance, note the finely decorated *base course* all round the tower and extending across the end of the s. aisle, with flint-knapped *flushwork* set into the panelling. The three-light sound-holes in the belfry stage are unusual. Like the tower, the body of the church is largely C15. Inside, it is immaculately decorated and beautifully looked after. There is a striking *Decorated* C14 *arcade* of four bays – very elegant, and a lovely chancel arch, complemented by the contemporary and beautiful tower arch at the opposite end. Very puzzling is the oddly-shaped and ramblingly large 'blind' arch on the nave n. wall; as is the odd 'loop' on the easternmost arcade arch. Very well preserved *rood stairs* and loft entrance. Nice C13 octagonal font – embellished on the e. face with the rude inscription

'Alice Nettleton baptised the 14th day of April 1692'

... naughty relations, no doubt, carried away by the joy of the day: wonder what the incumbent of the time had to say about it? Roofs and benches modern throughout, though a few old *poppy-heads* have been re-used. Heavily restored chancel, with a *piscina* niche and a *dropped sill sedilia* on s. side. In the s. aisle are *Royal Arms*, dated 1740, altered from 1712 – but that's an alteration too: for though it may have the initials AR for Anne, her motto was 'Semper eadem' not 'Dieu et Mon Droit' as here. Probably it was originally for Charles I. A very good stained glass window in the tower (west window) by *Charles Eamer Kempe* (d.1907); and from a little earlier, a splendidly bold one behind the pulpit, designed by *Sir Edward Burne-Jones* (d.1898) and produced by the *William Morris* workshops, showing Faith and Hope vigorously treading underfoot, respectively, Unbelief and Despair. Spare a moment too for the memorial tablet to Captain Marryat – who lies in the churchyard outside under the windy trees – and his son Frederick, who went down with his ship a year before his famous father's death. Captain Marryat was the author of those staples of childhood literature until not so long ago, 'Children of the New Forest', 'Masterman Ready' and others. He lived for some years at Langham Manor and farmed there: but his house has long since disappeared.

Lessingham, All Saints (F4): A tiny, unpretentious, welcoming little church, marooned in fields up a narrow lane. The neat tower has an early *Perpendicular* (mid to late C14) upper stage, but the lower half is early *Decorated* (nearer 1300) with a w. window whose Y-tracery just might be original – a questionable assumption, however, as the identical nave windows are all Victorian replacements, put in when the nave walls were rebuilt in 1893. The simple and appealing Decorated tracery

of one n. window looks original, as is the Decorated n. doorway. There is no chancel: it became ruinous some time this century and was walled off. Inside, the nave has a most handsome modern panelled roof, with *arch-braces* and 'battlemented' cross beams and *wall plates*. The C13, octagonal font, standing on a modern base, has faint double-arcading round the bowl, a common feature. Unusually on the n. side of the sanctuary is a *dropped sill sedilia*, which must be Victorian; adjoining is the narrow entrance to the old *rood stair* (the turret can be seen outside). On s. side, a simple *piscina* has the suggestion of an *ogee* head. The little *Jacobean* pulpit, of about 1650, with its tiny backboard, and a *tester* with hanging pendants, is really charming. There are remnants of *brass* inscriptions, one dated 1505, in front of the altar.

Letheringsett, St Andrew (C3): An attractive, compact church, set off by its round *Norman* tower. This has a C14 top with neat *Decorated* two-light bell openings. The nave and *clerestory* windows are simple *Perpendicular*, and those of the chancel have most attractive geometrical tracery of the Decorated period. The s. porch was added in 1875. Inside, most beautifully maintained. No chancel arch. The continuous roof is modern, but very good, and much enhanced by the 1979 redecoration of the church. Impressive display of candelabra (for candles, not electricitiy!), seven hanging, eight wall mounted. Like those at nearby Glandford, they were brought back from Italy at the end of the last century by Sir Alfred Jodrell, of Bayfield Hall. The nave has lovely *Early English*, C13 *arcades* with, unusually, full columns and capitals offset from the aisle e. walls, to most eye-catching effect. At w. end of arcade, notice the intriguing *corbel* heads – one a flat-faced visage like a 'bruiser', the other a weird grotesque with arms and legs growing from its massive head. Super little font, octagonal, C13, in Purbeck marble.

Interesting early Victorian barrel organ, originally at Hindringham Church, then in a private house at Holt, and installed here in 1956. In n. aisle, a *piscina*, and entrance to the old *rood stair*; also a modern *aumbry* put in by the Rev. Charles Linnell – that tireless chronicler of Norfolk churches – during his rectorship here in the 1950s. In both n. and s. aisle windows there are good examples of stained glass by the eminent Victorian artist in this field, *Charles Eamer Kempe* (d.1907). The s. aisle has a nice piscina (C14?) with a modern bowl (1956-58); a lovely little C17 communion table brought here from North Barningham church in 1957; a stately-phrased wall tablet to William Hardy, (d.1842), aged 72 . . .' . . .zealous promotor of gospel truth . . . impartial magistrate . . . upright landlord' (The Hardys were squires here, living at the hall immediately next door, until not many years ago); and in s.w. corner, the death mask of Johnson Jex (d.1852), the village's celebrated blacksmith, inventor, watchsmith and self-taught scholar, whose magnificently worded gravestone just near the gate into the churchyard should not be missed. . .

'Insensible to the voice of fame, he lived and died a scientific anchorite'.

The chancel is simple Decorated, early C14, and most appealing, with some good remnants of C15 Norwich glass in s. window. Magnificent Victorian *reredos* in alabaster, erected to the memory of Adela Monckton Jodrell by her three children – the same lady for whom her son Sir Alfred entirely rebuilt Glandford Church. Plain C14 *angle piscina* and *dropped sill sedilia*. A tiny filled-in doorway on n. side is only about 4ft high – presumably the chancel floor was originally much lower. Priest's door opposite looks *Tudor*.

Limpenhoe, St Botolph (F6): A restoration in 1880 which was virtually a rebuilding. There is a blocked *Norman* s. doorway, and the typical zigzag and scallop mouldings can be seen from the outside. The base of the C15 tower is more or less as it was, although an early C19 engraving shows that there was then a big square window in the w. face and a tiled pyramidal roof. The font is C13 Purbeck, its canted sides having shallow arcading, and resting on eight columns and a centre shaft. A fine Flemish tapestry of the Sacrifice of Isaac is framed on the s. wall and came from the nearby ruined church of St Edmund's, Southwood.

Lingwood, St Peter (F6): The base of the tower is C13 but its upper stage, with the porch and chancel, is early C14. There is a big *scratch dial* on the e. side of the porch entrance, and although the *headstops* of the arch are very worn, you can see that one was a figure holding a battle axe. Inside, the nave has an *arch-braced* roof which, with no intervening chancel arch, comes to an abrupt junction with the ugly flat ceiling of the chancel. Above the tower arch the *Royal Arms* of George IV are cut to outline and there is the head and shoulders of a big *St Christopher* on the n. wall which must have been rather fine in its entirety. There are two bench ends in the chancel with figures on the arms, and a set of simple but robust C17 communion rails. The *piscina* is a shallow *trefoil*-headed recess which has had the projecting section of its bowl chopped away.

Little Barningham, St Andrew (D3): Very prettily placed on a green mound above the village street, with a broad grassy path leading up to the gate. Subjected to extensive restoration in the C19, much of the exterior is in dressed flint. Inside, all is starkly simple, the chancel in duck-egg blue and no mural tablets at all. What does catch the eye is the panelled pew at the front of the nave on the l. dated 1640; it has an 18in carved skeleton standing

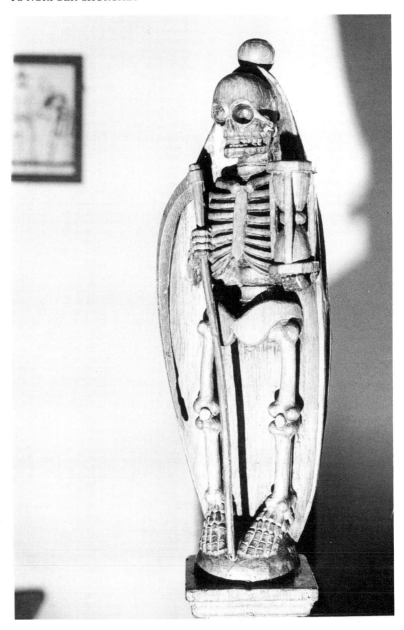

upright on the outer corner of the panelling, wearing a shroud and holding scythe and hour-glass. Two inscriptions are carved below in curious conjunction:

'For couples joynd in wedlock my freinds that stranger is. this seat did I intend. built at the cost and charge of Steven Crosbee'.

'All you that doe this pace pass by As you are nowe even so was I Remember death for you must dye And as I am soe shall you be Prepare therefore to follow me'.

What one might call friend Crosbee's version of the 'skeleton at the (marriage) feast'.

Little Plumstead, St Protase & St Gervase (F5): A dedication unique in England, to twin brothers martyred in Milan in Nero's time. The church is tucked away in the grounds of what is now a large hospital, centred on the old hall. A small, round flint tower, narrowing towards the top; almost certainly *Norman*, though authorities disagree, and it has been suggested that it is pre-Conquest; it has plain, pointed modern bell openings and a brick parapet. The body of the church, which overall is very heavily restored, is *Perpendicular* in character, though the fabric is obviously much older – a fascinating patchwork of flint and stone and of bricks of many hues and sizes. Standing, fittingly, outside the porch – for it looks more like a garden ornament than a piece of church furniture – is a fluted C18 font. The porch itself is predominantly brick, and rather pleasing, especially its brick outer arch, which looks C16 (similar to the one at Hemblington, nearby). The inner arch is very plain Norman, with a coarse *billet* moulding over the top. Inside, starkly plain and much restored, with spartan modern pews; roof modern also. But a round-headed n. doorway, and a massively thick wall-arch into the tower, speak of antiquity. Three *hatchments* hang on the nave walls. At

head of nave, s. side, is a remounted *brass* to Sir Edward Warner, 1565 – very good, showing fine Elizabethan armour. In the chancel, a grandly pompous monument, something of an C18 throwback, to Thomas Penrice, of Yarmouth, 1816, and his wife Hannah, 1829, complete with funerary urn on top and coat-of-arms underneath the inscription.

Little Snoring, St Andrew (B3): At first sight across the fields the tower looks like a very large pigeon-cote, with its conical cap (added about 1800), weather vane and tiny dormer-like openings. This sits on top of a round tower, *Saxon* in origin, adapted by the *Normans*, evidenced by the remains of arch and facia, which led formerly into the nave of a now disappeared church. The tower stands about 6ft clear of the present church, which rewards an observant walk around its exterior, for the range of windows here is a selective text-book in stone of 400 years of architectural styles. Note on stonework of chancel s.e. window a scratch or *mass dial*. On n. side, a lovely little *Early English* (C13) filled in doorway, with an an odd little inset above it – a bit of spare tracery popped in as an afterthought? Entering the church through the charming *Decorated* porch of about 1300, with its rudely carved outer arch, we are confronted by a fascinating curiosity. This is the inner doorway, where a Norman arch, with bold zigzag ornament, was crammed into Gothic, pointed conformity, no doubt by some C13 'new wave' enthusiast. The lovely carved capitals are Early English, but each keeping its Norman abacus – the flat bit between arch and pillar. Supremely plain and uncluttered inside, with nave roof of almost barnlike simplicity and practical sturdiness. Westernmost n. and s. windows, like castle arrow slits, are Norman, as is the superb font, round and richly carved. The other nave windows range through Early English *lancet* (mid C13), Y-traceried geometrical of the early

Decorated period (around 1300); at centre of s. side, Decorated of about 1330; and opposite, fine *Perpendicular* (late C14-early C15). Note splendid and rare *Royal Arms* of James II, dated 1686, above s. door (a brief reign and his 'Popish' inclinations ensured the scarcity of his Arms). Pulpit, neatly panelled in mahogany into a corner, is handsome C18. Through the wide and dignified Early English arch (about 1250) into the chancel, brilliantly light and airy – a real pleasure with its deeply set, separated lancets forming the e. window, each marked with slim shafts; and square headed *Tudor* windows (late C16), to each side, that on the s. having a *dropped sill sedilia* below it (see outside how it has been filled in and panelled) adjoining a very attractive C13 *angle piscina*. Note the *ledger slab* – s. side between the pews – to a parish priest 'as good perhaps as ever lived'.

Little Walsingham, St Mary (B3): This fine church was gutted by fire on the night of July 14-15 1961, leaving only the tower with its pretty lead covered steeple, and the s. porch intact. A very beautiful and effective rebuilding, of great care and taste, has been achieved, all colour and light – and giving an impression of what many medieval churches would probably have looked like in their original state. A treasure saved from the fire was the *seven sacrament font,* described by *Sir Nikolaus Pevsner* as 'Almost the perfect Norfolk font – it would be, if it were better preserved'. This splendid C15 piece, beautifully carved with the seven sacraments and the Crucifixion, with round the shaft the four Evangelists and the *Four Latin Doctors,* stands on three tracered steps in the shape of a Maltese cross. Its graceful *Jacobean* cover, given by the wife of Sir Henry Sidney, was alas destroyed in the fire. Sir Henry and his lady have a fine alabaster monument, 1612: their figures have been remounted 'step fashion' under the w. window in the n. aisle, with Arms below. He was Lord

Chamberlain to Elizabeth I, and cousin to Sir Philip Sidney, Elizabeth's celebrated courtier, soldier, poet and statesman and 'most perfect example of the Renaissance gentleman'. On n. wall of chancel is an appealing little Jacobean tablet, showing the front of a four-poster bed with the curtains drawn, and announcing simply:

'Dormitorium Edwardi de Fotherbye – 1632'. 'Here sleeps. . .'

Eternal rest indeed! Another monument worth noting is the *cartouche* on the s. aisle wall to Robert Anguish (of an important Norwich family of the time whose charity bequests to educational activities are still very generously active today), with its cleverly compact wording and dating – 'E.R. 1590 XXXII': ie the 32nd year of Elizabeth Regina's reign.

Little Witchingham, St Faith (D4): You might say that St Faith's has drawn back from the grave. *Cautley* described it (in 1949) as 'disused', and *Pevsner* (in 1962) as 'disused and ruinous' – and so it was until nine years ago. The problem is that, although there are a handful of houses nearby, the focus of the village has now shifted down to the valley, and thus the odds against the building surviving were high. But help came just in time from the Norfolk Churches Trust, through whose financial aid roofs, windows and floors were repaired and replaced. Restoration goes quietly on, with their help, though this simple little early C14 church of tower, chancel and nave with s. aisle, all under one roof, remains in parish care. The unbuttressed tower, with its frieze of *flushwork* below the battlements, has been repointed and has new louvres in the bell openings; here are new fall pipes from the gutters; the walls have a deep gravel-filled trench against them, and all the windows have been reglazed with clear glass in oblong leaded lights. More than that, inside, the remnants of a complete scheme of medieval paintings have been uncovered, and their

NON·ME·PVDET·EVANGELII·CHRISTI   VIVAT·REGINA·ELIZABETA·

reclamation by Mrs Eve Baker in 1975 won the church an award during European Architectural Heritage Year. All the designs are in a dark red, and a pattern of foliage scrolls reaches up 8ft from the floor. Above that, there are traces of figure groups and one is tolerably clear on the n. wall. The *arcade* arches between nave and aisle have a zig-zag pattern painted on the outer chamfer, and in the *spandrels* on the s. side there are two fine and very large roundels – one with the lion of *St Mark*, the other of *St Matthew*, both with lettered scrolls. A most exciting discovery. There is now a font again, a spiky brass lectern of the 1860s, a ringable bell, and a vested altar. Parts of the interior walls are still scabrous and more help is needed to complete the restoration, but it is heartening to see the march of decay halted. In your circuit of the outside, don't overlook the fragment from a preaching cross with a Crucifixion carved on it, which is set in the s. wall of the chancel. Near it, John Mountain's epitaph (1774):

'We daily see Death spares no Sex nor Age,
Sooner or later All do quit the Stage;
The Old, the Young, the Strong, the Rich & Wise,
Must All to Him become a Sacrifice'.

Ludham, St Catherine (F5): The village's connection with St Benet's Abbey – whose ruins are nearby on the bank of the River Bure – goes back to before the Conquest, and successive Bishops of Norwich spent much of their time here. Partly because of this no doubt, the church is large and fine, with ample C15 *arcades* and a range of *clerestory* windows to match, leading the eye forward to a great e. window, the head full of *reticulated* tracery. The wheel emblem of the patron saint can be seen in the *spandrels* of the *hammer beam* and *arch-braced* roof. The C15

Ludham: Royal Arms & screen.

font is unusually enriched by having two ranks of figures below the bowl, and there are two lions, a wild man with shield, and a wild woman, standing round the stem. The *piscina* and *sedilia* form a very rich composition of profusely *crocketted, ogee* arches, and on the other side of the chancel hangs a good C17 *Decalogue Board* painted in oil and tempera on canvas. The *tympanum* filling the chancel arch is of exceptional interest. It lay hidden for many years in the blocked-up *rood stair*, and was discovered in 1879 by an Archaeological Society outing, (on which they dined-out for years no doubt!) On the w. side is a roughly painted rood, with two angels flanking *St John*, the Virgin, and two soldiers. This was probably a makeshift alternative put up in the short reign of Mary Tudor, to replace the original. The whole was then reversed, and the arms of Queen Elizabeth substituted. These now appear on the e. side, inscribed:

'Non me pudet evangelium Christi' (I am not ashamed of the Gospel of Christ).

Below there is one of the best *screens* remaining in the county. The middle rail has a diagonally folded label that gives the names of John Salman and his wife Sicilie who gave £14 in 1493 for its construction. Below, in intricately decorated panels are fine paintings of (from l. to r.) *Mary Magdalene, St Stephen, St Edmund,* Henry VI, the *Four Latin Doctors, Edward the Confessor, St Walstan, St Laurence,* and *St Appolonia*. Delicate detached buttresses grace the front of the screen. Restoration of both screen and *tympanum* was completed by Miss Plummer in 1972. Note a label brass (inscription) to Christopher White (d.1652) which is brief and to the point:

'Hodie mihi, cras tibi' (Today for me, tomorrow for you).

Marsham, All Saints (D4): Entry is by a tall, thin s. porch, which now has a jolly

red and olive-green ceiling. The C14
hammer beam roof is a very nice piece
of work, although the picture is confused by heavy transverse beams.
These were inserted after a great gale in
the C18 which caused the s. wall to
move, and the *arcade* on that side still
has a distinct list. The *seven sacrament
font* is very good, and can be dated
c.1460 by the ladies' headdresses.
Clockwise from the e., the panels
are Baptism, Confirmation, Extreme
Unction, Last Judgement, Penance,
Matrimony, Ordination, and Mass.
The *rood screen* has 14 painted saints in
the panels, most of whom can be identified by their attributes, although all the
heads are defaced. From l. to r. they
are: *St Faith, St James the less, St
Thomas, St James the Great, St John, St
Andrew, St Peter, St Paul, St Philip,*
four saints without emblems, and a
bishop. The *gesso* work is reminiscent
of Aylsham and Cawston, and the
screen probably dates from about 1500.
There is an interesting framed pastel
on the n. sanctuary wall, showing the e.
end in 1842 – classical *reredos, Laudian*
rails, and two statues – now all gone. In
the centre aisle floor, the epitaph of
Mrs Margarett (d.1698) admits defeat:

> 'whose worth & goodnesse cannot
> be expressed within the limits of a
> gravestone'.

Close by is an uncompromising piece
of honesty: Sarah Bear (d.1757) aged 58.

> 'To die I must
> To stay I'd rather
> To go I must
> I know not whither'.

Martham, St Mary (G5): Large enough
to have been dubbed 'the cathedral of
the Fleggs' (the Fleggs being the crisp
name of this locality of Norfolk) the
C15 church has a great west tower
topped by a spirelet. The s. porch has
two storeys and a *groined* roof, and
much of the carving of the lovely doors
is original. Beyond them is an enormous
tower arch and a *seven sacrament font,*

mutilated but understandable: clockwise, starting from the e. face – Extreme
Unction, Mass, Matrimony, Baptism of
Christ, Ordination, Penance, Confirmation, Baptism. At the w. end also, a
bier of 1908 – good honest workmanship, carefully restored. The s. aisle
chapel is dedicated to *St Blide* (who is
said to be buried here at Martham),
mother of *St Walstan,* the Norfolk
patron saint of farm workers whose
shrine was at Bawburgh, just west of
Norwich. The remaining medieval
glass is set in the e. windows of the
aisles, with a particularly nice figure of
Eve with her distaff, in a green meadow
(s. aisle, bottom pane). The chancel is a
C19 disaster or delight, according to
taste: either way, it will remain in the
memory.

Matlask, St Peter (D3): To drive
through this pretty village on a sunny
day and come suddenly upon the
church with its rough, round tower, is a
pleasure indeed. The tower is *Norman*
(part of the original church, built
between 1066 and 1189) with traces of
tiles in its construction which *Pevsner*
thinks are Roman. The octagonal top is
C14 *Decorated,* with window-openings
of neatly text-book tracery. The attractive n. porch has a mellow Decorated
arch; nice square-headed *Perpendicular*
windows in nave; the pretty s. porch,
with depressed (flattened) outer arch,
has been blocked off to serve as a
vestry. No chancel: on the morning of
March 19th 1726, while the rector was
celebrating communion, it suddenly
collapsed – but outwards, so miraculously no-one was hurt. Inside, this
little church is a pleasure of light and
calm, simplicity and order, and merging
colours of masonry and colourwash.
The neat modern roof is supported on
medieval *corbels* carved with rustic
faces: so distinctive they are, that it
would be agreeable to think that they
are portraits of the masons and
labourers who built the church – be sure
not to miss them. Severely simple C15
font; carved cover of same date;

massive C14 chest under tower; good old benches and *poppyheads* in nave of 500 weathered years; *Royal Arms* of George III, glowingly restored to former glory in 1969 by local artist Mary l'Anson. *Jacobean* side-table in nave aisle (beside attractive, square-headed *piscina*) was formerly the main altar table. The two *hatchments* at the w. end are interesting – they are of the Gunton family, of Matlask Hall, dated 1794 and 1804, one carrying the often-seen and confident assertion: 'Resurgam' – 'I will rise again'.

Mautby, St Peter and St Paul (G5): The round *Norman* tower has a C15 octagonal top like many others in the county, and a long thatched roof covers both nave and the early C14 chancel. When the nave was restored in 1884 and new windows inserted, the *arcade* in the s. wall was uncovered and it is the only trace left of a C13 south aisle. A pity, because Margaret Paston (writer of the famous *Paston Letters*) directed that her body be buried

> '. . . in the ele of that cherch at Mauteby, byefore the ymage of Our Lady there, in which ele reste the bodies of divers myn auncestres'.

She was at Mautby before her marriage and came back here after her husband's death in 1456, writing many of the letters from her childhood home. The tomb of one of her forebears – probably Sir Walter (c.1248) is now in the s. wall within the easternmost arcade, having been moved there when the aisle was demolished after the *Reformation*. Under a fragmented canopy is a monolithic figure of a Knight Templar in square-topped helm and chainmail, with sword and shield. The cross-legged effigy has been harshly treated and only the little paws show that a dog or lion once lay at his feet. The old Crusader's bones were actually handled by an antiquary in 1822 and are still there in the stone coffin. The C15 *screen* has good tracery, and when it was restored in 1906 the *rood* was added. It

has a *squint* cut in one of the panels, which indicates that a nave altar stood on the s. side – the *piscina* for it is in the wall by the chancel arch. In the chancel itself, the pleasing *cinquefoil* arches over the *sedilia* and piscina have small animal heads as stops to the *hood moulds*. Note that the piscina has two drains. This was general practice 1250-1350, when the priest's hands as well as the chalice were washed there. On the opposite wall, an excellent architectural tablet to Richard Gay Lucas (d.1771). It has a coat of arms over it, lively swags of flowers, a cherub's head below, and is a subtle exercise in varying the planes to take full advantage of shadow. C15 font of good proportions, with slim traceried panels between the shaft columns. Only the *crocketted* ribs of the candle-snuffer cover are original but they show that it was made at the same time.

Melton Constable, St Peter (C3): By the e. lodge of the disused hall, trees on one side and a great vista of open fields on the other. This is a small but fascinating church. The central *Norman* tower retains its big undecorated arch to the nave, and above it, set within an outline replica of the arch below, a double arch separated by a massive round pillar. Beyond is a very short C15 chancel which has big figures as roof *corbels* in the corners – one of the Virgin crowned. The whole is oddly reminiscent of an opera set, an impression heightened by the Hastings pew in its own s. transept approached by a staircase. The altar *reredos* is a Flemish triptych (Gethsemane, Crucifixion, Deposition) brought into the church during this century, which everybody is careful to describe as 'attributed to Rubens'. But the chancel's unique contribution is the *low side window*. The lower half is still unglazed and there is a stone bookrest and hollowed-out seat beside it; this is the clearest indication anywhere of the true purpose of these windows – to enable the sacristan to ring the *sanctus* *bell* at the Elevation of the Host. To the s. of the chancel arch is an elaborate recess with a large *ogee* arch where there was once a nave altar. There are still traces of colour in the mouldings and there was much more before the war memorial was set in the back. On that, the list is headed by the squire's son (writ twice as large), which brings us back to the Hastings pew. The short flight of stairs (steps would be too flimsy a word) is dated 1636 on the newel (post) and leads up to the white panelled front of a gallery. Twin doors, each emblazoned with a coat of arms, are topped by crimson plush-padded canted sills matching the rest of the frontage, on which lie folio 1721 Prayer Books bound in sheep skin, each labelled 'Melton Constable Chapel'. The gallery is large enough to take four carved walnut upholstered carvers and a dozen gilt and cane occasional chairs without overcrowding. Behind a low screen there is an area for the servants with its own door to the outside world. The white wainscot panels have up-wards of forty numbered coats of arms emblazoned in miniature, with genea-logical notes in careful gilt of the ramifications of the Astley/Hastings family. Above them, a splendid array of marble tablets. Portrait medallions adorn the memorial to Sir Philip Astley (d.1779) and his wife to *Robert Page*. There is a lovely baroque *cartouche* in the corner to Isabella (1741) – all shells, scrolls and undulations. On the e. wall, Anna Maria Astley (d.1768) has asym-metrical rococco striving rather too hard, while Lucy and Judith's epitaphs have a curtained canopy supported by *putti*. The two recent additions to the collection are beautifully executed, and look like well-moulded plastic pastiches of their C18 neighbours. In the silence, the weight of an ancient family obsessed by lineage is almost oppressive, but this church must have known that valiant old Royalist Sir Jacob Astley, victor of Edgehill:

'O Lord! thou knowest how busy I must be this day: if I forget thee, do not thou forget me'.

Nobody in the great house now, but plenty of memories here.

Metton, St Andrew(E3): The C14 tower has a processional way (n. to s.) beneath it, and the scaffolding *put-log* holes are open all the way up. Inside, the church is homely with boarded ceilings. There are some *brasses*, including a good one of Robert Doughty and his wife dated 1483. The chancel e. window contains roundels of Flemish glass, and close by is a *piscina* with the unusual addition of a grotesque head to support the bowl. The small C19 organ has a nice classical mahogany case, although the attached striplight is a pity. By the door is a dumpy Parish Constable's staff of the 1830s.

Morston, All Saints (C2): The church stands castle-like on a knoll, no trees or vegetation around to soften its lines. A chunky, square tower, largely C13, but part rebuilt in red brick when it was struck by lightning in 1743. Interesting and unusual *clerestory*, with little *quatrefoil* windows, perhaps as early as C12; above, partly battlemented. The window tracery all round is specially interesting and attractive, for here we have C13 *Early English* hover-ing in transition on the edge of early C14 *Decorated*. The chancel, s. side, has one window with classic interlacing pattern of Y-tracery extended to three lights, of about 1300, with its other windows further advanced into tran-sition. Look closely at the tracery in the s. aisle windows – this is *plate tracery*, where the pattern is pierced through the masonry, as distinct from *bar tracery*. Entering through the C15 s. porch, we find ourselves in a light, white, refreshing interior, with a C13 *arcade* of simplicity and beauty with its slim round pillars indicating an earlier Transition, that from *Norman* into Early English (see glossary, *Styles of Architecture*). Incidentally note from here the small window in the w. face of the tower – it is a pointed *lancet*, but the distinctively wide-to-narrow splay in which it is set must be Norman! Returning to the arcade, see that its arches at each end rest on *corbel* heads carved with highly individual faces – gossip with tongue out; a bulbous-nosed boozer? a half-wit? – and a moustached gent of undoubted 'county' rank. Above the lovely chancel arch (also C13) are the *Royal Arms*, 1823, *Decalogue*, creed and Lord's Prayer – a faithful return to old usage of this filled in arch or *tympanum*. Below, the *rood screen*, dated 1480, has remarkably well preserved painted figures – on the left, the four Evangelists with their symbols, on the right, the *Four Latin Doctors*. The *Evangelistic symbols* are also carved (with more devotion than artistry) on the good C15 font, where they alternate round the octagonal bowl with four seated saints. Above the paintings on the screen are particularly fine carvings . . . small figures, a *pelican*, feathered angels, a bird with a crest, a dragon. The chancel has a coarse *angle piscina* and a *dropped sill sedilia*; opposite, what was presumably an *aumbry*, now adapted with a modern tracery head. Under the altar – to where it was moved for safe keeping a few years ago – is a fine *brass* to Richard Makynges, 1596, rector here for 40 years – a rarity, for there are few brasses to Elizabethan clergy, and this is the only one in Norfolk.

Mundesley, All Saints (F3): A complete rebuild, between 1899 and 1914, of what for a century had been a deserted ruin – and most successful it is. Every remnant still in situ, or discovered in the churchyard and round about, appears to have been re-used with imagination and affection: note diagonal buttress of nave (to left of porch) with pleasant old *Tudor* roses; nave and chancel window tracery, using as far as possible the original materials; the attractive buttress at s.e. angle of chancel, with its *Decorated* statue niche. Inside there is a real air of antiquity, accentuated by the fine 1904

rood screen below the reconstructed C15 chancel arch and, to left, the *rood loft* entrance. Facing as one enters by the s. porch is a tiny *Norman* slit window – probably the oldest visible part of the fabric – but with a pointed head. There's a nice *Jacobean* pulpit with *tester*, which came from Sprowston, near Norwich; a massive plain C14 font, and the arms of Queen Victoria.

Neatishead, St Peter (F4): Over the w. door a tablet in the head of a medieval niche states that the church was rebuilt in 1790. What is left is basically the chancel of a much larger church. The w. face also has three little kneeling figures, flanked by shields, which may have come from the original porch. Further work in 1870 re-arranged the windows. The C14 font has shallow panelling reminiscent of window tracery, and there is a good *piscina*.

Northrepps, St Mary (E3): Although there are traces of earlier work (ie the chancel *lancet* windows), and the *arcades* are C14, the rest of the church is mainly C15 in style, with a good deal of C19 restoration. The tower is a compact design with good detail. The C15 *rood screen* was rescued from a barn and eventually restored to its proper place: although much of it is new work, it does have the original inscription mentioning its donor, John Playford and his wife. The C16 benchends are conventional except that the westernmost *poppyheads* are halved and squared-off intentionally – unusual. Under the tower is a 'Gallas' plough: these were famous throughout C19 Norfolk, and were made at the local foundry here.

North Barningham, St Peter (D3): A church without a village, by the side of the road that runs from Gresham to Baconsthorpe, it is now in the care of the Redundant Churches Fund. Heavily damaged in 1714 and restored in 1893, it has again been put in order and contains a number of good things. The early C14 *piscina* and *sedilia* are badly damaged, but were unusually rich and have inlays in the buttresses and arches. In the n.e. corner of the sanctuary is a tomb chest to John Palgrave (d.1611) with a number of shields, and three small alabaster figures representing Justice, Toil and Peace, which are fine despite their loss of heads. Nearby is the elaborate wall monument to Margaret Pope, who died Christmas Day 1624. She kneels beneath a canopy and between 2 angels, and of her it is said:

'The most of her life she past in Virginitie,
But alwayes had care to serve well ye Trinitie,
Her that so ernestlie servd God on earth,
Christ tooke into Heaven the day of his birth'.

In the n.e. corner of the n. aisle is a splendid monument to Sir Austin and Lady Elizabeth Palgrave (1639). Within an elaborate surround, rich in heraldry, are two marble busts. He is bearded and faintly quizzical; she will brook no nonsense. Her double chin rests nicely upon a massive ruff, and is smooth to the touch. In front of this monument is a *brass* to Henry Palgrave (d.1516) and his wife – elegant figures with two groups of children below. The four shields are modern replicas. The enigma of the church is the circular design in brick and stone set in the nave floor e. of the font, reminiscent of a rose window. There has been no convincing explanation offered and it may have been purely decorative in origin.

North Barsham, All Saints (B3): A little church – just chancel and nave, of mainly *Decorated* work, standing high and windy in a meadow. During restoration in 1897-8, the *rood loft stairs* were exposed: you can see them set in the exterior buttress on the s. side. Note head and base of C14 niche re-set over w. door outside. Three of the four nave

windows and the e. window are restored; one square-headed brick mullion window in s. wall of chancel is original. Inside, there's a C13 Purbeck marble font (only the bowl is original) and the C17 pulpit, into which you have to climb to read the lovely wording of the monument to Philip Russell, who 'spunne out his thred of time, in ye dimention of 66 years' etc and whose 'exanimated body' (sic) went to 'ye common mother of us all' in December 1617.

North Walsham, St Nicholas (E3): A grand town church, packed with so much of interest that these notes can only touch upon them. The grimly ruinous tower, like a collapsed cliff, used to be 147ft high – but on May 16, 1724, the s. and w. sides fell, bringing down the steeple too . . . 'and no-one getting any mischief . . . Thanks be to God', as the parish register recorded. Another 100 years went by before the next collapse, in a storm in February 1836. Rebuilding plans have come and gone – save for the vestry of lavatorial ugliness built into the base. Move on quickly to the magnificent late C14 porch, luxuriously carved, decorated and pinnacled, with three figure niches containing modern figures of *St Benet,* the Virgin & Child, and *St Nicholas.* In the *spandrels* of the outer arch are the contemporary arms of Edward III (r.), 1322-77, and his son, *John of Gaunt,* (d.1399), who owned great Norfolk estates. Inside the lofty porch (it never had an upper room) the roof beams have fine original *bosses*; set into the walls below are, again, the arms of John of Gaunt, and opposite, of St Benet's Abbey (the ruins are a few miles away, near Ludham), once patron of the living. Inside the church is one vast hall, the noble seven-bay *arcade* of clustered columns and eloquent pointed arches hardly seeming to interrupt it, and light streaming in from the great aisle windows with their simple tracery (of the same period?). The e. windows, in the French 'flamboyant' style, are

Victorian replacements. Things to note: glorious C15 painted cover over the font, soaring up to its (very rare) original suspension beam; nearby, a couple of old *misericords*, variously carved, including *woodwoses* (wild men); in s.w. corner, a huge C15 iron bound chest, with seven locks; over the tower door, another rarity – *Royal Arms* with Charles II on one side and Cromwell's king-killing Commonwealth on the other; at w. end of n. aisle, a *lancet* window indicating an earlier, C13 church; in n. aisle pavement, a *chalice brass* to Sir Edmund Ward, Vicar, 1519; nearby, an inscription to Dame Margaret Hettercete, 1397. At e. end of s. aisle, brass to Robert Raunt, 1625, with arms of the Grocers' Company; a few feet away, an inscription to John Page, 1627 . . . by which time brasses were almost out of fashion (see glossary). Further e. in aisle chapel, another chalice brass, this one to Sir Robert Wythe, Chaplain, 1515, next door to an inscription to William Rous, 1404; the chapel's altar table, whose inscription text comes from the Edward VI prayer book, dating it between 1549 and 1552. All that remains of the mighty *screen* which would have extended between the two *rood loft* entrances in the two aisles is the lower part, with a fine assemblage of painted saints. The darkly impressive pulpit is pre-*Reformation*. Laid against the wall in the n. and s. chancel aisles are pieces of another screen, probably C14, the panels blanked but with excellent carving in the spandrels. In the sanctuary: handsome *piscina* and triple *sedilia*; and opposite, the ornate and pompous tomb of Sir William Paston, 1608, founder of the local grammar school, Sir William reposing full length in armour, comfortably propped on an elbow. A meticulous man, he erected this extravaganza himself before he died.

Ormsby, St Margaret (G5): The church has a good-looking tower with stepped battlements and a nice *base course*.

There has been much heavy restoration, but the solid *Norman* doorway with its four friezes of *billets* and zig-zags indicates the building's true age. In the chancel of the s. side the C14 *piscina* and *sedilia* group nicely under arches with fine *headstops*, and there is an ornate tomb of the same period on the n. side which doubtless served as an *Easter Sepulchre*. A similar recess was moved to the e. wall of the new n. aisle in 1867. There is a *brass* effigy of Sir Rober Clare (d.1529) on the n. side of the sanctuary, and another half figure of Alice Clare (d.1538) has now been laid in the floor of the nave at the s.e. corner. Parts of a brass to Robert Clare (d.1446) are mounted on a board in the chancel. Glass of the 1920s and '30s in the chancel shows how style and taste were changing, moving towards the modernist interpretation in the n. aisle w. window by Stammers of York, 1964. The Lacon mausoleum n. of the church looms like a wartime bunker, surmounted by an uncompromising cross.

Ormsby, St Michael (G5): A small compact church, obviously cherished. The C14 tower and much of the rest of the exterior has been recently restored, and most of the windows have been renewed. The thatched nave has a good *arch-braced* roof. The octagonal font is C13 and has a ring of Purbeck marble shafts. Recent additions include a thatched and glazed s. porch, both sensible and decent, and the arms of Elizabeth II. The chancel windows have glass spanning 1898-1920 on the themes of Faith, Hope and Love, and are very pleasing. There are good wall tablets to members of the local Upcher family in the chancel ('Memory . . . the most sacred tablet on which departed worth can be recorded'). Outside, don't miss the line of C18/early C19 headstones by the path to the priest's door. They have carved tops with cherubs and ships, and some affecting verses.

Oulton, St Peter and St Paul (D4): A

quiet and isolated little church. It had n. and s. chapels halfway down the diminutive nave, but only the arches now remain. On the wall opposite the door, a cheeky-looking fish is all that remains of a *St Christopher painting*. As with many minor churches of little apparent interest, there is still something to catch one's eye; this time, it is a little *brass* in the nave floor:

'Here laye Edmund Bell
An Katherin his wife
Who thirty six yeares
Did live man and wife
Thay had three sonns
An daughters three
Farwill our freinds all in
Heaven we hope to see'. 1636

Overstrand, St Martin (E2): A rather confused mixture of rebuilding and restoration. The roof of the original church collapsed in the C18 and the nave was partitioned, leaving the e. end and chancel to decay. Then in 1859 a small church (Christ Church) was built on the site, and this was in use until summer congregations outgrew it. In 1911 the old building was restored/rebuilt and enlarged. We now have the original C15 tower and nave; a new n. aisle and chancel; and the old n. porch moved over to the s. side. The original n. doorway remains in position and makes a nice surprise as you come across it. There is an old *wafer oven* in the base of the tower. Buried here is Sir Thomas Fowell Buxton, who composed the long verse epitaph for his son John (d.1830, aged 16) to be seen in the n. aisle.

Oxnead, St Michael (E4): The church is approached by an estate road and lies close to the last great house of *the Pastons*, Oxnead Hall. The *lancet* in the ruined n. chapel, the base of the tower and the s. door point to a C13 origin, but the building is now a hybrid, with late C16 brick e. gable, n. porch and top of the tower. The C18 s. porch is also brick

with cement rendering. The chancel holds all the fascination. Here are the Paston monuments – well restored under Stanley Wearing in 1956 with the aid of the Pilgrim Trust. Sir Clement Paston built Oxnead and died in 1597. His sumptuous alabaster tomb chest is in the n.e. corner; a calm bearded figure in full armour, resting upon a thick rush mat which is rolled to support his head. Except for the hands, the effigy is perfect and still has traces of colour. Below him, his wife Alice kneels. As befits a widow she was all in black and died in 1608. Her ruff frames a grave and lovely face with high cheekbones. The floor in front has her brass inscription:

'. . . who for great hospitallitie and bountie to the poore was the honor of her country. . .'

Sir Clement, whom 'Henry VIII called his champion, Protector Somerset his soldier, Queen Mary her seaman and Queen Elizabeth her father' has a long epitaph which is worth the reading. Forty years on we have Lady Katherine, daughter of the Earl of Lindsey and wife to the fourth Sir William Paston. A large monument by *Nicholas Stone* who, although he did much work for the Pastons as well as the Coke monuments at Tittleshall, is not at his best here. It is a rather characterless bust with little expression in the smooth face. Perhaps that was a true reading, but on twin tablets her husband extols her virtues in Latin and English in measured periods

'. . . that future Ages might from it collect
Her matchless merit and his true respect'.

Paston, St Margaret (F3): An almost exclusively C14 building, presenting a lovely range of windows in several *Decorated* period styles, from the simplest Y-tracery through to the lovely four-light e. window: all are worth a careful look. The porch is C15 – but quixotically with a rounded outer arch. Rather gaunt interior, accentuated by the darkly discoloured roof of the nave with its C14 scissor-braced beams. On the n. wall are some contemporary wall paintings (uncovered in 1922) including a 12ft tall *St Christopher*, bearded and patriarchal, holding the Christ child aloft in his left hand; further on, vague skeletons are all that remain of a *Three Living and Three Dead* sequence; and finally, remnants of what could be a Scourging of Christ. There's a Victorian *Royal Arms*, 1831, over the filled-in tower arch; a battered, iron-bound chest, said to be C14; and of similar period, an octagonal font carved with plain arcading. By the organ stands a lovely old carved reading desk, topped with *poppyheads;* the first pew on the s. side is splendidly carved with the *Paston Family* coat and crest; and on the n. side, sixth pew from the front, note the devil with his tongue out. The *rood screen* is basically C15 but much restored – and much varnished. Behind the pulpit the entrance to the *rood stair* is exposed. Paston family monuments dominate the chancel, notably the enormous confection (which cost at the time a staggering £340) in black, white and pink-flushed alabasters, with pillars, arches, a coroneted skull and mourning figures 'to the reviving memory' of Dame Katherine Paston, 1628: the Dame, sumptuously dressed, reclines with her right elbow propped on a tasselled cushion, looking composed and amiable and indeed . . . 'expecting a joyful resurrection' (her father, by the by, was Sir Godfrey Knyvitt, who in 1604 discovered Guy Fawkes setting his trail of treasonable gunpowder). Next to it, by the same sculptor, *Nicholas Stone*, is the monument to the Dame's widower, Sir Edmund Paston, 1632 . . . it is 'faultlessly classical' – and massively ugly. There are two more tombs to Pastons, abutting into the sanctuary, one of them shoved rudely into the ancient triple *sedilia*, adjoining which is a beautiful *piscina*, with a *credence shelf* and its drain mounted onto a neat little

pillar. In front of the altar, the figure of Erasmus Paston, 1538 (father of Sir William, founder of the grammar school at North Walsham) is all that remains of the *brass* to himself and his wife. Note, either side of the e. window, the lovely slim *jamb* shafts topped by exquisite little foliage capitals, C13; and the communion rails, with their pompous little balusters and dumpy posts . . . all put together in 1843 from the staircase of a 'great house' somewhere in Norfolk.

Plumstead, St Michael (D3): Nice late C15 *Decorated* tower, with neatly contrasted flint-knapped and panelled battlements, with badly eroded pinnacles and *gargoyles*. The only carving to be seen in this simple church, and very agreeable too, is the *flushwork* panelling at the base of the tower. Body of the church fairly shrieks 'over-restoration', with its ugly nave window tracery dating from a general restoration of 1873. A s. nave aisle became ruinous in the C18, was demolished and the line of the *arcade* filled in. But inside the arcade is still there in outline, very simple and respectable *Perpendicular*. For some reason the *clerestory* above was blocked in too. Plain C14 font with good modern cover. Nearby, a *Stuart* table, formerly the altar table. In the chancel, of about 1300, remnants of a small *Easter Sepulchre*, now crudely coloured; tiny coats of arms to either side are interesting – replicas of ones formerly in the church of the Plumstede family, Lords of the Manor here for 300 years up to the early C17. To right of altar, heavily restored *piscina* and outline of dropped sill window. Especially note old glass fragments – C15 Norwich in the e. window, the best being lower centre, *St Agnes* with her lamb – and sword in breast; and C16 Dutch in s. windows, including a lovely smug angel, levitating and 'look, no hands'.

Postwick, All Saints (E6): Chancel of

the C13; nave with *Decorated* and *Perpendicular* windows, but whose original fabric seems to be earlier; and a good Decorated tower with *flushwork* around both base and battlements, make up this calm, simple village church. Chief feature here is the windows of the nave: s. side has a lovely C14 Decorated example whose 'flowing' tracery, even if rather stiff (a local mason doing his best?) is most attractive, with next to it a super Perpendicular example with battlemented *transoms* (cross pieces) dividing the tracery. This one is twinned by another opposite, where there is also another Decorated window with tracery of elegant *reticulated* shapes. Though the chancel fabric is C13 *Early English*, its side windows are later and the e., Perpendicular. Set into the base of the window at the s.w. corner is a *low-side window*, complete with shutters. Inside the church, where all is beautifully cared for, the hand of a restoration of 1866 lies heavy, not least in the 'Victorian Early English' chancel arch and the 'false' tower arch, whose columns have been plonked straight onto *ledger stones*, as has the C14 font (Decorated, octagonal, crisply carved). In chancel, a good double *piscina*, of text-book C13 pattern – though its authenticity is open to question; *aumbry* opposite with modern door. In nave, lavish Victorian stone pulpit inset with chips of coloured stone brought back from the Dead Sea by the rector of that time, Sir William Vincent. In tower, a stained glass window and enormous wall brass to the 4th Earl of Rosebery, (d.1868), whose family (who sold off Mentmore Towers in 1980's much publicised 'Sale of the Century') were closely associated with Postwick. The tower contains a most interesting clock mechanism, recently described by one expert as about 300 years old and similar in date and mechanism to one at Dover Castle.

Potter Heigham, St Nicholas (G5): One of the nicest Broadland churches. The C12 round tower has a C14 embattled octagonal top which is superior to most in the county. All the roofs are thatched, and the six late C15 *clerestory* windows are sumptuous for a church of this size. The combination of flint and pale pink brick around them is strikingly good. Local bricks are very much a feature here; not only do they figure in the s. porch, but the C15 font is made of them. It stands solidly on two steps, and the rare roller pulley that used to support its cover can still be seen in the fine *hammer beam* roof above. The *rood screen* is of high quality. Although the heads of the figures are defaced, the panels are rich in the original red and gold. The third panel from the r. depicts St *Eligius*, patron saint of farriers, holding his claw-hammer emblem. Above, the *rood beam* survives, and behind the modern crucifix the outlines of the original rood group of figures can be seen. There are many traces of medieval wall paintings, but only the *Seven Works of Mercy* in the s. aisle can now be understood with any ease. The chancel has a well restored set of *Laudian* altar rails, and in the floor a stone recalls 17 members of the White family:

'. . . lovers of ye church, Loyal to their Prince, True to their Words'.

Rackheath, All Saints (E5): Rescued recently from disuse, decay and vandalism, this pretty church, all alone in the fields, is now cleaned up, alive again and open for occasional services, as a place of meditation and the venue for activities diverse as a Japanese tea ceremony and children's art exhibitions. Largely early C14 *Decorated*. The aisle roof is pitched so that, oddly, it cuts in half the small *quatrefoil, clerestory* windows. Inside, a charming C13 *arcade*. Interesting memorials to Sir Horatio Pettus (1746) by the Norwich sculptor *J.C. Chapling*; and to another Sir Horatio (by *Thos. Rawlins*, of Norwich) who married the granddaughter of a famous Dean of Norwich, Dean Prideaux; the baronetcy died with him in 1772. The estate was bought, about 1785, by Sir Edward Stracey – whose family is recalled by the popular pub on the Acle road to Yarmouth, which bears their name and arms.

Ranworth, St Helen (F5): Although there was a previous church on this site (see the fragment of a *Norman* arch re-set in a buttress on the s. side), the present building dates from the late C14 – early C15. The tower has a chequered *base course*, sound-holes, panelled battlements, and a fine view of Ranworth Broad from the top. The church is justly famous for its *screen*, and a report of the Society of Antiquaries says:

> 'The magnificent painted Rood Screen and *reredoses* of the nave altars form a composition which is unequalled by any now existing in a district famous for its screens. As a whole, it may be said that there is nothing of the sort remaining to equal it in England'.

The vaulting and base of the loft are in situ, and there are twelve panels with painted saints below. On either side, the nave altars have their own *reredoses* with saints, and there are side partitions, again with figures in the panels, surmounted by delicate flying buttresses. The quality of the work is not to be equalled in the county, and the recent restoration by Miss Plummer and her assistants (completed in 1975) has revealed even more. In particular, neither the debonair and fantastical St Michael nor the gorgeous embroidery of the female saints' dresses should be overlooked. A rare Cantor's desk stands before the screen, and may have been used in the *rood loft* itself. It has a versicle of plainsong painted on the front, and the eagle of St John on the back carries the first words of the Evangelist's Gospel on a scroll. Some of the stalls have simple *misericords,* and there are the remains of a wooden *Easter sepulchre* on the n. side of the sanctuary. The C17 altar rails are tall

and very pleasing. In a case by the door is the exquisite manuscript Antiphoner of 1400 (see glossary, *Antiphonal Lectern*). Illuminated by the monks of Langley Abbey – the remains are on farmland near Loddon, s. of Norwich – it disappeared in 1552, and by 1852 was part of the collection of Henry Huth (the Victorian merchant banker and bibliophile who collected together and published many early English and European manuscripts). Recognised in a bookshop in 1912 as belonging to Ranworth, it was happily brought home, and here it is on view, a priceless treasure to delight the eye.

Reedham, St John Baptist (G6): The village has drawn away from the church much as the sea has retreated from the village. The Romans had a lighthouse here and tiles embedded boldy in the n. wall exterior may well bear witness to that. St Felix, Bishop of Dunwich built a church here in the C7 and so Reedham has one of the longest known Christian traditions in Norfolk. As befits the village, the church is entirely thatched in reed – even the porch and the attractively long slope of the vestry roof. The main structure dates from c.1300, but the nicely proportioned tower was built in 1447 and Margaret Paston records in one of her letters (see glossary, *The Pastons*) that she had contributed 8s 4d to its cost in acknowledgement of childhood memories of Reedham. The interior is curious at first sight – an *arcade* that once separated nave and s. aisle has gone, but the s. aisle chapel of *St Helen* remains, so that you see two big arches side by side under a single roof with, in effect, two chancels beyond. The chancel proper has blank arcading of two bays in the n. wall and beyond it, an early C14 door to the vestry with an attractive *ogee* arch. The ends and panelling of the range of choir stalls are original but they have evidently been rebuilt. By the stripped pine pulpit, have a look at the chancel arch headstop – a pensive king supporting his chin with his hand. The s.

chapel was enlarged (see the extra arch at the e. end) to become the chapel of the Berney family, and the late C15 *brass* in the sanctuary to Elizabeth Berney has her wearing a butterfly headdress and fur-trimmed gown – her husband's brass has gone. The tomb to Henry Berney (d.1584) and Alice his wife has a strange mixture of period forms – a *Tudor* arch over the recess, but flanked by classical columns, and with a coat of arms above which is contained within a purely Gothic ogee arch. The family kneel conventionally in bas relief, five sons behind him and four daughters behind her, all white-washed over. The e. window of the chapel has some interesting glass, probably Netherlands C16 – a Holy Family with *St John the Baptist,* the Magi, *St Michael* with his foot on the neck of the Devil, and an unusual Benjamin with his brothers delving into the sacks of corn. The arms are those of Berney and de Cartaret Leathes. Before leaving, see the rough wooden *cartouche* to Robert Melling on the n. wall of the nave, with his arms above and skull resting on an hour-glass below. He was one of 200 who died in the Great Plague year of 1665, when Reedham's position on the river made it vulnerable to the pestilence from London. Another and much older connection with the sea is the little mermaid on the hood of the priest's door outside the Berney chapel, and on the left of the path leading to the churchyard extension, seek out the grave of Richard Pottle. He lived out his 108 years here, dying in 1840, and the stone was 'erected by those who, knowing his worth, supported him in his declining years'.

(Since this entry was prepared, Reedham church has, tragically, been gutted by fire.)

Reepham and Whitwell, St Mary and St Michael (C4): There are a number of cases where two churches stand in one churchyard, but Reepham is unique in having three, although Hack-

ford church has been ruined since the C16, and only a portion of wall remains. St Michael's, Whitwell, is westernmost, nearest the marketplace. It has a good C14 tower, with finely proportioned buttresses and a delicately traceried parapet. The rest of the exterior has been unsympathetically restored and the interior, with the exception of an outstanding C17 pulpit, has little of interest. The chancel of St Michael's joins on to the s.w. corner of St Mary's, Reepham, and there is a connecting door. Entrance is via a s. porch which stands rather eccentrically w. of the s. tower. At the w. end, a square C13 Purbeck marble font and nearby, a fragment of a churchyard cross, with figures set beneath the arms. The tower door has elaborate C15 ironwork, and by the door into St Michael's is a fine set of James I *Royal Arms* in carved relief. In the centre of the chancel is a large *brass* to Sir William Kerdiston (d.1391) and his wife. His effigy has lost one and a half legs and much of the canopy has gone, but what remains is of high quality. The memorable feature of this church, however, is the tomb of Sir Roger de Kerdiston (d.1337) in the n.e. corner of the chancel. The large mailed figure lies on a bed of cobbles, possibly of some allegorical significance. One hand is on his sword, and his feet rest on a very plump and very large lion. Apart from a chipped nose, the effigy is in near-perfect state, and is set beneath a tall and elaborate canopy. Below it, the eight small weepers still have nicely varied attitudes and dress despite their mutilation. This is a fitting memorial to one who, to judge by his church at Ewerby in Lincolnshire, was a distinguished patron of architects.

Repps, St Peter (G5): Originally the church had the more usual dedication to both St Peter and St Paul. The round *Norman* tower has a pleasing C13 octagonal top stage. The two-light bell openings are linked with bays of

Reepham St Mary: Kerdiston tomb.

matching blind *arcading*. Apart from the C18 brick chancel, five restorations in the last twenty years of the C19 have left their mark and little else. One of them uncovered a *stoup* by the door and a pedestal and a niche by the *rood loft* stairs, but all is smoothed and cement rendered. At the w. end by the wall is a C11 or C12 coffin lid. The worn, slightly coved top has a large plain cross, with a shield beneath one of the arms, and traces of scroll work above. There are three C15 label *brasses* (inscriptions) in the nave. The C15 font is octagonal with simple decoration, and parts of the *rood screen* remain. The stairs that led to the loft lie behind the deal door in the s. side.

Ridlington, St. Peter [F3]: A good-looking early *Perpendicular* tower with a pronounced 'cobbly' look to its flint work; topping its corners, in place of pinnacles, are the four *Evangelistic symbols*: but these, like the tracery of the bell openings, are much ravaged by wind and weather. Though the body of the church is mainly of C15 date, most of its windows are replacements, with plain intersecting tracery (wooden, and not pretty, in one n. window!), including of course the e. window where the whole end wall has been rebuilt in red brick. The n. door to nave, and nice priest's door on chancel s. side, are both *Decorated*. On n. side of chancel, what looks like a *low side window*. Inside, a charmingly simple village church, with harmonium and gas lights; modern roof and fittings; upper entrance to *rood loft* outlined to l. of small, trim chancel arch; C13 octagonal font of the locally common variety, arcading carved on bowl panels, with modern stem and cover. The chancel has an old and sturdy *arch-braced* roof; an attractively clumsy *piscina* and adjoining *dropped sill sedilia*. There is a particularly large *holy water stoup* by the main door.

Rollesby, St George [G5]: The round

Norman tower has two C14 upper stages rather than one, and the unused s. door of the same date has an exceptional, richly carved arch. A fine chancel was added in the C15 with corner pinnacles, topped by heraldic *talbots*. As you pass through the n. porch, look for the *Nine Men's Morris* frame incised on the left-hand bench. The *rood loft* stairs s. of the chancel arch have a blocked *squint* which used to pass right through them. In the s.e. corner of the sanctuary is a small arched enclosure which remains a mystery; it may well have housed relics originally. In the n.e. corner lies Rose Claxton, her effigy sumptuously dressed in Elizabethan ruff and embroidered gown, poses uncomfortably on its side. One hand supports her head precariously, the other clutched a prayer book until it was chopped off.

> 'Know Freindly Passenger that this smale roome,
> Rose Claxtons bodie onelye doth intombe
> Her bewtye love & gracefull modestye
> In her freinds hartes shall lyve etarnallye
> Her soule redeemd from sinns captivitye
> In Heaven lyves crownd wth immortallitye'.

Opposite is a good alabaster monument to Leonard Mapes (d.1619) with 14 kneeling figures.

Roughton, St Mary [E3] Stands finely exposed on a ridge above the main road in a big rough grass churchyard. The *Anglo-Saxon* tower is an interesting example, with a lot of the red Norfolk *carstone* laid herring bone fashion, and triangular heads to the belfry windows. The *clerestory* range is nice, with interior shafts rising from bases which have carved heads. There was a n. chapel – the arches can be seen outside in the chancel wall, and a plain square-headed *piscina* has been reset below them. The font is not the usual East

Anglian type and a number of churches in this area were obviously supplied from the same source; it has eight attached shafts with tracery between and around the bowl, and dates from the late C14.

Salhouse, All Saints (F5): It seems that a rebuilding was begun here but not completed. The low n. arcade has nicely carved capitals, of large foliage designs, except one that has heads. The later C15 tower was placed off-centre in anticipation presumably of a larger church, but it was never finished, and goes no higher than the sound-holes. The *rood screen* has been restored to the extent that most of it looks new, but judging by its position and method of hanging, the little *sanctus bell* on the top may be original. If so, it is a very rare survival. There is one *misericord* on the s. side of the chancel, with a large and fine bearded head, and an *hour-glass stand* is fixed to the pulpit. There are two C12 or C13 grave slabs set in inner w. wall of the tower.

Salle, St Peter and St Paul (D4): Standing almost in open fields, this is a mighty church which draws one back again and again, by virtue of its exceptional interest and great beauty. Historically, it is important because it can be dated very accurately. In the line of shields above the w. door, the third from the r. carries the arms of Henry V as Prince of Wales, i.e. 1400-13, and the building of the transepts is documented as 1440-1444. The tower has a richly decorated w. door, and there are carved angels with censers in the *spandrels*. Above, there are big, intricate sound-holes, and a beautifully traceried and battlemented parapet. Both porches have two storeys, individual stair turrets, and *groined* ceilings with *bosses*. The n. porch is particularly grand, and the chapel chamber above has a large window, a *piscina*, and a series of bosses which have been re-coloured. The upper door

has a massive bar which drops into slots when turned by the centre handle. (Virtually all the doors in the church are original.) The main parish footpath passed close by, and records show that this porch was often used to transact parish business. Entered now by the great w. door, the interior has a memorable ambience of calm and peace. The slender clustered columns of the *arcades* rise to roofs that are superb. The nave roof is *arch-braced*, and has angels at all the intersections, while the rafters retain their decoration of sacred monograms and crowned 'M's. Aisle roofs have great traceried spandrels, and the transept roofs are beautifully panelled. The chancel roof of 1440-50 is outstanding, and it is calculated that of the original 276 angels, 159 still remain. Apart from huge flowers at the intersections of the panelling, a line of carvings representing the life of Christ are spaced along the ridge. These have the appearance of bosses, but are actually carved blocks hung from the roof by hooks. Binoculars are helpful here to appreciate the high quality of the wood sculpture. Over the chancel arch can be seen the *corbels* that carried the *rood beam*, and below, the bottom half of the *screen* remains. Figures of four Apostles flank the two doors, on which are the *Four Latin Doctors*. The other eight panels apparently carry their original priming paint, and it can be inferred that altars stood before them. The stalls in the chancel have a fine set of *misericords*, and minor carving on the arms is worth studying – animals and birds on the n. and human heads on the s. The head on the stall nearest the screen doors could well be a portrait of the rector of that time, and certainly Thomas King (rector 1628-57) left his initials on the end of the desk. The pulpit retains the alternating red and green colour scheme common to the whole nave, and is interestingly combined with the clerk's pew, reading desk, and *tester* given by Lord Knivett in 1611, thus forming a *three-decker*. Under the tower is a ringers' gallery which supports a huge

Salle St Peter & St Paul

bracket, from which the tall font cover is suspended. The fact that the cover has lost the tracery between its sixteen slender buttresses gives it a lightness and delicacy that cannot have been intentional. The font stands on two steps, the lower inscribed:

> 'Pray for the souls of Thomas Line and . . . his wife and Robert their son chaplain and for those whom they are bound to pray who caused this font to be made'.

The *seven sacraments* round the bowl have a unique addition. Under each can be seen the relevant symbol, carried by an angel. Of the many *brasses*, two at least should be seen:– in the nave, that of Geoffrey and Alice Boleyn (1440), and in the n. transept, that of Thomas Roos (or Rose) and his wife. They stand

with their twelve children on a fine bracket which was once part of an elaborate design. Thomas was the donor of the transept in 1440, and his *rebus* (a 'T' enclosing a rose) can be seen in the roof bosses. Note that Thomas wears his hair short. Fashion changed, and his sons' hair is longer and brushed forward, a style that lasted until 1480.

Salthouse, St Nicholas (C2): Standing high and grey on its hillside above the village, looking broadside down to the open sea, the church gives an instant impression of clean architectural lines and of crisply ordered design. It is a handsome example of late *Perpendicular*, having been built in Henry VII's reign, and completed in 1503, by Sir Henry Heydon (member of a family powerful hereabouts for around a century, their seat being not far away at

Baconsthorpe). The tower is from the earlier church, with attractive *Decorated* bell openings. The aisle windows to n. and s. are unusual – very tall and narrow (perhaps a precaution against the tempestuous winds on this exposed coast?) with neat little tracery heads which suggest 'Dec' rather then 'Perp'. Inside – light, lofty and impressive; a single 'hall' with no chancel arch, the whole topped by a fine C15 *arch-braced* roof, with handsomely carved and panelled *wall-plates* and deep *wall posts* resting on 'battlemented' *corbels*. The posts frame a range of neat, small *clerestory* windows – eleven in all, twice the number of the bays of the elegant *arcade* with an extra one for the sanctuary. The aisle windows are let down to make seats (as at Cley, Wiveton, Tunstead and others). Each aisle has a *piscina* at the e. end, indicating the former presence of chapels there (see glossary, *chantry/guild chapels*); that in the n. aisle is let into the easternmost column of the arcade, its bowl having been put back there some years ago when it was discovered built into a brick oven in a cottage in the village. The delightful old door and arch in this corner leads into the vestry which, after being ruinous for many years, was rebuilt earlier this century. In the s. aisle is displayed a 1613 Authorised Version of the Bible, brought back here to its original home from Kelling in 1959. Also a contemporary copy of John Jewell's 'The Defence of the Apology of the Church of England', of about 1564, when all churches were instructed to provide a copy of the book: but few remain now, so this is a rarity. The splendidly preserved C15 font carries on its panels the *Symbols of the Evangelists*, the *Instruments of the Passion,* and a *Tudor rose*. Back to the e. end now, to a chancel dominated by its soaring e. window – though those to l. and r. of the altar are somewhat at odds with its Perpendicular majesty, their simple, graceful Y-tracery heads harking back to around 1300 and suggesting that they were retained in the 1500 rebuilding. Of special remark

is a piscina set into the sill of the e. window – most unusual. In floor of chancel – a lovely little *chalice brass* to Robert Fevyr, 1519, the church's first rector. High on n. wall, traces of painted texts, dated 1638. Soon after Sir Henry Heydon built his church, a great *rood screen* was erected across the first bay from the e., and *parclose screens* across the arches between chancel and aisles. As late as the C18, according to *J.C. Cox*, this was all dismantled and cut up – 'barbarously', he says, and he's right! The major portion is now at the back of the nave pews, where among the brutally disfigured paintings one can make out *St James the Less*, with spear (l. of font) and *St Jude*, with boat (r. of font, behind pillar). Another section is behind the pulpit, where *St Thaddaeus*, with a fish, can be identified. More pieces make up the extraordinary, itsy-bitsy choir stalls which – having accepted the implicit vandalism – one must say are really rather charming in their cobbled-up way, together with their masses of graffiti and scratched-in ships; the coloured bits on the s. side were parclose panels, stencilled with flowers and mitred 'Ns' for the church's dedicatory saint, Nicholas. Yet more remnants comprise the ricketty side-table immediately behind the n. side choir stalls. Born at Salthouse and baptised in this church was *Sir Christopher Myngs*, the celebrated admiral who died in action against the Dutch in 1666.

Saxlingham, St Margaret(C3): Village, churchyard and church alike here have a pleasing air of being cared for and cherished. Plain tower (C14? – the severely simple *plate tracery* of the bell openings would appear to indicate so), the rest of the church in C15 *Perpendicular* style. At the end of the last century the church was in so delapidated a state that the architects recommended complete rebuilding. Sir Alfred Jodrell of nearby Bayfield Hall, nonetheless undertook restoration and renewal in 1898, just as he did at neighbouring Glandford a year later. Inside, the effect is of a Victorian Gothic, rather than a medieval church, but it is done with such good taste that it is very acceptable. Though perhaps it is a little too zealous when, as in the s. transept behind the organ, the *dropped sill window* and three *piscinae* (this number in a very small space perhaps being a legacy of the guilds of St Margaret and St John the Baptist, who in medieval times had their altars in the church) have been 're-done' like new! Happily, the sedately carved, octagonal C15 font at the head of the nave is as the centuries handed it down. Of special interest here: set in a niche in an arch leading into the n. transept is a kneeling alabaster figure of Mirabel, died July 15th, 1593, wife of Sir Christopher Heydon; in the e. wall of the opposite transept is a curious little alabaster bible, carved with a quotation from a pre-C17 translation of the bible. These two remnants are all that remain of what must have been a most amazing monument which Sir Christopher, a scholar and astrologer, erected to his lady. *Blomefield* describes it graphically in his 'History of Norfolk' as 'a sumptuous monument, which takes up almost the whole area (of the chancel) . . . being raised in form of an Egyptian pyramid, of marble and stone, supported by pillars, and reaching almost to the top of the chancel'. In turn, the pyramid, in an arch of which knelt Lady Mirabel, was surrounded by effigies of her eight children and four large 'Dorick pillars'. It was removed in 1789, on the grounds (a good excuse?) that it was 'delapidated and dangerous'. Note the strange corbel head also in the s. transept wall, of a bearded, vinegary faced man. The organ here is worthy of mention, a fine example from the Jevington works, and originally in St Barnabas' Church, Kentish Town.

Saxthorpe, St Andrews (D3): The church stands high and handsome, with a solid outside stair turret, with *carstone*

quoins (corner stones) on the s. side of the C14 tower; and with pretty *clerestory* windows with pointed heads. The nave and aisles were rebuilt in 1482 by the lord of the manor and his tenants, and the fine tall *arcades* rest on big octagonal pillars. The older chancel has a *low side window* with a long wall seat below it. The C14 font has a plain bowl, but the panels of the stem are delicately traceried. Its cover is a neat little *Jacobean* piece marked 'A.P. 1621'. The C15 *screen* has been badly defaced, but one can see that the original painted brocade patterns were rich in colour and design. Unlike the rest, the front bench on the n. side of the nave has a traceried back. An Agnus Dei is carved in the recess on the double width end, and this crest of the Page family can be seen on *ledger stones* at both ends of the nave. A crowned 'P' is carved on the bench end opposite for Peter Page, vicar from 1482 to 1536, who lies buried e. of the font. The C17 communion rails are distinctly eccentric. The uprights have large turned balls at the top, and the heavy top rail curves down between them, with flat supports that look rather like chair splats. Under the tower is a most interesting combination of *Royal Arms* and commandment, or *Decalogue* board. Used originally as a *reredos*, it has the arms of Queen Anne flanked by the Decalogue, Lord's Prayer and verses from the psalms – all of it on canvas and in a wooden frame. It is faded and sadly torn in places, but the design and execution are all exceptionally good.

Scottow, All Saints(E4): This church is quite some way off the road and the approach is through a farmyard. Hens forage unconcernedly in the churchyard under the limes, against a background of constant noise from R.A.F. Coltishall next door. Here there is an interesting mixture of styles. The porch – groined with a *Green Man* centre *boss*, has battlemented capitals on the outer arch which match the s. *arcade* piers, and the aisle itself goes with the tower – all *Perpendicular*. The n. aisle has rather later square headed windows, but the n. arcade rests on slim *quatrefoil* (four-leafed) *Decorated* pillars contemporary with the chancel. The big e. window has flowing tracery, and a late elevation of the sanctuary on three steps has put the *piscina* at floor level. A pity, because it has pretty, open tracery in the arch and can no longer be used. By it, an old 3ft x 2ft *mensa* (altar slab) has been framed on a stand as a memorial, and not far away there is a small *chalice brass* to a priest, Nicholas Wethyley c.1520. On the n. side is a great grey and rather ugly obelisk to Davey Durrant (d.1757) by *George Storey of Norwich* on one of his off days. There is no chancel arch, but the *rood beam* survives and the *rood stair* to the s. has remnants of the original wooden treads. The nave has a set of plain deal *box pews* and in front, a C17 double-sided oak lectern which swivels on a turned shaft. Carved overall, it even has an openwork door at one end and came from a London church in 1876. The organ case is clad in a rich array of carved *Renaissance* panels dated 1641 and 1649 which have also been brought in from elsewhere. The font cover is a jolly C17 affair of thin painted dolphins supporting a centre shaft. There are ten *hatchments* of the Durrant family, the *Royal Arms* of William and Mary on the s. aisle w. wall, and above the s. door, the arms of Elizabeth II. These are remarkably good and look more like C18 work – possibly an update.

Sea Palling, St Margaret (G4): Early unbuttressed w. tower, and what was a C14 nave, aisles and chancel arrangement – the aisles have gone, leaving blocked windows to the west. C14 font with shallow tracery round the bowl like an exercise in window design. A large *banner stave locker* hides behind the organ, and there are *rood loft* stairs with square-headed doorways and an

associated *piscina*. A series of boards listing lifeboat rescues 1860-1929 are propped up behind the decayed remains of the *rood screen*. Most of the s. door is original C15.

Sharrington, All Saints (C3): The C14 tower has a curious set of small windows set above the more conventional bell-openings. Entrance now through the base of the tower from the w. end. The church formerly had aisle and transepts, and when these were pulled down in the late C18/early C19, the C13 arcades were filled in to form the present nave walls. Chancel and vestry rebuilt in 1880 and the roof and fittings, including the font, date from then. Good brass to John Daubeney (mounted on s. wall of chancel with others) He died in 1469 defending Caister Castle for the Pastons against the Duke of Norfolk, and wrote some of the famous *Paston Letters* for Margaret Paston. At the time of writing, the church is out of use, with the e. end under repair.

Sidestrand, St Michael and All Angels (E3): Clement Scott – best remembered as the fiery drama critic of the 'Daily Telegraph' in the 1860s and fierce enemy of the 'new wave' plays of Henrik Ibsen, rather than as a commentator on rural byways – brought fame to this old poppy-strewn churchyard by calling it 'the garden of sleep'. But the last of the old church which he knew slipped into the sea in 1916. The present building was erected in 1881 by Sir Samuel Hoare. He duplicated the former church and re-used much of its fabric. The winged angel above the s. doorway came from there, and so did the strange cross in the nave e. wall. The inscription refers to a man of the C15, but it looks much older. The organ case of mixed Georgian/Gothic design dates from 1800, and the war memorial set in the n. wall made use of a niche found in an antique shop. Headstones from the old churchyard line the wall by the road.

Skeyton, All Saints (E4): On a windy upland with big fields all around and but one house for company. The *car-stone* quoins (corner stones) in the s.w. corner point to an early date and although the nave windows are C15, the tower and blocked n. doorway are C13 and the foundations of a n. aisle were found in 1845. One of the old *lancet* windows is blocked up at the side of the porch, and the door you enter by is C15 and has a fine robust knocker. This was one of the first Norfolk churches to exchange its *box pews* for benches in 1846, and the font at that time was apparently a wooden affair painted red and yellow! The replacement is a stiff uncomfortable piece with a shallow octagonal bowl. The cover is better – in the style of Salle with radiating fin buttresses and well proportioned. The little cast Victorian *Royal Arms* are painted and gilt and look well.

Sloley, St Batholomew (E4): The ground plan is a little unusual. The tower is offset to the n. and its base seems to be the same date as the chancel, which has a blocked n. window and *piscina* c.1300. There were extensions in the first half of the C14, and a late C15 rebuilding produced the stately arches of the *arcades*. Above the matching chancel arch can be seen the line of its predecessor, offset to the n. – so everything had been pushed sideways. The outstanding thing here is the *seven sacrament font*. It is quite the best surviving example with very little damage to the panels. Clockwise from the e. they are: Baptism of Christ, Ordination, Matrimony, Baptism, Mass (one figure ringing the *sanctus bell*), Confirmation (illustrating the common medieval practice of infant confirmation), Penance (the devil of sin pushed away by an angel), and Extreme

Unction. Angels display shields in the corona under the bowl, and shaft niches have standing figures, and the *Symbols of the Evangelists* crouch at the foot. In the s. aisle chapel is the recessed table tomb of Oliver le Gros (d.1435). He was Lord of the manor and in one of the *spandrels* the arms are encircled by the double 'S' collar of Lancaster, and all the achievements have been picked out in colour. The nave has a homely set of C18 *box pews* with a two-decker pulpit en suite – all grained light oak. Apart from painting the doors a jolly canary yellow, the present church generation's contribution is polythene sheeting on removable frames to blank off the s. aisle. Well, it must be pretty cold for a small congregation in winter.

Smallburgh, St Peter (F4): St Peter's tower fell in 1677, taking with it the w. bay of the nave. This was replaced in 1902 when the bell-cote was added. The e. window is Victorian, but those in the nave are pleasing late C14 work. The roof is a High Victorian version of *hammer beam* with tie beams (see glossary, *Roofs*). Painted red and cream, with a running text on the *wall plate*, it even has at its e. end a 'celure' as in medieval times – an adorned and decorated section of roof over the *rood loft* – although there is no rood to go with it. The bottom half of the C15 *screen* has a good deal of its original colour, but the saints in the panels are heavily defaced. Some can still be identified: far l. *St Anthony*, l. of the opening *St George*, r. of opening *St Giles* and *St Lawrence*. The back has traces of a pretty brocaded design. The *piscina* is very decorative, with a *cusped* arch and pierced *quatrefoils*. On the n. side of the sanctuary is a very elegant memorial by *Thomas Rawlins* to Richard Oram (d.1762). The plain tablet has a curvaceous surround and top, with a cherub's head below. Before you leave to go down the attractive little avenue of sycamores, have a look at the door. It is C15 with remains of applied tracery at the head.

Southrepps, St James (E3): This is a big church which was even larger before the aisles were pulled down in 1791. The *arcades* can still be seen. The commanding 114ft tower is beautifully proportioned and one of the best in Norfolk. The *base course* has the shell emblem of *St James* (adopted as a badge by pilgrims to his shrine at Compostella in Northern Spain), and the large w. door is flanked by nice niches with shields and tracery above. The sound holes have a delicate lattice design, and above the large three-light belfry windows is a fine parapet. Inside, the panels of the C15 *screen* have their original colouring – a diaper of crowned 'M's on alternate red and green grounds. The priest's door in the s. wall of the chancel has a lovely *hood mould* terminating in demi-figures of laymen with most expressive heads.

South Walsham, St Mary (F5): The C15 tower and s. porch catch the eye for the unity of their design and the quality of their execution. The porch has a fine frontage, with the Virgin and the Angel of the *Annunciation* in the *spandrels* of the door. Over it, a lovely little niche contains a small sculptured group which probably represents the coronation of the Virgin. In the s.e. corner of the sanctuary is a large incised slab which was from the tomb of a C15 Abbot of St Benet's Abbey (whose ruins are on the banks of the River Bure, not far away from here near Ludham). After use as a doorstep in the palace in Norwich, long since disappeared, of the *Dukes of Norfolk* (see glossary) it came home to the abbot's birthplace in the 1940s. The C15 *rood screen* has the distinction of retaining its original door handles, and has a most interesting inscription in a mixture of Latin and English:

> 'Pray for the souls of John Galt and his wives the which have done painting this perke'.

Galt was a serf who, having gained his freedom, had the screen painted in gratitude. The wall behind the pulpit shows how the decorative pattern of the screen was continued beyond it in paint. In a showcase in the n. aisle are photocopies and transcripts of the *Solemn League and Covenant* entries from the parish registers. Parishioners were ordered during the Cromwellian period to sign the Covenant – but at the *Restoration* the offending or embarrassing pages were nearly everywhere torn out. South Walsham's are the only example left in Norfolk. In the huge churchyard are the remains of a second parish church. St Lawrence's tower once outshone St Mary's, but it has gone, and the rest of the building is derelict. Windows are knocked out, and it is a sad and sorry sight.

Sparham, St Mary the Virgin (C5): This is a church where rebuilding has resulted in some curious anomalies. The early C14 chancel 'weeps' slightly to the s. and must always have done so, because the two easternmost *arcades* of the nave match it in date. At that time there was a lower roof and the *clerestory* had small *quatrefoil* windows. Two of them can still be seen blocked up, above the arches at the e. end. The tracery of the window at the w. end of the n. aisle shows that it too was built at the same time. The present C15 tower has buttresses on the inside – a sure sign that it was free-standing when built, but when the nave arcade was extended to meet it the original setting-out proved to be faulty and the western-most bays had to be stretched to bridge the gap, and heavier pillars were used. The s. aisle was added in 1481, and the detailing of the s. porch matches the clerestory. A *scratch dial* on the l. hand *jamb* of the inner door shows that it was in use before the porch was built. The tower is handsome and has an unusually rich niche over the w. door. Designed no doubt for a statue of the Virgin, it has a nodding *ogee* arch with canopy, and attendant lions on top of slim pillars. The C15 clerestory stops short one bay from the e. end and a big gable window was used to complete the top lighting. The arch-braced roof has little angels under the ridge bearing shields, looking for all the world like birds in flight. The chancel is now nicely open, with modern stalls incorporating old bench ends set well back. The original C15 screen is no longer there, but four of its panels have been framed and stand in the n. aisle. They are of quite exceptional interest and two of them are illustrations from the Dance of Death – a unique portrayal in screen painting. In one, a shrouded skeleton rises from a tomb by the font in a church, and the text on the scrolls is from the Book of Job, chapter 10:

'I should have been as though I had not been born. . .'

In the other, a macabre pair of corpses are dressed in the fashionable clothes of Richard III's day, with another paraphrase from Job:

'Man that is born of woman hath but a short time. Now he is. Now he is not. . .'

The two other panels have St Thomas of Canterbury, and the local St Walstan of Bawburgh, who was believed to be of royal blood – witness the crown and sceptre. Just by these panels is a good brass to a rector, William Mustarder (c.1490) in mass vestments. While still in the n. aisle have a look at the lengths of carving on the e. window ledge. They probably came from the wall plate of the original roof. The C18 Royal Arms have been well restored and are now over the n. door.

Spixworth, St Peter (E5): The church presents an odd outline, with a tiny unbuttressed tower at the s.w. corner which was rebuilt in 1804. The nave and chancel are in one, separated from the s. aisle by an arcade set on thin octagonal columns. The e. window has a nice variation of tracery, with a spray of leaf forms springing from the centre above the panels, two of which have ogee heads. The C15 piscina and sedilia

are grouped under a single square label. On the other side of the chancel is a splendid monument to William and Alice Peck (1635), by Edward Marshall. The two marble figures lie in shrouds, one above and behind the other, below a canopy. A helm is fixed to the wall above. There are verses below, one of which reads:

'Tread soft, tis holy ground, the dust lyes heere
Was once pure flesh, the relique of a cleere
And noble soule, which because, free and rare
Heav'n did translat, and there it shines a starre,
But this sad earth's below, which being dust
Did heere fall downe & this kind ground in trust
Keepes till it starts refind; for then this clay
Shall ev'n a sunne appeare at that great day'.

Sprowston, St Mary and St Margaret (E5): Almost entirely of the Perpendicular period, though the tower (good, restrained brickwork) is C18, and everything heavily restored 1889-90. The porch has C18 sun dial and four mass dials on s.e. buttress. Inside, the arcades are C14, s. earlier than n. There are Royal Arms of George III on canvas. An attractive, traceried C15 piscina has, erected across it with scant regard, one of the unusual number of monuments here. This splendid one is to Sir Thomas and Lady Adams, 1667 – he was Lord Mayor of London, an intimate friend of Charles II, and bought the Sprowston estate from the last Corbet baronet (see below) in 1645. The sober Latin tells that Sir Thomas suffered from calculus and that, after death, a stone was taken from his body which weighed 25 ozs (a learned ecclesiologist, we read with amusement, was much disconcerted on viewing the monument by 'this minutely indelicate catalogue of his ailments'). In startling contrast is the simplicity of the adjoining small tablet to Dame Anne Adams who, poor lady, had ten children and died in 1674 giving birth to the last of them, when only 33. In the n. chapel are the Corbets: John, 1559 – half his body missing, but four sons and six daughters still in attendance; Thomas, 1617, High Sheriff and father of one of the regicides of Charles I; Miles, executed 1662 – a very good monument; and an earlier Miles, 1607. Also fine is a monument in the n. aisle to Christopher Knolles, 1610 – even though he, wife and nine offspring are all decapitated. Others are a brown and white marble piece, good, to Nathaniel Micklethwaite, 1757, by *Robert Page of Norwich*; and a grand marble work by the younger *John Bacon* to Lady Maria Micklethwaite, 1805, symbolising her death in childbirth. As you leave the church, note the lovely group of yews to the east.

Stalham, St Mary the Virgin (F4): A big, *Perpendicular* town church with a massive, squat tower. An outline in stone indicates that the tower once had an enormous w. window, but there is now only a modest one in Perpendicular style. The s. aisle windows are impressive Perpendicular, but those on the n. side have Y-tracery, which if original puts them about a century earlier. While outside the n. aisle, note at the e. end the strange interlacing triple-head stone carving. . . sharing four eyes; and near it, on the *clerestory* corner, a carving of what looks like a lovable bear! The e. end windows of the two aisles have lovely flowing tracery of late *Decorated* style, which is reproduced in the chancel, which was rebuilt in 1827. Entering through the s. porch (a Victorian restoration) we find ourselves in a spacious, uncluttered interior. The eye is drawn at once to the fine octagonal C15 font, standing high on its three traceried steps, its rich carvings round bowl and stem magnificently intact – during the last century it was found, partially buried and covered in plaster, thus its happy preservation.

The bowl carving shows a lovely Baptism of Christ, God as Trinity, and pairs of saints, with more saints around the stem. The five-bay *arcade* and above, the clerestory with its deeply inset *quatrefoil* windows, are Decorated, as are the soaring tower and chancel arches. To either side of the latter are two enormous *squints*, but these no longer, as originally intended, look direct from the side chapels to the high altar – for the chancel has been stripped and cleared and the altar brought forward to the centre: it looks impressive, and admirably serves for today's family communion. In the s.e. corner is a splendidly pompous tomb, all swathes and cherubs, to Katherine Smyth, 1718. Mounted on the s. wall are five restored panels from the old *rood screen*, l. to r., Saints *Andrew, Thomas of Canterbury, Edward the Confessor, Edmund . . .* and *Roche*. The latter is a very rare representation. . . he draws aside his robe to display his particular and unpleasant symbol, plague spots on his left leg. The s. aisle has a beautiful *angle piscina* and a *dropped sill sedilia*. In front of the altar are two tiny figures from a C15 *brass*. Beside the n. aisle altar an *aumbry* shows hinge marks of its old door in the stone. As you leave, note by the s. door the remains, still opulent, of what must have been a remarkably grand *holy water stoup*.

Stibbard, All Saints (B4): A pretty village church within a peaceful curtilage of trees, the lead cap (rather French!) on its stumpy, C14 and recently well restored tower being visible above the foliage as you approach. The tower's red brick, Victorian buttresses surprisingly set it off rather well, even the one slapped over the w. window. The range of windows here is quite fascinating: simple, attractive *Perpendicular* in nave s. wall; a curious, but appealing pair in the n. aisle, one pointed, the other square headed; the irregular, and rather charmingly heavy-handed tracery over the aisle altar. In n. wall of chancel, there's a lovely little *Decorated* window containing a lot of fragments of C14 glass, made up into a mosaic of venerable colour; and the best of them, the chancel e. window – five slim lights of interlacing tracery, but with a *quatrefoil* slipped in interestingly at the top . . . most individual. Note especially the *rood beam*, probably original, which would have supported the *rood loft* in pre-*Reformation* times, and now bears a modern cross: above, fragments of original painting on the wall. Pleasant Perpendicular *arcade*. Base of an old *screen* remains; some nice carving on the (battleship grey painted!) pulpit; some lovely old battered C15 *poppyhead* bench ends, with assorted carved figures.

Stiffkey, St John Baptist (B2): Tucked away below the seaside ridge where this picturesque village clings, this church surprises at once with its impressive parapets to the nave, in chequerwork flint, punctuated by tiny pinnacle-columns rising from the buttresses; and by its handsome porch, with a good *Decorated* outer arch with shields in the *spandrels*, above it a figure niche; and the upper gable end delightfully chequered in red brick and flint. The upper room to the porch has gone but the octagonal turret at this corner was the stairway to it. An architecturally similar turret stands at the opposite diagonal corner (s.e.) of the nave: this was, unusually, a rood turret, giving entrance to the *rood loft* by a still-existing outside door and stairway. The church's interior is bright and light, the spacious nave lit by large C15 *Perpendicular* windows (in the centre-s. window are fragments of ancient glass). The chancel arch has *corbel* portrait heads and most interesting capitals – one is carved with floral motifs, but the other has heads of two women and a man in fashionable headgear, the former in 'butterfly' headdresses. The chancel has an attractively coarse *piscina* with a lop-sided arch; and nearby, three old *misericords*

(though the carved seats have gone). At extreme r. in front of communion rails, only a small inscription remains of the *brass* to Margaret Branche, 1479. Opposite, set low in the n. wall, is a deep recess with a pointed arch: its purpose intrigues – an *Easter Sepulchre* perhaps? Nathaniel Bacon's large monument is restrained, in black marble with coloured shields in alabaster; the date 1615 is squeezed in, in miniscule script . . . the monument having been erected by Nathaniel before he died, and the date added later. Note the chancel n. window – an example of *plate tracery* (see *Styles of Architecture*). The e. window is in the late Decorated flowing style, but it looks like a replacement.

Stody, St Mary (C3): The church stands prettily on its small hill, approached by narrow winding lanes, with a house or two nearby. The round tower has C14 bell-openings but may well be *Saxon* in origin. The chancel windows have good and varied *Decorated* period tracery, while those in the nave are later. Best of all is the composition of *arch-braced roofs*, culminating in a timber *rib-vault* at the crossing of nave and transepts – most unusual in a church of this size. The remains of a *St Christopher* have been rather boldly re-coloured opposite the door and provided with a painted frame.

Stokesby, St Andrew (G5): A field path from the n. (where you can run your hands through the ears of corn in the summer), or a grassy track from the s. leads to the well kept churchyard lined with beech and lime. Altogether a delightful spot, and the church itself is very attractive. The roofs are thatch, the C13 tower has triple-stepped battlements of the C16, and there is a porch in warm red brick which sets off the white slatted outer door. The s. door proper has a C14 ring handle with long wrought iron decorated straps, and on its inside face, a most eccentric placement for the Victorian arms painted on a semi-circular board. The C14 nave has a *scissors-braced* rood left open to the thatch, but the chancel now has a coved ceiling in pale blue – that and its white-washed walls mark it off clearly in the absence of the customary arch. At the w. end there is an interesting set of benches with *poppyheads* and traceried backs; the ends, (one with initials 'E.W.') have big figures carved on the arms. There are dogs, a lion holding a shield blazoned with the arms of Berney, a griffin, a mighty odd eagle, and the best is a lady kneeling at a desk on which she has laid her rosary. On the chancel floor (s. side) a *brass* to Edmund Clere (d.1488) and his wife – he in armour with a fawning greyhound under his feet, she in a low cut dress with arms akimbo. The sanctuary now has a raised board floor and the brass to Anne Clere (d.1570) has been lifted and screwed to the wood (s. side). This is a very good figure in cloak, hood and ruff, with lots of character in the face. Her five sons and six daughters are grouped on two separate plates. At the sanctuary step look for the *ledger slab* of John Wace, rector here for 60 years while his brother James served nearby Filby for forty. On the e. wall is an interesting evasion of the low church prejudice against prayers for the dead – the Rev. William Taylor Worship's memorial:

> '. . . Reader, offer, if not a prayer, at least a kind wish for the welfare of his soul.'

The enigma of the tall blue pole at the end of a front pew is solved if you know that it was put there recently to help a blind parishioner find his accustomed place.

Stratton Strawless, St Margaret (E4): The squat C15 tower was probably planned to go higher, but was finished off at an intermediate stage, and has seated figures at the corners, two of which have been recently renewed. The aisle was rebuilt in the C17, and is divided from the nave by a gothicky *screen* beneath the *arcade*. It houses the monuments of the Marsham family. At the e. end is Thomas Marsham (d.1638). His marble effigy reclines gracefully on a black sarcophagus, one hand negligently lifting aside the shroud, as the eyes look heavenward. A coat of arms is supported by improbable swags of fruit, and is flanked by trumpeting angels. Evidences of mortality peep out of the grill below. On the s. wall, the family of Henry Marsham kneels. Henry (d.1678) sports a full wig, son Henry is in long buttoned coat with stylish pockets, and wife Anne is demure, with a pearl necklace under a plain cap. They all kneel on cushions, but so shallow is the ledge that they are without benefit of legs below the knee, and the effect is of a family of amputees. Baby Margaret in swaddling bands is upright on a pedestal. By the n. wall is the effigy of a late C13 woman wearing a wimple, and in the heads of two of the n. windows there is some fine C15 glass. The easternmost window contains figures of the four Evangelists – note *St Luke* in his role as painter of the Virgin's portrait. The nave is dominated by a magnificent brass chandelier, with 25 branches in three tiers. It is said to have come from Russia, and looks to be late C17 or early C18.

Strumpshaw, St Peter (F6): The continuous roof over nave and chancel has been lowered and flattened, to the extent that the outer line of the tower arch to the nave shows above it. This gives the C15 tower a remarkably gaunt look, particularly from the e. when the w. buttresses cannot be seen. It is handsome nonetheless, with stepped battlements bearing St Peter's initials and a flourish of eight pinnacles. The rest of the building is of the late C14 with Y-tracery in the chancel and later square-headed *Perpendicular* windows in the nave. The nave roof interior is moulded and painted, and there is no chancel arch. The bowl of the C15 font has alternating shields and roses in the panels and deeply overhangs the shaft, around which sit six lions. A fragment of a former C13 font sits at the bottom of the thin *banner stave locker* e. of the n. door. The *rood screen* is good and has delicate tracery above the *crocketted* arches, with much of the colour remaining. The lower panels are painted in alternate red and green, patterned with ornament. That to the left of the opening incorporates little 'R's which may indicate that the nave altar on that side was dedicated to *St Edmund*, King and martyr. There are clear indications that additional sections projected westward to flank the altars, in the manner of the more famous screen at Ranworth. The *Early English* double *piscina* has beautiful *trefoiled* arches and an engaging dragon in the foliage of one of the stops.

Suffield, St Margaret [E3]: A big church standing high and almost alone in gently rolling open country. The top of the C15 tower is severely plain like Cawston, but has very decorative sound holes and a chequered *base course*. The C16 s. door is handsome with a succession of cusped panels round the edge. Inside, the *arcades* and aisles do not match – the n. side is in straightforward *Perpendicular* style, but the s. side is coarser work, possibly late C16. The late C13 chancel has an unusually tall *lancet* where one would expect to see a *low side window*, and a double *piscina* with little arches springing from a Purbeck shaft. The early C16 *screen* (only the lower part remains) has a fine variety of livestock in the *spandrels* of the panel tracery, including a pig playing the harp, eagle catching a rabbit, and an owl. Eight of the panels have painted figures: l. of the opening, the *Four Latin Doctors,* to the r. *St Luke, St John, Sir John Schorne,* and *St Heiron.* The rather battered tomb chest in the s. aisle is that of John Symonds (d.1504) and his coat of arms in colour on the front features a sprightly dolphin.

Sustead, St Peter and St Paul [D3]:

W. of the village in an exposed position, with a single house for company. Round tower with a neat brick battlemented cap. The C14 porch is particularly pleasing, and has diagonal hooded buttresses, two large *flushwork* crosses, and an unusual decorative jeu d'esprit at the top of the arch. The outer *jambs* have C17 and C19 graffiti including a large hand-in-glove outline. The chancel s. windows are excellent – leaf terminations to the hoods outside, and inside, stiff-leaf foliage surmounting delicate shafts. The double *piscina* has a satisfying combination of clustered shafts and steep arches, but the *sedilia* design is oddly broken into by the window above, although of the same period. The C14 n. transept has gone, leaving a fine blank arch, and an *ogee*-headed doorway is also blocked. The simple C17 pulpit with little angel heads came from the redundant church at N. Barningham. The C15 font has an interesting set of armorial shields round the bowl, including those of the Calthrop and Palgrave families. There are fragments of high quality medieval glass – in the head of one of the s. windows look for the angels playing instruments, particularly the engaging bagpipe player, whose instrument has a lion's head at the junction of pipe and bag. There is a C15 exterior *rood loft stairs* in the s. side in warm red brick, with a little two-light window and decorative (diaper) patterning in flint.

Sutton, St Michael [F4]: Much restored, but most attractive and lovingly maintained in its orderly churchyard. Interesting range of windows: the three in the s. aisle have Y-tracery of around 1300 and at the w. end, a simple intersecting pattern, with restored *cusping.* The tower (C14, with nice *Decorated* bell openings) has a neat and simple *Perpendicular* w. window; also Perpendicular, but square headed, are the n. side windows. The e. window is Victorian restoration. The late Perpendicular porch is most attractive, using red brick freely, in particular for the splendid outer arch, which is squared off with a hood; the porch formerly had an upper room, but is now open to the roof. Inside, the church is serenely uncluttered and appealing, with white-washed walls and gleaming woodwork. All the furnishings are modern, except the pulpit and combined reading desk below it, an endearingly simple *Jacobean* piece; on the rail of the modern steps has been 'planted' an ancient kingly head. An old wooden carved frieze, with tiny *Tudor* roses, plus two more well-carved heads and *poppyhead* fragments, have been added to the low rail dividing off the spaciously wide chancel. A low, plain nave *arcade* of the C14, an earlier tower arch, and a dignified font – octagonal, on eight shafts and also C14 – complete this pleasant and welcoming church.

Swafield, St Nicholas (E3): Standing clear above the village, a handsome small *Perpendicular* building with fine, large windows. The nave windows have most unusual carved *corbels* to their *dripstones*: all alike, not quite grotesques, yet what? Seahorses? The priest's door in chancel, s. side, and the blocked n. doorway have unusual arch heads, cut from just two pieces of stone. The beautiful little porch has a lovely outer arch (and an early coffin slab as door step). Massive inner door with original C14 knocker and plate, but much rusted away. Inside, spacious, wide nave with fine *arch-braced* roof, enormous *bosses* carved with portraits and *Tudor* roses, still showing hints of original colour; and deep *wall plates* and plain *wall posts*. A tasteful idea to use the filled in n. doorway, with wooden steps added, as a war memorial. Nearby a crucifix of stark beauty, in sombre colour, hangs on the n. wall – it was found in separate pieces over a two week period in spring 1937 on Walcott beach, each piece being thickly caked with clay. It is thought it must have been buried, when or why unknown, in nearby cliffs

which had collapsed in a storm shortly before the discoveries. Behind the organ is the entrance to the old *rood stair*. Most attractive 1900 lectern: an angel bears the bible rest, which is convex in order to hold the book open. Very plain chancel, a plain C15 *piscina* with imposed Perpendicular tracery head, and a *dropped sill sedilia*. The base of the old *rood screen* remains, with some very good panel paintings of saints with their symbols: *Andrew*, cross; *Peter*, keys; *Jude*, ship; *Simon*, fish; *James the Great*, staff and club; *John*, chalice; *Thomas*, spear; *James the Less*, book and fuller's club (see glossary, *Saints*). Particularly note on the screen's central door posts the decorative colouring, in floral motif, of great beauty.

Swannington, St Margaret (D5): One of those churches where a series of rebuildings and adaptations over the centuries has produced an interesting mixture. The n. doorway is C13, as is the shallow Purbeck bowl of the font – now in the s. aisle. The nave *arcades* date from c.1300 and the *Perpendicular* tower was built into the existing church so that the aisles flank it. This gives a nice space at the w. end, with big double-depth arches on three sides. The late C15 porch has a *base course* of crowned letters, and I.H.S. NAZARENES in matching *flushwork* above the door. The dragon from the legend of *St Margaret* crouches in one of the arch *spandrels*. The fine C14 *sedilia* in the chancel have *cinquefoil* arches with shallow carved vine, oak, and lily leaves in the spandrels – all neatly enclosed in an ornamented band. The surprise of the church is there too – a Norman pillar *piscina*. It had been hidden in the *rood loft* stairs and was discovered by the rector in 1917. Most piscinas of this type are plain, but this one has lovely little carvings on the cap; *St George* slaying the dragon, and a knight charging into battle with his lance and shield who might have stepped straight out of the Bayeaux

tapestry. While in the chancel, look at
the late Perpendicular roof – panelled
overall, with carved flowers at all the
intersections, and supported on massive
cambered tie beams which have tracery
above them. The richly carved communion table came to the church in
1846. Although the top and stretchers
are new, it is a fine piece, dated 1635.
The sanctuary rails were given in 1912
and are excellent. They have heavy
mouldings above and below, and the
six-baluster clusters at the ends are an
original touch. Below the n. aisle e.
window there is a stone panel with
traces of colour, and this would seem to
be the original reredos for an altar,
although it looks as though it was used
subsequently for a mural monument. A
plan of the church in 1892 shows how
times change – then there were 'raised
seats for the band' below the tower.
(See also Galleries, in glossary). Things
are still changing, and the w. end has
recently been divided off from the body
of the church by tall panelled screens,
each with a solid door. This is well done
and has created a useful meeting area.
Full marks too for the modern kitchen/
cloakroom built onto the side of the
church, with access via the old n. door.

**Swanton Abbot, St Michael and All
Angels** (E4): The C14 tower has angle
buttresses and a square outside stair
turret reaching to the top. The rest is
C15 rebuilding and the 29ft wide nave
proved too much for the arch-braced
roof – it had to be completely reconstructed in 1953. The s. door is medieval
but is probably not as old as the ring and
plate which may be C13. The C14 font
has a thick panelled stem with heavy
mouldings and heads at the angles
under the bowl. The screen is rather
extraordinary. Between 1906 and 1913
the octagenarian Rector rebuilt it, and
the majority is 'his unaided work'. Very
competent too, but for some unknown
reason he reversed the panels and the
faded paintings of the saints now face
the altar. From l. to r. they are: Saints
Andrew, Peter, John, James the Great,

Jude, Simon, James the Less, Philip,
Anthony and Thomas. In the chancel
there is a good brass to Rector Stephen
Multon (d.1477). 18in long, it shows
him robed for the Eucharist. The
sanctuary has been raised and clad in
encaustic tiles – a Victorian blunder
that reduced the piscina to floor level
and made it quite unusable.

Swanton Novers, St Edmund (C3):
Remote from its tiny village, peacefully
surrounded by forest and farmland,
with Barney Church visible a couple of
miles away across the fields – a beautiful spot. A very heavily restored church
however. The tower was rebuilt in
1821. By 1960, it was again in such bad
condition that 'one good hard kick', it
was said in the village, would have sent
it tumbling. In fact the whole church
was in so parlous a state that the
question of abandoning it and building
elsewhere was examined. Happily, the
parishioners refused to take that course
and faced up to the considerable restoration task before them. The job was
done – and today St Edmund's is beautifully cared for. Old materials were
evidently reused in the tower rebuildings, including the Decorated   bell
openings and the w. window, with its
uncluttered Y-tracery and a nice old
statue niche below it. The n. aisle and
the s. porch were added in the 1880s,
during another thorough-going bout of
restoration. The chancel is a Victorian
rebuild too. On the outside wall of the
nave you can make out the outline of a
round-headed doorway, long since
blocked. The masonry, says wise old
Nikolaus Pevsner, suggests it to be
Norman. Inside the church, the effects
of successive restorations are doubly
severe. But of great interest is a curiously carved, ogee-headed piscina in
the chancel, with a 'W' carved on each
side, each surrounded by a circle
studded with Tudor roses. Those same
'W' carvings appear on the C15 font,
where they occur on shields surrounded
by thorns, punctuating other panels
bearing the Symbols of the Evangelists.

Taverham, St Edmund (D5): Up to 1970, both nave and chancel were thatched, but in that year the nave roof was tiled. It is on record that the nave was destroyed by lightning in 1459, which dates the present one accurately: but a *Norman* doorway of the same period as the base of the round tower (the octagonal top was added in the C15) remains on the n. side. The chancel is *Decorated* in style. The church was heavily restored in 1861-63 when the porch and s. aisle were rebuilt. Inside there's a fine C15 *Perpendicular* font, with exceptionally good figures round it (Saints *Edmund, Lambert, Giles* with doe, *Margaret, Anne, James the Less, Agnes* and *Leonard*); a nice C15 screen which could do with a good clean; a *Jacobean* chest; and – one of the best things in the church, some lovely fragments of a C14 screen, probably from some other church, formed into an altar rail. Unfortunate that the modern rail above this delicate filigree tracery does not do it justice. A fragment of the *sedilia*, and *piscina* of the same date, remain in the chancel.

Themelthorpe, St Andrew (C4): There are all the signs of a C13 building here – slim unbuttressed tower, *lancet* windows in the chancel and tower, and the re-set *jambs* in the outer porch doorway, but the foundation is older. There are no dressed quoins (corner stones) at the nave corners and the herringbone pattern of masonry points to this. The nave and chancel are one, and although there were the remains of a *rood screen* as late as the mid C19, they have gone. There is a simple trefoil-headed *piscina* and a stepped-sill *sedilia*. *Poppyheads* have been rescued from the C15 benches and re-used in recent work. By the font there is a good *brass* to William Pescod (d.1505), a 13in figure in a long gown with deep sleeves and an inscription below. Three other brass inscriptions are screwed to the n. wall. Fresh paint and lovely flowers.

Thornage, All Saints (C3): Perched above the village street, the church was rather brutally restored twice at the turn of the century, and the interior is bleak. Outside there are indications of Saxon *'long and short'* work at the n.w. angle of the tower, and *Norman* windows remain in the nave and chancel. The s. aisle has disappeared, but the arcade can still be seen. There is a *Renaissance*-style tomb chest of Sir William Butt (d.1583) on the s. side of the chancel, opposite the very pretty little 1812 chamber organ by Thomas Elliot: with its mahogany case and gilded pipes, it was made for Squire Atkinson at Swanton Novers Hall. See also the *ledger stone* slab to Rector Francis Fesquet (d.1734) 'who left his Native country for the sake of the true Protestant Religion'.

Thorpe Market, St Margaret (E3): In 1796 local magnate Lord Suffield engaged a Mr Wood to build him this little exercise in 'churchwarden's gothick', and although it has attracted abuse in the past ('the ugliest place of worship I ever entered' was local historian *Walter Rye's* comment) it is delightful for those who have some feeling for the period. A plain rectangle with twin porches on the s. side and corner turrets, dressed overall in faced white flint, its interior is beautifully kept. The pale blue coved ceiling is picked out in yellow and red, and the windows have a pleasing pattern of blue and orange diamonds. The most surprising thing is the arrangement of two tall *screens* – slender wood columns with glazed panels at the top. That at the chancel end has painted glass panels of Moses and Aaron plus a recent addition of George III's arms in the centre, while the other has another set of *Royal Arms* dated 1796. The font was saved from the old church and so were the excellent memorials in the chancel. One on the n. wall is to Sir Thomas Rant:

'... his sovereign Charles ye first was driven from London by the tumult when retireing into his native countrey he lived hospitably and honourably in composing differences between his neighbours and was chosen a Member of the Healing parliament'.

The tablet opposite to Robert & Elizabeth Britiffe (1712) is an outstanding piece by John Ivory. Good architectural composition with three cherub heads below and a curly pediment with arms above – very like his Mackerell monument in St. Stephen's Norwich.

Thrigby, St Mary (G5): The C14 tower has an odd mixture of bell openings. Two of them are the same period but of differing shapes, while the other pair are a late *Perpendicular* design. The sound-holes are tiny *quatrefoils*. There was a wholesale restoration in 1896 when the nave walls were raised, chancel arch constructed, and the *Decorated* windows put in the chancel. Look for the three little *Norman* or even *Saxon* fragments set in the wall above the chancel arch. The four windows in the nave have wooden mullions and look to be late C18. Best feature of the church is the C14 doorway. The deeply moulded arch has a trail of flower ornament at the outer edge, and big headstops (one has been heavily re-cut and given quite a sultry Hepburnish expression). *Royal Arms* of George III are opposite the entrance above the n. door and are nice enough to merit a better position on the s. wall – they could then be seen with the light instead of against it. The chancel has two big *consecration crosses*, the one on the e. wall retaining its colours. In the base of the tower there's a reminder that communion wafers were sometimes baked in the church – the square recess in the n. wall was an oven, and still has its flue.

Thurgarton, All Saints (D3): Now closed to the public (extensive scaffolding inside) with the thatch in a dreadful state and standing in a riotously overgrown churchyard, alto-gether an unhappy sight. But worth a passing look from the outside for the beautiful, clean-lined C14 *Decorated* windows to the nave, with their *reticulated* tracery; and the curious little passageway under the buttress thrusting out from the s.e. corner of the chancel. At the time of writing, there are hopes that the church will be taken into the care of the Norfolk Churches Trust.

Thurne, St Edmund (F5): The C14 tower has a most curious feature in the ground floor chamber. A circular peephole some 8in in diameter runs through the w. wall at eye level. It aligns with St Benet's Abbey, one and a half miles away across the river, and the suggestion is that it was used to summon the monks in time of need, by lighting a candle within the tower. The interior of the church is plain, with an unpretentious *arch-braced* roof. There is a simple late C13 double *piscina*, and the original *rood beam* divides nave and chancel. The late C17 communion rails are solid, with good balusters, and would be even better for having the old black paint removed. The e. window has good panels of mid C20 glass – the risen Christ and Mary at the tomb, with flanking roundels.

Thurning, St Andrew (C4): In a pretty situation, with one cottage for company. C14 unbuttressed tower and three attractive *Decorated* windows in the s. nave wall. There was a chancel, but by 1719 only the n. wall was left, and the rector was excused by faculty from rebuilding it. Its late C13 e. window, with lovely *reticulated* tracery, and the blocked priest's door are re-set in the present e. wall. So we have an C18 reduced church and what a delightful example it is. The n. aisle is furnished with a range of *box pews* which were allocated to the various village farms, the squire, and the rector. The Hall and Rectory servants had their own pews at the w. end, and these still have the brass uprights for draught-excluding curtains. The corners of the servants' pews are rounded, and the joinery throughout is excellent – fielded panels, crisp mouldings. The body of the nave has plain open benches, and as late as the '20s the congregation still clung to the old convention of 'men on the right, women on the left'. The *three-decker* was moved across to its present position in the 1830s, and the pulpit itself was made up out of panelling from Corpus Christi, Cambridge. William Wilkins pulled down the old chapel there in 1823 to make way for his new design, and Thurning (being a Corpus Presentation) had, through the good offices of Sir Jacob Astley of Melton Constable, the benefit of its discarded fittings designed by 'that ingenious architect' *Sir James Burrough*. And very good they are. Not only the pulpit, but a lovely set of three-sided communion rails, with slim turned balusters, a broad inlaid top rail, and a deep plinth – plus the sanctuary panelling wherein are set the *Decalogue* and Lord's Prayer. On the e. wall a tablet to William Wake (d.1750) is a potted biography of an Indian nabob who died on the way home before he could fully enjoy his rich rewards, and also on the same wall, an excellent tablet in variegated marble to Caleb Elwin (d,1776). The lettering is particularly good, as it is on Elizabeth Wake's memorial in the nave (1759) by *William Tyler*. This has a big scrolly pediment supporting a shell and, again, coloured marble panels. The hat pegs for the men and boys, which cost £2 18s 0d in 1840, still line the s. wall. No wonder C18 churchmen preferred worship in such surroundings to the draughts, muddle and dirt of the average church of their fathers. Here are dignity, intimacy, and comeliness, with a proper regard for the niceties of social distinction – the age caught like a fly in amber.

Thursford, St Andrew (B3): Nothing unusual about this church as you approach it down the park drive to 'the

big house'. Assorted gothic, it seems, with an elegant early C14 tower. But inside it's rather extraordinary, rather gloomy – and a Victorian chancel which either exasperates or enchants. High Victorian pantomime piers, two-deep, look through to a resoundingly ugly transept raised about 6ft higher than the rest of the church, like the public gallery in a courtroom. This was, in fact, the family pew of the Chadds of Thursford Hall, its elevation explained by the fact that their burial vault is underneath. Back in the chancel, typical Victorian *encaustic tiles* cover the floor, and a dominant mosaic *reredos* backs the altar. If you like Victorian glass, then here you will find some of the finest, that in the e. window in particular, of about 1862 ('One of the most beautiful of its time in England, or indeed Europe', enthuses the normally cool and analytical *Pevsner*). In the nave, a central column holding up the n. arcade defies (courteous) description: 'a Victorian disgrace' (Pevsner again) suffices. On the other side, the *arcade* looks original, but is so individual (a long tradition, evidently, at Thursford) that one hesitates to place it, but the s. aisle itself is mainly C15 work. Under the tower, a good marble monument to Sir Thomas Guybon, 1666, signed by the London sculptor, *William Stanton* (1639-1705). Don't miss, in the vestry, the small, stained glass Arms of England, inscribed for Elizabeth I, 1579. A pity it's tucked away there – a most interesting item. As you leave, note the fine doorway – it's the oldest part of the building, said to date from the early C13. Walk round outside (you'll probably have to climb sheep fencing – at time of writing, the churchyard was grazed) and see the wildly fanciful *gargoyles* which complete the Chadd chancel.

Thwaite, All Saints (D3): The round *Norman* tower is smooth and tapers slightly up to the C14 bell openings. There is a blocked doorway low down on the s. side and inside, the outline of a tall and narrow original arch can be seen. The C15 *rood screen* has been cut down to the middle rail, but the remains of *gesso* decoration show that it must have been beautiful. Little canopied figures on the buttresses are very like those on the screen at nearby Aylsham. The plain dark tall pulpit, backboard and *tester* are dated 1624. Somebody later unfeelingly put the steps in and cut half across the screen in so doing. The builder of the aisle chapel was John Puttok (d.1442), and a *brass* to him and his wife Alice lies before the altar there. The same family's arms can be seen on the end of the *box pew* at the front of the nave, which, like the rest, has very crude *poppyheads*. For such a small church the size of the chest is extraordinary and it's completely swathed in iron bands. Equally lavish is the C19 Sunday school room. Complete with fireplace and hat pegs at all levels, it opens off the chancel on the n. side. For some reason a window in the s. aisle attracted the local graffiti specialists. Among other mementos scratched on the glass one reads: 'J. Spurgeon Aldborough January 26 1832 Glazier.' – his version of a trade card!

Trimingham, St John the Baptist's Head (E3): The dedication of the church is most unusual. Before the *Reformation* swept away such things as saintly relics, a local Will mentioned the head of St John the Baptist at Trimingham Church. But had that been so, this would have been a place of pilgrimage to rank with Compostella in northern Spain. In fact what was almost certainly kept here was one of the alabaster representations of the Baptist's head, which were manufactured at Nottingham and Burton-on-Trent in alabaster mined nearby in Derbyshire. As it was, records the 'History, Gazetteer and Directory of Norfolk', 1854, in ancient times Trimingham was visited by pilgrims who 'came to see the head of St John the Baptist which the wily priests pretended they had got'. Which is probably very near the mark. A pleasant

church this is today, mainly in the *Perpendicular* style, with some earlier work built in, and a solid squat tower dating from about 1300. The C15 *rood screen* at once impresses: amazing to learn that it was lost for many years, rediscovered in a farm barn about 1865 and then carefully restored. Notice that its meticulous carving is in a double-layer. Then it has lovely paintings, date about 1500, of eight saints: l. to r. – *Edmund, Clare, Clement*, John the Baptist (holding aloft his own head on a dish, underlining the church's very rare dedication, there being only one other such, in Kent), *Petronella, Cecilia, Barbara* and, again, *Edmund, King and Martyr*. The chancel arch above is beautiful in its simplicity, as is the lovely little pink stone double-headed *piscina* by the altar. Those wooden braces across the angles of the walls, to either side of the altar, are puzzling, with their original-looking *billet* moulding – until you realise they are artistic cosmetics to hide metal braces doing a practical wall-holding job. Note the fairly rustic chancel windows, square headed within Perpendicular recesses. The font is C14, early Perpendicular. All around the church are highly distinctive carvings, all the work of the Rev. Reginald Page, rector here from 1909 to 1923 ... including his own memorial in the chancel, dated 1953 which – unless someone is a very clever style copyist – he prudently carved for himself 'in advance'.

Trunch, St Botolph (E3): A trim, neat church with a fairly plain tower (the little cross-shaped slits in the s. face are air/light holes to the tower stair). A *Perpendicular* church throughout, though the tracery in some of the aisle windows is so *Decorated* in its flowing character that it must be very early Perpendicular – compare with the 'pure' version of the style in the chancel, particularly in the fine e. window. The *clerestory*, still later, has flattened

Trunch: Interior from e. end.

arches of *Tudor* character. On the s. side of the chancel, note the charming and unusual feature of a Perpendicular porch over the priest's door, with a buttress 'seated' on its roof (see also Warham St Mary); the doorway itself is earlier, of the Decorated period. Once inside the church (via the C15 Perpendicular porch) there is no question about what dominates the attention – the astonishing and beautiful oak font canopy, one of only four of its kind in England (the others are at St Peter Mancroft in Norwich, Luton and Durham), a carved, crested, canopied and gilded creation standing on six legs set around the plain C15 font, and richly carved in foliage, flowers, birds and animals (including a pig wearing a bishop's mitre) – a memorable sight. Above is a fine *hammer beam* roof, adorned with angels, with lush carving in the *spandrels*, and long *wall posts* between the clerestory windows (note some remnants of ancient glass in the centre window, n. side). The four-bay *arcade* is of the Decorated period; at the e. end, in both aisles, are slots in the arcade pillars which indicate where *parclose screens* were once fitted to enclose side chapels. On the top stone of the pillar facing into the s. aisle chapel is a faded 'star' outline which could possibly be a *consecration cross.* Below the tower is an open ringing floor, supported on a splendid painted wooden arch – was this, perhaps, formerly part of a west gallery? (see glossary, *Galleries*). The chancel *screen*, dated 1502, is very good, with painted saints in 12 panels, with really beautiful carving above them. The saints and symbols on the l. side are *Thomas,* spear; *Philip,* loaves; *James the Less,* bible and fuller's club; *Matthew,* axe; *James the Great,* shell; *Peter,* keys. on the r. are *Paul,* sword; *Andrew,* cross; *John,* chalice with snake and palm branch; *Jude,* ship; *Simon,* fish; *Bartholomew,* flaying knife. The chancel is full of interest: on n. side, note *squint* through wall (more probably to a sacristy than to an anchorite's cell); set into the base of a window, what

looks like an *Easter sepulchre*; on the s. side, over the priest's door, an intriguing monument to Robert & Ann Thexton, whose initials stand outside a circle containing the *Instruments of the Passion*; two *piscinas*, one angled with an *aumbry* above, built into the base of a window, the rest of which is let down as a *sedilia.* The carvings and scratchings all over the friendly old choir stalls probably date back to a period around 1700 when the chancel was used as a schoolroom (note the ink-well holes!). More interestingly the stalls are raised up on sounding-boxes, to give more resonance. There are half a dozen good old C14 *misericords,* carved with grotesques, angels, winged animals and a devil.

Tunstall, St Peter and St Paul (G6): Once a large and beautiful church to serve this hamlet on the edge of the marshes, but now the tower is riven, its top like a rotten tooth, and grass grows between ivy-laden walls of the ruined nave. Even in 1704 the parish petitioned the Diocesan Chancellor 'to sell the bell in the decaying steeple to repair and adorn the chancel', for 'by reason of dilapidations and fall of roof no service has been held for 40 years'. Ruined churches are not a new thing in Norfolk. They did repair the chancel, and in fact extended it eastwards in red brick, so that the C13 double *piscina* with its simple *cinque-foiled* arches and centre column is now outside the sanctuary and partly masked by pews. The chancel arch was bricked up and a stone table over the little door reads:

> 'This rebilt by Mrs Elzabeth Jenkinson the relict of Mils Jenkinson of Tunstul esq and Mrs Anne Kelsall daughter of ye said Miles and Elizabeth 1705'.

It was repaired again in 1853, and it looks as though the bowl of the C15 font with its good tracery was re-cut then. There was once a chapel s. of the chancel, and the arches of the *arcade* show on the outside. This little building still suffers, and some window glass has been broken, but it is used and cared for, and the Norfolk Churches Trust has given some support.

Tunstead, St Mary (F4): This is another of the great churches raised on the rich back of the medieval *wool trade* in this part of Norfolk. Building went on from 1327 until the *Black Death* called a halt in 1349. Work started again in 1371. The s. facade is striking; where one would expect a *clerestory*, there is a band of blank *arcading* in *flushwork*, and the chancel is almost as tall as the nave. The windows of the aisles and chancel match in size, and a prominent *drip course* runs below them for the whole length, giving a strong unity to the design. It is interesting to see how the flowing (technically, *reticulated*) tracery of the *Decorated* style in the aisle windows was used in conjunction with the tall and slender *Perpendicular, quatrefoil* piers in the nave – an example of how architectural fashions merged and overlapped sometimes. The C15 *arch-braced* nave roof had tie beams added in 1683 but they were not enough to prevent the arcades being pushed outwards. This forced a major restoration 1952-56 when the n. arcade was taken down and rebuilt. The n. aisle wall still has a decided list. The feature of the church (unique in England) is the stone platform at the e. end of the chancel. It has a door on the s. side by which one descends into a barrel-vaulted chamber running the whole width and lit by an iron grating in the top. The platform is reached by steps on the n. side, and no one has produced a definitive answer as to its function. It may have been used for the exhibition of relics, with the chamber serving as a strong room; the presentation of mystery plays has been suggested and scorned in equal proportion. There was once a painted stone *reredos* for the high altar and fragments are preserved in situ behind glass. In 1771 the e. window was bricked up in desperation because the village children persisted in throwing stones at it (nothing changes!), and now a huge cross worked in dried flowers, grasses and foliage hangs before it. The *rood screen* of 1470, tall and very like the later one at Worstead, has much of its original colour, and the paintings of the named saints on the panels are virtually untouched. The floor of the *rood loft* is still there and above it the *rood beam* itself, standing on large brackets and with most of its colour intact. Lastly, be sure not to miss the quite exceptional C14 ironwork on the s. door. The ring is at the centre of a 4ft cross fantastically decorated with curly tendrils from which spring little *trefoil* leaves.

Tuttington, St Peter and St Paul (E4): Apart from the round *Norman* tower with a spike on top, the church was rebuilt in 1450, although some of the window tracery takes earlier forms. The shallow s. porch is two storied but has had its upper floor removed. The chancel has no step and the few stalls are set well back to promote a welcome feeling of space. The *rood loft* stairs are in the n. wall and one of the stone *corbels* for the beam itself remains. The C15 font has shields round the bowl and rests on a very short panelled stem. The 1638 cover is a pleasing design of scrolls radiating from a centre post. The pulpit is dated too – 1635; it has barleysugar balusters to the stairs and is fitted with an hour-glass stand. In the chancel lies Ann Elwin (1697) who seemingly died somewhat preoccupied with lineage:

> '. . . only daughter & heires of Thomas Scamler of Heveingham Esq., & great Grand daughter of Edmund Scamler, formerly Lord Bishop of Norwich. . .'

(it *might* help I suppose). But what one remembers about Tuttington are the bench ends. They have a splendid variety of unusual carvings on the arms which are full of character – the Elephant and Castle has a face peeping out of the window, men play lute and tabor, a milkmaid regards her churn, a fox steals a goose, animals thieve from

a woman's basket – a little gallery of fable.

Twyford, St Nicholas (C4): That this was a Norman church can be seen by the w. wall mixture of flint and carstone, and there is a lancet window with a deep splay. The w. wall is uneven up its centre line and there were traces of a door in the C19, so the original building probably had a western tower, although this suggests that the window has been repositioned. Now, there is a homely brick C18 tower serving as a s. porch, with a most engaging cupola to house the bell. Backed by great trees it is a beautiful combination. Nave and chancel are one, but the e. end is largely undisturbed C13 work, with a fine triple lancet window and a simple piscina. The chancel roof was given a ceiling in the C18 and one mourns the upholstered box pews and three-decker pulpit that were here then. The C13 font is a massive cube relieved only at the corners, standing on four pillars with a centre column. Small is beautiful and so is the hymn board – don't overlook it. It has an inset limewood panel carving of a branch of the vine, with grapes and a tiny butterfly perched on the stem. A sinuously carved pelican in her piety is set upon the top. Exquisite. Admiral Sir Edward Ellis (d. 1943) is commemorated thoughtfully:

> 'Life is eternal and love is immortal, and Death is only an horizon and an horizon is nothing save the limit of our sight'.

A table tomb near the porch illustrates a very likeable trait – Robert Framingham was a shoemaker. His grandson, Henry, became Mayor of King's Lynn and High Sheriff of Norfolk, but he built a fine tomb for his 89 year old grandfather who died in 1683.

Upper Sheringham, All Saints (D2): With the original Sheringham village

clustered comfortably about it, some little way from the sea, All Saints is basically C14 and improved and enlarged a century later. At that stage the handsome s. porch was added, with its excellent flushwork, crocketted pinnacles and fine outer doorway. Inside, the really exciting feature is the rood loft. The C15 screen is good but not unusual – it is the survival of the loft front parapet and floor that is remarkable, together with the original bottom door to the stairs, complete with ring handle. There are carved dragons in the spandrels of the loft, one with the head of a crane. Many bench-ends with good large grotesques on the arms – cat with mouse, mermaid, griffin, chrysom child, monkey, etc. There was originally a large cover for the C14 font, and the painted beam from which it was suspended remains above. Wall monument in the chancel to Abbot Upcher (d.1819) – a cold but impressive piece by Bacon & Manning (who often exhibited at the Royal Academy) commemorating the owner of Sheringham Hall, who never lived to see Humphrey Repton's landscape work completed – his widow weeps disconsolate upon a fallen column.

Upton, St Margaret (F5): The tower had been ruined for centuries before its rebuilding in 1929, and the rest of this C15 church has been extensively restored. It is memorable for its magnificent font which is unusually interesting. Dating from about 1380, it stands on three steps, and the shaft is surrounded by richly canopied figures. They represent the two Sacraments of Mass and Baptism, and godparents flank the mother with her swaddled baby, while priest and bishop occupy the other side. Little angels in the corona above hold rebec, crowth (an early square form of two-string violin), and an open music book with the ancient four line score. All the figures are of high quality. The base of the rood screen has painted panels of the Four Latin Doctors, and

Tuttington St Peter & St Paul

Saints *Etheldreda, Helen, Agatha* and *Joan of Valois* (the latter a very rare bird – how she came to Upton is an interesting query). The way the two outer panels have been cut away suggests that the screen originally stood further west. There is a nice pair of *piscinas*, one in each aisle chapel, with prettily pierced tracery heads. On the way back to the gate, see the memorial on the e. wall of the s. aisle to John Cater (d.1781) which has two attractive cherubs, and this verse:

> 'Afflictions sore long time I bore,
> Physicians were in vain.
> Till God was pleased to give me ease,
> And free me from my pain'.

great skill after being splintered open by vandals. In the lovely, lofty chancel (from where the screen looks even better) there is an excellent modern *reredos*; and a really spendid *piscina* and triple *sedilia*, each with its traceried arch and little clustered columns. Don't miss, in the chancel floor, an eccentric *ledger stone* – across the top, in text in Hebrew script; then, in Latin, a long eulogy to John Collingnes, Doctor of Divinity, died January 1690. . .

> 'protagonist of truth, the hammer of error, but not unworthy example of human courtesy'.

Finally, following his 31-line citation is added for good measure a goodly text . . . in Greek.

Walcott, All Saints (F3): An elegant church, all of a piece in its late *Decorated* and *Perpendicular* lines, standing straight against the blustering coastal winds. The big and impressive C15 tower has stepped battlements, finely decorated with *flushwork*; and below, a good flush-panelling *base course* all round; the big bell openings have tracery which, though Perpendicular, cannot quite let go of the Decorated idea. An unusual feature, on the tower's s. side, is the V-shaped stairs turret. The splendid nave windows are eloquently Perpendicular – but the n. door is equally clearly Decorated . . . as are the flowing traceries of the n. and s. windows of the chancel; the e. window, in sympathetic style, is Victorian replacement. Inside the church is spacious and light. But alas damp is affecting the sturdy *arch-braced* roof of the nave, and creeping down the walls. The C15 *screen*, though much restored, is most agreeable and restrained, the delicately carved upper part having faded to that lovely soft look of very old wood. The little screen under the tower arch is a patch-up job, but the main posts and the simply turned little balusters to l. and r. look *Jacobean*. Nearby is an enormous and individual C17 chest, recently repaired (December 1980) with

Warham, All Saints (B2): The tower has gone (stubs can still be seen) as have the aisles, excepting their last bays, which remain as transepts with their C14 *arcades*. Walls are partly *Decorated* period, but with several *Perpendicular* and later windows added. Chancel, early C14. All heavily restored by the Rev. C.F. Digby, rector 1874-1923, who was thorough and Victorian – pitch-pine pews, floor tiles and all. There is a stiff and spiky alabaster *reredos*, 1897, 'in memory of those who have entered into rest' . . . which makes a change from 'the Dear Queen's Jubilee'. Overall, however, something of a contrast with the taste and refinement of the 1800-1 restoration of the village's second church, St Mary's. Note that here at All Saints there are two fonts: a square *Norman* one, which came from St Mary's, and in the n. transept, another old Norman font, rescued from a nearby rockery! In chancel, a *low side window*, a simple *angle piscina* and a *dropped sill sedilia*. Interesting *brass* to William Rokewode, 1474, a nice little 18in figure in armour (near s.w. door). In s.e. corner of sanctuary, a big stone effigy – unusual for Norfolk and pleasing, though defaced – of a civilian, about 1300, carrying what could be a horn or a roll.

Warham, St Mary (B2): *Decorated* tower with later battlements, attractive in flint and stone, and some *Norman* work at base (plus a blocked n. doorway). Rest mainly Decorated with some *Perpendicular* windows inserted. There is a delightful priest's door, good early Perpendicular, on s. side of chancel, with a buttress rising immediately from its top. Inside the church a pleasing surprise awaits: 'This lovely interior, calm and moving, is one of the most memorable in the whole of East Anglia', said Mark Chatfield in his 'Churches the Victorians Forgot' (Moorland Publishing, 1979). It is, in point, a *Prayer Book Church* arrangement, of which there are few left in Norfolk. It has its C18 high *box pews* and *three-decker pulpit*, plus its 'bird bath' font – as it was called by Sir John Betjeman, who loved everything here – and the *Royal Arms* on canvas of George III. There's some fine glass, splendidly glowing Flemish work, mostly of the early *Renaissance* (enormous popes, cardinals and kings) and English medieval glass, all collected by the rector, the Rev. W.H. Langton, who in 1800-1 'beautified' the interior – and who lies in the chancel. There's a strange, melancholy mausoleum to the Turner family, probably dating from the same time as the pews and pulpit. In the sanctuary note the *brass* to James Wigfall, priest, 1638. A nice homely touch – the 'chapel hat pegs' (C18?) on n. wall of nave.

Waxham, St John (G4): The parish is obviously having a struggle against the decay of its church. Although repaired at the top, the tower has its windows boarded and bricked up, and the chancel has been a ruin long since. Inside, the walls all cracked and scabrous. There are *Norman* and C13 windows and a *banner stave locker* oddly placed halfway along the n. wall. Close by the blocked chancel arch is a large recessed monument to Thomas Wodehouse (d.1571). It has classical details

and the painted inscription can still just be read.

Wells-next-the-Sea, St Nicholas (B2): On Sunday morning, August 3rd, 1879, the church was struck by lightning and in two hours completely gutted by fire, leaving only the walls and tower. It was wholly restored – nicely done, but a bit dull – on its original C15, *Perpendicular* lines. Two side windows in the chancel retain old tracery, and a chancel doorway re-uses old mouldings. Over this doorway is a *brass* – text only, no figure – to Thomas Bradley, rector, 1499. The *rood loft* stair remains on the n. side within the wall. There's a large coffer-type, iron-bound chest dated 1635; and a fine medieval brass lectern, an eagle with three lions at its feet, all smoothed by the centuries and with that lovely buttery look of old brass.

West Runton, Holy Trinity (D2): The heavy western tower is *Early English* with a w. *Decorated* window. Apart from the s. range of C15 windows (two in the chancel unusually large), most of the others are Decorated. The e. window and the roofs are C19, and it was then that the former *clerestory* disappeared. The *sedilia* and *piscina* in the chancel are rather ponderous C14, but the font is a fine member of the late C14 'family' which crops up in this district (eg., Roughton and Sheringham) with eight attached shafts below a traceried bowl. There is a pleasing portrayal of worshippers down the ages in a n. aisle window by H.J. Stammers of York, dated 1959.

West Somerton, St Mary (G5): Round tower with C14 octagonal top, thatched nave and porch. Of the many traces of medieval wall paintings, only the Last Judgement on the s. wall remains to any extent. In it, a king and a bishop wake, along with the hoi-polloi, to the sound of the Last Trump. There is a good early C15 screen, with a *crocketted* centre arch. By it stands a contemporary pulpit with unusual concave panels: note the hinge at the bottom of one of the front uprights, showing that the door has been repositioned. Outside, look in the n.e. corner of the churchyard for the C19 grave of Robert Hales, the Norfolk Giant. He was 7ft 8in tall and turned the scales at 33 stone. Also a headstone on the way to the porch with its chatty epitaph to a good lady who 'toiled and muddled through her life.'

Westwick, St Botolph (E4): The church lies just within the park of Westwick House, and tall trees hug it close on three sides. The late C15 tower is well proportioned and has a *base course* of shields carrying Passion emblems. The sound-holes are particularly attractive, each with a shield encircled by little *quatrefoils*. The outside of the rest of the building has the slightly petrified look common to restorations done in the 1840s. There is a good early C16 font with the usual four lions squatting round the shaft and the bowl decorated with foliage. The *rood* and *parclose* screens have been extensively restored and then grained, but there are painted panels of the Apostles. The chancel had its n. windows blocked to accommodate Burney and Petre monuments which are worth looking at, and for this it is well that the priest's door has been replaced with leaded lights to brighten the gloom of the e. end.

Weybourne, All Saints (D2): The present church grew out of a C13 Priory of Augustinian Canons, which itself took over the site and building of an earlier church. The impressive ruins of the *Saxon* tower remain to the n. of the present chancel and much of the outlines of the Priory can still be seen. The canons added a s. aisle for parish use and the old nave forms the present n. aisle. Handsome tower with nice sound-holes and *flushwork* added in the C15, as was the porch. This is prettily chequered and had an upper chamber

used as a chapel – note the blocked *squint* which gave a view of the high altar. An impression of the old Priory seal is displayed on the s. wall of the nave.

Wickhampton, St Andrew (G6): This was once a prosperous community when, like other villages round about, it lay on the banks of the great tidal estuary. When C16 reclamation formed the grazing marshes Wickhampton declined, and now the church with its cluster of cottages and farm buildings stands on the very edge of the level meadows that stretch away to Breydon and Great Yarmouth in a windy solitude. The chancel was originally *Norman*, but you can see from the outside that there were *Early English lancets* before the C15 e. window was inserted. The present nave was built about 1300, and both the s. door and the windows on that side have charming headstops – one man and one woman to each. The tower details are a mixture of *Decorated* and *Perpendicular* and it dates from the late C14. The *base course* is very like that at Halvergate, a mile away across the fields, and the tiny window in the tower stairs matches the Halvergate sound-holes. Here there are regulation-size sound-holes, and two of them (n. and s.) have excellent and varied tracery with traces of carving on the moulded surround. The corner pinnacles each have a weather vane – unusual in this part of the country. Wickhampton's treasure, however, is inside. Open the door and you are faced with one of the finest ranges of C14 wall paintings in the country. They cover most of the n. wall and are in three parts. At the w. end there is the legend of *The Three Living and the Three Dead*; under the skeletons a hare runs from the leashed greyhounds held by a youth in the centre, and the King on the right has a hawk on his wrist. Next, there is a huge *St Christopher* (10ft x 5ft), and then a fine series of *The*

Seven Works of Mercy, each set in a 3ft x 3ft architectural panel, with rudimentary perspective. The eighth panel is a Resurrection scene. There are useful water colour drawings of 1849 with annotations, framed below the paintings. The series was uncovered in the 1840s but deteriorated badly until they were described a century later as 'almost indistinguishable'. Happily, the Pilgrim Trust financed their restoration in 1963 when much more detail was brought to light. Another treasure in the chancel – two splendid C13 effigies lying under restored *crocketted* canopies. They are Sir William Gerbrygge and his wife. His 6ft figure has a lion at the feet, and he is dressed in short tunic and carrying a shield which has his coat of arms in relief. He wears sword and spurs and his head rests on two pillows. His wife, in plain gown and wimple, has a pug dog minus nose for company. Sir William was Bailiff of Yarmouth in 1271 and patron of this church. Between his hands he holds a stone heart (inscribed by some C19 oaf 'RMD 1832'), and this wove itself into a local legend which surfaced in Glyde's 'Norfolk Garland' – too long to quote here, but the extract is neatly typed and framed by the tomb. Don't overlook the little C19 chamber organ in the chancel – it has a very fine mahogany case with an extraordinary number of panelled doors.

Wickmere, St Andrew (D3): Lonely and in a big churchyard where the grass often lies flat in the wind. The round tower and the nave w. wall have much *carstone* and may be pre-Conquest. The aisle and chancel windows have pretty *Decorated* tracery and although renewed, the alternating circular and two-light *clerestory* windows are strikingly attractive. The facing between them and also on the s. porch is of dressed white flint which flashes in the sunshine. Inside, some of the benches are medieval, and one in the s. aisle has a carved and painted inscription for the donors, with the lily emblem of the Virgin in a shield on the *poppyhead.*

Another at the w. end of the nave has a mutilated satyr figure on the arm, and on the l. hand stall in the chancel a little man plays the lute with his legs crossed negligently. The C15 *screen* has been largely restored, but four of the panels retain their paintings of saints, although only *St Andrew* with his cross can be recognised. The pulpit dates from 1938, and the two panels with C15 paintings of donors came from Wolterton Hall and were probably taken from the screen of St Margaret's, Wolterton which has been ruinous for some 300 years. As a result, the Walpole family adopted Wickmere and their *hatchments* hang in the chancel. There too, is the *ledger stone* of Horatio Baron Walpole

'. . . a useful Co-adjutor to his brother (the famous Sir Robert) in directing the Councils of England and the Peace of Europe'.

In the n. aisle, the fifth Earl of Orford (d.1931) has a massive tomb chest with robed figure attended by angels on top. The crown of his head already has a faint sheen and one feels that the whole effigy may gently weather in time. (Sir Robert Walpole was created first Earl of Orford. The title became extinct with the death of the fifth Earl. The Barons Walpole of Wolterton continue at Wolterton Hall). The most memorable memorial in the church is a white marble *cartouche* with cherub heads at the corners, on the wall at the w. end. It is to Henry Spelman (d.1765) who, 'having distinguished himself by his Intrepidity and Conduct as a Soldier at Dettingen and Fontenoy, died at Calcutta in ye Kingdom of Bengal'. Two of his friends brought back the standard 'under which he has often bravely fought', and its bamboo shaft with pointed filigree head is still there on the wall above. As you go out, admire the excellent C14 ironwork on the door.

Wighton, All Saints (B3): There are many similarities with Great Walsingham here. The body of the church is all

C14 and has an impressive range of large, three-light *clerestory* windows giving a spacious and airy feeling to the interior. Everything is on a large scale, with a chancel arch some 20ft across. The early C14 tower collapsed in 1965 in a gale, and for eleven years the church presented an unfamiliar silhouette on the skyline. Then, from over the Atlantic, came Canadian businessman Mr. Leeds Richardson, whose ancestors had worshipped here at All Saints, who paid for the tower's rebuilding in 1976. His generosity did not end there: in 1980 he paid for a peal of six bells to be hung in the tower, including the one original Wighton bell, first cast in 1657 and now, in its recasting, inscribed with the fitting words: 'With determination, success is inevitable'. The other five bells came from a redundant church in Maidstone. Inside the church there is a good *rood loft staircase* and the font has a range of shields around the octagonal bowl, with the *Instruments of the Passion* included in the subjects. Sheep graze in the churchyard around the timbers of the medieval bell-frame from the old tower.

Winterton, Holy Trinity and All Saints (G5): A very lofty (132ft) tower, begun in the C14 and completed or remodelled in the C15. The design has a satisfying unity, due partly to the clever variation on the corner buttresses, from square at the bottom to diagonal at the top. The *base course* and the parapet with its *gargoyles* and pinnacles are of high quality. In late spring, yellow wallflowers bloom in patches all up the s. face – not good for the fabric perhaps, but endearing. The C15 porch is a large ambitious piece which now lacks its upper room. The carving in the arch *spandrels* has come to look like a sponge, but the dedication inscription above the door can still be read, and the coats of arms point to a connection with Sir John Fastolf of Caister Castle (Shakespeare is said to have based the name of his memorable character Fal-

staff upon him – though not the character himself, for this Caister Sir John was a fine and noble soldier). There was a full-scale restoration of the church in the 1870s and little of the original work in the C14 chancel and C15 nave can be seen: but the interior is impressive, and the modern roof spans no less than 34ft. Just beyond the *screen*, on the chancel n. wall, is a memorial with an unusual Christian name – 'Persis', the wife of John Lens. The modern communion rails have flame tracery of very high quality. At the w. end of the church is the unique Fisherman's Corner, where everything is made from ships or has been to sea.

Witton (near Norwich), St Margaret (F6): A tiny, well-cared for church, only a step from the busy A47 yet seemingly in deepest, peaceful countryside. Heavily restored and re-roofed in 1902, with a chancel rebuilt in 1857, little of its early fabric is in evidence – the nave's original structure is probably C14, but the window traceries are replacements. Presumably there was originally a western tower, as can be seen from the layout inside (tower arch and stair turret) but there is now a rather attractive octagonal bell turret perched on the w. gable of the nave – possibly C17, says one authority. Inside, the Victorian chancel in the *Early English* style, including the somewhat overstated chancel arch, is rather agreeable, with plenty of colour. In the nave, the pulpit is modelled on one at Croydon designed by the celebrated Victorian architect and Gothic revivalist, Sir Gilbert Scott (the same who built St Pancras Station!). The neat font is crisply carved with miniature 'windows', largely showing detailed *Decorated* tracery at its high phase. *Pevsner* says it's C14, but perhaps one should question that. Nearby, by the entrance door, a nice little figure brass to Juliana Anyell (or Angell?), about 1500, with an inscription revealing her as a widow and *vowess*. There's a rubbing of it on the n. wall adjacent.

Witton-by-Walsham, St Margaret(F3):
Distant from its village, this attractive
church has a fine round tower, the
lower part possibly *Saxon* (opinion
varies), the upper section – where flint
is delightfully mixed with sun-glowing
pink brick – is a C15 addition. Very
probably Saxon too, tucked in behind
the tower, are the s.w. quoins (corner
stones) of the nave, large rough blocks
of *carstone*. The nave n. side presents
an intriguing prospect: there is a *clerestory* range with rather coarse Y-tracery,
early C14 – but no aisle below; above
the modern vestry (built around the
ancient n. door) are two tiny round
windows, deeply splayed, which are
thought to be part of a range in an
earlier Saxon church of C10, or even
late C9 date; then come two nice square
headed *Perpendicular* windows (C16).
The *Decorated* style chancel windows
are all renewed. The church's interior is
serene and full of interest. A good,
sturdy *arch-braced* roof to the nave,
with simply carved *wall plates* and
heavy, deep *wall posts* descending
between the clerestory windows. The
tower stair juts into the nave, rather
castle-like. Simple C15 font. Attractively unpretentious *arcade* on s. side,
C14 like its aisle. The easternmost
column of the arcade looks earlier,
possibly C13 *transitional*, contemporary perhaps with the remains of a
filled-in window immediately behind
the C15 chancel arch. The aisle has
pleasant early Decorated window
tracery in three windows, a fourth with
Y-tracery. The easternmost window is
cut away to form a low-sill seat, with an
appealing *piscina* adjoining, its plainly
carved head cut from one piece of
stone. In this corner are some rudimentary old *box pews*. The chancel is
graced by a most beautiful two-seat
sedilia of the C13, with graceful arches
and *dog-tooth* moulding. Below a
starkly simple piscina niche are two
brasses, one of especial interest. It
reads:

'Heare lyeth berried the boddyis of
Thomas Parmenter and Francis his

wife who weare maried 47 year
together, and Thomas Paramenter
died 12 days before Hollimvs 1631.
His wife died one St. Stevens day
1627'

– note that word 'Hollymus' for Christmas – an early hint of Puritan 'anti-
Christmas' feeling? Nearby is an
inscription without date to Henry
Hemsley, once vicar here. To l. of the
altar, a third inscription, invoking
prayers for Thomas Calke, 1519. On
the n. wall are two splendid C18 monuments to members of the Norris family,
that to Elizabeth Norris, 1769, being as
opulent and unusual in its design (all off
centre, supported by a single cherub on
one side and piled with carved books,
sacred and secular, on the other) as in
its wording . . . a moving and timeless
offering of a husband's radiant love and
devotion to his young wife, for Elizabeth –

'She looked like Nature in the world's
first spring'

– died aged 28.

Wiveton, St Mary (C2): A most handsome building in the *Perpendicular* style
in its early phases – possibly within 20
or 30 years of the *Black Death* of 1349-
50. Look closely at the tracery in the
big, fine windows – its flowing forms,
though contained within Perpendicular
mullions reaching to the top of the arch,
yet seem to suggest a harking back to
the *Decorated* forms which burgeoned
before the 1349 catastrophe. Contrast
with the *clerestory* windows: these are
later Perpendicular, C15, more stylised
and disciplined. They include an e. end
nave window, which before the *Reformation* would have lit the *rood loft*.
The tower is basically earlier than the
body of the church – those windows at
the belfry stage are the giveaway, with
their Y-tracery of about 1300. The large
e. window in the chancel, with its
graceful, simple interlacing tracery, is
of the early part of the C14. While

standing outside the e. window, look at the most interesting flushwork panelling set into the chancel walls; *Pevsner* suggests that it could be some of the very earliest on record, possibly as early as 1316. The church has two fine porches, n. and s. Inside, St Mary's is severe but grand. Roofs are splendidly simple *arch-braced*; the nave has a great, five-bay *arcade* and matching tower arch; all C15. Minimally different, but possibly of the same date, is the chancel arch. Over the chancel arch – *Royal Arms* of the Hanoverians. Below the arch, the sorry remnants of the old *rood screen* which is said to have been in its original place across the chancel arch until a little over 100 years ago, when it was torn out in a Victorian 'restoration', hacked down and planted in its present position. The dignified octagonal font, on its carved and canopied base, is C15. In the aisles, note that all the windows are set within arcades, and in turn are let down to provide seats – as at Cley a stone's throw away, at Blakeney and at Tunstead. A magnificent brass candlechandelier, known to have existed here in 1760, hung at the e. end of the nave until the summer of 1980 – when it was stolen! In s. aisle, a huge iron-bound 'charity chest'; and above it on the wall, a *brass* to Raulf Grenewey, 1558, citizen and alderman of London, with merchants' marks, arms of the Grocers' Company, and his bequests to Wiveton which still operate. In chancel, a *piscina* and *dropped sill sedilia*; the lovely e. window has slim *jambs*, with tiny, moulded capitals – typical *Early English*. The church has some good *brasses*: before the pulpit steps, a fine set, complete with coat-of-arms, to George Brigge of Letheringsett, 1597, and Ann his wife; beside the pulpit, a macabre 'cadaver' brass (skeleton in shroud) for George Brigge's great-great-grandfather, Thomas Brigg, 1470; nearby, in centre of chancel, an attractive little brass to a priest, William Bishop, 1512. Outside, several headstones in the churchyard are worth examination.

Woodbastwick, St Fabian and St Sebastian (F5): There is no other church dedicated jointly to these saints in England, and it is picturesquely sited by one of the most photographed village greens in Norfolk. It underwent a thorough-going restoration by *Sir Gilbert Scott* a century ago, and apart from the tower sound-holes and the C14 chancel windows, not much of the old fabric can be identified. The high thatched roof is terminated by pretty crowstepped gables in red brick, and within, it has braced *kingposts* which are not often seen in Norfolk. Scott inserted an unusual *tie-beam* across the chancel to delineate the sanctuary. The C15 *screen* has a beautifully solid look at the head because the two layers of tracery of the arches have an infill cut to shape between them. The tracery above the arches is beautifully delicate and reminiscent of Scarning, near East Dereham. There is a series of very well designed modern mural tablets to the Cator family who were Lords of the manor.

Wood Dalling, St Andrew (C4): A big church struggling to combat the effects of damp and decay. The C15 tower is very handsome – four *drip courses*, good sound-holes and, like the *clerestory*, dressed white flints. The chancel is C13, with three *lancets* in the n. wall and a tall priest's doorway akin to that at Castle Acre. The e. window has good flowing tracery and the *ogee* arch of the *piscina* has an exceptionally nice headstop – the finely moulded features are perfect. The C15 s. porch has an upper chamber reached by a stair which ends at a door 6ft above the floor, a possible indication that it was used as a treasury. The e. window of the s. aisle has a space below it designed for a reredos but no trace remains. There is a fine recumbent effigy of a priest at the e. end of the n. aisle but the head, neck, and hair have been re-cut. There are *brasses* to Robert Dockyng (d.1465) priest, (s. aisle), John Crane (d.1507) – a 17in figure by the pulpit, and to John and Thomas Bulwer (1517), (e. end of nave). The last has only the inscription and two attendant children, and the stone was used again in 1726.

Wood Norton, All Saints (C4): The tower has a warm red brick C18 upper stage with battlements, and the arched bell openings are filled with honey-comb screens of brick. The C14 s. porch is of much better quality than the rest and probably came from a wealthy donor. The arch is tall and thin, and there are *crocketted* pinnacles, angle buttresses decorated with little hoods on the *set-offs*, and the porch has its own *gargoyles*. The bowl of the C14 octagonal font has an unusual curved profile and stand on a short plain stem; its C17 painted cover is topped by a gilt dove. Just why a wicker bath chair is in attendance is not clear. The chancel is C14 but the angle *piscina* with its slender column is about 1300, and so is the priest's door. There is a big head of a pig with extended tongue as a stop to the blocked arch in the s. wall. The pulpit is a curious Victorian essay – three panels on a plinth that was going to be the real thing but then lost confidence. The fragments of C15 glass in the w. window mentioned by *Cautley* and *Pevsner* are no longer there. Instead, there are hardboard panels, and one hopes that the loss is only temporary. For epitaph hunters the churchyard yields a rich harvest – mainly C19 but some C18, ranging from the quietest

> 'This Mortal must Put on Immortality'

(Susan Dewig 1713 s. of nave) to

> 'Dear George is safe, all his sorrows are o'er. . .'

(George Wright 1868 s. of nave).

Worstead, St Mary (F4): William *Paston*, 1378-1444, wrote to his cousin Robert, 'I shall make my doublet all Worstead, for the glory of Norfolk.' Though the riches of the wool trade that made the name of this village known throughout the world have long since gone, its church is very much a part of 'the glory of Norfolk'. Apart from the mid C15 vestry, the whole church was built in one continuous operation from the chancel in 1379 to the tower twenty years later. It replaced a smaller predecessor and the size is impressive – 130ft long. The 109ft tower with its big sound-holes is splendid; a double *base course* is topped by *flushwork* arcading and the w. door and window are linked within a single composition. The n. door has no porch but is embellished with flower carvings and a line of shields above. Entry is by way of a sumptuous s. porch, two storied with its own stair turret. There are triple niches over an arch enriched with decoration and the *groined* ceiling has a Coronation of the Virgin on the centre *boss*, with the *Symbols of the Evangelists* around it. Once inside the church, the impact is one of great space and light. Improvements in the C15 gave the whole building more height when the chancel arch was lifted and the great *hammer beam* roof inserted. The strain that this subsequently caused probably accounts for the afterthought *flying buttresses* over the aisle roofs. The chancel *screen* is one of the tallest in the county, and has a nice folded label inscription along the middle rail which referred to John Arblaster and his wife Alice who gave it in 1512. There is a little *brass* to him just in front of the screen, and it is a nice touch that it is protected now by a thick fleecy rug made locally. The paintings on the screen panels have been so confused by Victorian essays in restoration that a competent listing is difficult. Apart from the Apostles, the two at the extreme right are probably *St William* and *St Uncumber*. Both n. and s. chapels also have screens with painted panels; those on the n. are Saints *Bartholomew, Philip, Lawrence* and *Thomas of Canterbury*; those on the s. are Saints *Peter, Paul, John the Baptist,* and

---

Worstead St Mary

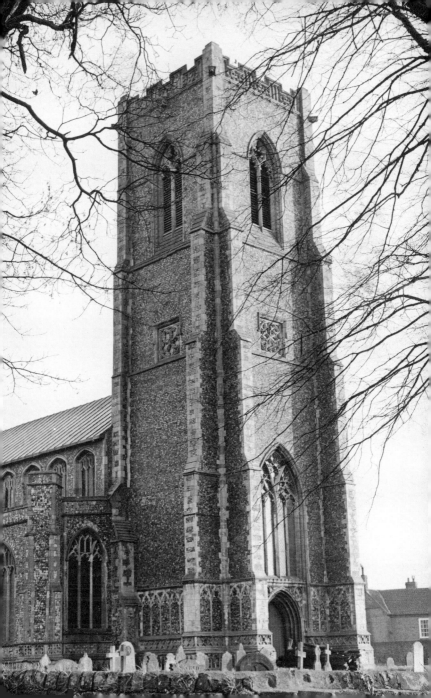

Stephen. Notice how the screens were originally linked by matching painted patterns across the walls and arches n. and s. of the chancel arch. The n. chapel has an interesting and unusual survival – the original altar *reredos* has gone, but the painted frame remains with a panel of beautifully varied decoration below it. The ringers' gallery under the tower has an elaborately carved front with an inscription:

> 'This work was made in ye yer of God MCCCCCI (1501) at ye propur cost of ye catell (probably meaning candle) of ye chyrche of Worsted callyd ye batchellers lyte yt God preserve wt all the benefactors of ye same now and ever, amen, then wer Husbondes (ie. wardens) Christofyer Rant and Jeffery Deyn.'

The screen below is beautifully delicate and could well be taken for original work, but an early C19 engraving does not show it and another of the same period describes it as 'lately erected'. This squares with the painted panels on it which are copies of Sir Joshua Reynolds' work at New College Oxford. The font stands imposingly on three steps with the top level in the shape of a cross, and the bowl has an overall pattern of *quatrefoils*. The cover is really only the skeletal remains of quite an elaborate construction, but it was well restored in 1954 and is very graceful in its present form. The nave has a most satisfying suite of oak C18 *box pews*. The interiors have been modified but the chest-high doors with beautifully made fielded panels are intact. The tall draught screens at the w. end have little fluted pillars at the ends. An arduous programme of restoration has been in progress since 1964 and there has been a gradual transformation. Work on the roof has been completed – it looks superb, and memories of leprous green stains and general decay have given way to clean creamwashed walls and general good health. It is a heartening example of what can be achieved by local initiative, faith and hard work, backed by national support.

Links with Worstead's famous past are maintained by St Mary's Guild of Weavers Spinners and Dyers, and there is a fascinating array of 14 looms in the n. aisle with much work in progress.

Wroxham, St Mary (E5): In one of the centres of the popular Broads holiday area, the church is quietly sited above a steep bluff, and looking west, the view is all treetops and greenery. The C15 tower has good angle buttresses, well defined *string courses*, and pretty four-leaf sound-holes. Entry is by way of a stunning *Norman* doorway with a deep blue colouring. Triple miniature columns with plaited rings carry capitals which sprout little grotesque heads and figures; the concentric rings of the arch have a whole variety of decorative carvings. The C15 porch had an upper room at one time, but only part of the stairs now remains. The entrance door is at least as old as the porch and the handle may be two hundred years older. The s. aisle was re-built in 1825, and the crude and graceless *arcades* may be of a like date but could be earlier. At the n. end of the n. aisle is a monument to Robert Blake-Humfrey, who lost a leg serving with the Buffs in the peninsular, but still survived to the ripe old age of 91. The glass in the e. window is dull in spirit, garish in execution, and dear at £101 15 0d in 1851. Much nicer is the 1882 s. window by Thomas Curtis: lots of flowers and foliage around Christ and Mary in the Garden – she with a great mane of crinkly hair. It's probably significant that the first essay in ecclesiastical gothic by the Victorian architect, *Anthony Salvin*, was the Trafford mausoleum of 1829 in the churchyard, n. of the tower. He went on to remodel Norwich Cathedral s. transept and Norwich Castle, with more enthusiasm than sensibility.

Glossary

Adam style: The four Scottish Adam brothers were distinguished architects and interior decorators. Robert and James developed an architectural style, distinctly their own, of elegance and charm and classical line (Robert, who was appointed architect to George III in 1762, had travelled widely in Italy and Dalmatia). They were especially renowned for their interior work – fireplaces, ceilings, furniture and other woodwork – which all showed a very Grecian influence. Together with their two brothers, John and William, Robert and James designed the district of London between the Thames and Charing Cross which is known as The Adelphi – the Greek for 'brothers'. (See Gunton, St Andrew.)

Angle piscina: See *piscina*.

Anglo-Saxon: The Anglo-Saxons were the Teutonic invaders who overran Britain in the 'Dark Ages'. Between the fifth and seventh centuries Norfolk and Suffolk were overrun – and were settled by the Angles, who gave their name to East Anglia. *Saxon* architecture, distinctive in its simplicity, existed until it was superseded by Norman building following the Conquest of 1066 (see *Styles of Architecture*).

Annunciation: Annunciation representations are a regular subject for stained glass scenes, as well as wood and stone carvings – when the Arch-angel Gabriel brought to Mary the news of the Incarnation, that she would conceive a child of the Holy Ghost (Luke 1, 26-38). A splendid Annunciation may be seen in fine C15 glass at Bale, near Fakenham, and a lovely C15 carving in the porch at Great Witchingham. The Feast of the Annunciation is March 25th – otherwise known as Lady Day, an important date too in the rural calendar, when tenant farmers' rents were due, and new tenancies were granted.

Antiphonal lectern: The antiphon (literally – 'before voice') is a sung verse immediately preceding the psalm, or the Canticle for the particular office or service (ie. before the Benedictus at matins, or the Magnificat at vespers or evening prayer). It was sung by the Cantor (the leader of the singing, whose equivalent in today's Anglican cathedrals is the Precentor) who during this office stood at the Antiphonal Lectern, on which his music was placed. (See Ranworth, St Helen.)

Arcades: A series of arches – ie., those down each side of the nave of an aisled church – supported by pillars. Sometimes arcades are 'closed', 'blind' or 'blank' – a decorative outline on a wall or tomb or furnishing; or when, as may often be found, an aisle has been demolished and the arcade bricked up, but leaving its pillars and arches outlined.

Arch-braced roofs: A roof carried on a simple, braced arch. (See *Roofs*, fig. 4. for full description).

Assumption of the Virgin: The translation of the Virgin Mary, body and soul, into heaven – a theme often represented by medieval artists in painting and sculpture. The Feast of the Assumption is August 15th, a festival first initiated in the year 582 by the Roman Emperor Maurice. The Eastern Orthodox Church, with a poetic touch, celebrates the Assumption as 'The Feast of the Falling Asleep of Our Lady'.

Aumbry: A small cupboard or recess in which were stored the Holy Oils used in Baptism, Confirmation and Extreme Unction (annointing of the dying person by the priest); also the sacred vessels/plate used for Mass or Communion. Sometimes the aumbry held the Reserved Sacrament – the consecrated bread, 'reserved' from a Mass (see also *Easter Sepulchre*). The aumbry is generally found on the north side of the chancel (opinions vary about medieval usage), but sometimes near the *piscina* – which is almost always on the south side – and in a few cases may be near the font. Originally very few parish churches had sacristies for storing the plate and valuables: the priest robed at the altar, his vestments meantime being kept in a parish chest, the vessels for altar and font being placed in the aumbry. Thus chest plus aumbry equals the later vestries. Occasionally the aumbry was used in the C15 as a safe for documents, not only belonging to the church, but to parishioners, as it would be secured by door and lock. Very few of these wooden doors remain today, though the hinge and latch marks in the stone can often be made out. One complete survivor, however, can be seen at Great Walsingham.

Bacon, John the Younger (1777-1859): One of the most representative memorial sculptors of his time. One of his grand marble monuments is at Sprowston Church, to Lady Maria Micklethwaite, 1805, symbolising her death in childbirth. Something of a child prodigy – he was already sculpting monumental works at the age of 11 – examples of his artistry may be seen in many churches throughout England.

Ball Flower: An early C14 decorative ornament in sculpture. See 'Decorated period' under *Styles of Architecture*.

Banner-stave lockers: In the late medieval period, *parish guilds* proliferated – St Peter Mancroft Church in Norwich had nine attached to it – and all had their banners to be carried in the processions which in medieval times were an important part of services on Sundays and Feast Days (see also: *Galilee porches*). Between times, the banners would be placed in the *guild chapels*, and the staves in their lockers – which explains the long, narrow upright niches in the walls of some churches which can seem so puzzling. A most unusual example is at Castle Rising in West Norfolk, where the locker is highly decorated, and its position and character suggest that it was used to house a processional cross rather than just the simple banner staves.

Bar tracery: Tracery in the heads of windows, constructed in separate pieces, as distinct from *plate tracery*, where the pattern is cut directly through the masonry. See 'Early English' under *Styles of Architecture*.

Base course: A horizontal layer of masonry, decorative in character, usually at the base of towers. See *Courses*.

Biers: Some churches – and particularly, for obvious reasons, those with a long path between *lych-gate* and church – have a platform to carry the coffin to and from the funeral service. These curious conveyances can often be seen, discreetly tucked away at the back of the nave or in a side aisle. Occasional ancient examples, but usually Victorian.

Billet: Billet moulding or decoration was particularly used in *Norman* work – it was formed by cutting notches in two parallel and continuous rounded mouldings in a regular, alternating pattern.

Black Death: Some time in the 1340s. an horrific epidemic of bubonic plague ('The Black Death' is a modern expression coined in the C19) began, possibly in China, and by 1348 it had reached the south of France where it devastated the Papal city of Avignon. By the end of the year it had crossed the Channel and begun the ravages which, in 12 months, would leave between a third and a half of the nation's population dead. It cut off in its prime the greatest flowering of English architectural beauty (see 'Decorated' under *Styles of Architecture*). Whether or not it destroyed whole village communities, and thus left their churches isolated, is discussed under *Isolated Churches.* On January 1st, 1349 the king, Edward III, issued a proclamation postponing Parliament because 'a sudden visitation of deadly pestilence' had broken out in and around Westminster, and by June the full fury of the plague had reached Norfolk. Hunstanton may serve as an example of what must have been repeated in scores of parishes. In the two months of September-October 1349, 63 men, among them the parson, and 15 women died of the pestilence; during the next six months, the total reached 172. In the dreadful year ending 1350, it has been estimated that at least half, and probably more, of the population of Norfolk and Suffolk were swept away. Plague broke out again at intervals over the next three centuries (the city of Norwich was ravaged by it after Queen Elizabeth's visit early in her reign) until the last major outbreak, culminating in the Great Plague of London in 1665, when a quarter of the inhabitants died. What is remarkable, in considering the Black Death in relation to our churches, is that it was followed by one of the greatest ages of church building.

Blank/blind arcading: See *arcades*.

Blomefield, Francis (1705-1752): was an historian and map-maker, who is best remembered for his vast undertaking, 'The History of Norfolk'. This was incomplete when he died and was carried to its conclusion by Charles Parkin, Rector of Oxburgh, near Swaffham. Blomefield, who was born at Fersfield, near Diss, in the south of Norfolk, began collecting material for his history while he was still at school at Thetford. But it was not until he became Rector of his home village in 1729 that the work began to take shape. He sent out a most comprehensive questionnaire to more than 200 people, and travelled extensively in the county, collecting and verifying information. It was he who first discovered the Paston Letters (see *Paston family*) at Oxnead. After many difficulties, he set up his own press and volume one of 'The History' appeared in 1739. He got as far as page 678 of the third volume – then was suddenly struck down by smallpox and died in 1752. The completed edition of his great work, which is still a source of valuable information today (many things which he meticulously recorded, or sources to which he had access, having since disappeared) was published in 1805-10.

Bosses: A boss is the carved ornamentation seen at the intersections of roof beams or of the ribs in vaulted (see *groining*) ceilings. Usually they represent foliage or grotesque animals or figures, but may often be intricately worked with biblical scenes, with portraits, heraldic arms and symbols, or lively scenes like that in the porch at Cley St Margaret, where a fox, chicken in jaws, is being pursued by an old woman.

Box Pew: Large pews panelled to waist height or higher, often with seats on three sides, and entered by a door from the aisle. Nicknamed 'box pews' from their similarity to horse-boxes or stalls. They came into favour in the late C17 and early C18 and were often embellished with curtains, cushions and carpets. Most disappeared in the wave of C19 'medieval' restorations. See also *Prayer Book Churches*.

Brasses: Brasses are incised memorial portraits, usually found set into the floor, though ancient brass inscriptions may be seen fixed to walls and furnishings. Brasses are made in an alloy called latten, a mixture of copper and zinc. This was chiefly manufactured at Cologne, where it was beaten into rectangular plates for export to Britain, the Low Countries and elsewhere. Such memorials were for long favoured by a wide range of classes, from the nobility, through the priesthood, scholars and monks, to merchants and families of local standing. The earliest brass to be seen in England is said to be that of Sir John d'Abernon at Stoke D'Abernon in Surrey, dated 1277 in the reign of Edward I. It was not until the first half of the C17 that the fashion finally petered out. Norfolk is particularly rich in brasses, with examples dating from the early C14 onwards, including a very late one at Acle, 1627, one of only six known from the reign of Charles I; North Walsham has a good inscription brass with coat-of-arms, from only a couple of years earlier. At a time when Norwich was, in wealth and consequence, the second city of the kingdom, it had its own prolific workshops of brass craftsmen, as well as drawing on the work of London workshops and of other provincial centres. But brasses are more than memorials: they are remarkable, pictorial commentaries on four centuries of our history, martial armour, manners, customs, dress and fashions. Among fine examples in Norfolk are those at Felbrigg, at St Margaret's, King's Lynn, and at Elsing, near Dereham. See also, *chalice brass* and *palimpsest brass*.

Browne, Sir Thomas, 1605-82: Physician, scientist, writer, scholar, antiquarian, philosopher, sage, and a distinguished son of the city of Norwich –

where he spent most of his life, and where he was knighted in 1671 during a Royal visit to the city by Charles II, in recognition of his steadfast Royalist loyalty and for his antiquarian scholarship. His writings are renowned for their sonorous prose and rich use of language, not least in his personal confession of Christian faith, 'Religio Medici', with its fascinating diversions upon all matter of things touching upon man's religious quest; and in the intimidatingly titled 'Hydriotaphia or Urn Burial', in which the ever inquiring mind of Sir Thomas, set off by the discovery of some ancient burial urns in Norfolk, contemplates the many and various ways of burial . . . and that Great Unknown which follows:

> 'But the iniquity of oblivion blindly scattereth her poppy. . .'

Sir Thomas's statue sits, deep in thought on a plinth in Norwich's Hay Hill (now turned into a horrid concrete yard, with litter floating in its water 'cascade', with as backcloth a modern store to which Sir Thomas's back is mercifully turned). His memorial is nearby in the sanctuary of St Peter Mancroft Church.

Burne-Jones, Sir Edward, (1833-98): Meeting *William Morris* (see separate entry) at Oxford University was a formative influence on Burne-Jones. Until then he was intent on entering the Church. Contact with Morris turned him to painting, and no doubt, also had something to do with the young artist's work being mainly of medieval and mystical subjects. His work, influenced by the Italian *Renaissance* masters, is notable for its medievalism, for its mystical and dreamlike air, and its exotic and symbolic themes – qualities which in his day earned him great popular fame and a baronetcy. He created numerous glass and tapestry designs for William Morris, which were executed in the Morris workshops. Among good examples of their collaboration in stained glass to be found in Norfolk is a typically brilliant one at Horstead (s. of North Walsham);

and a splendidly bold one at Langham (near Holt). These windows serve too, to illustrate the nostalgia for a kind of ideal medievalism which the two friends shared.

Burrough, Sir James, (1681-1764): Amateur architect, and successively graduate, don, master and vice-chancellor at Cambridge. His skill as an architect earned him a considerable reputation at the university, where he was responsible for many projects – new buildings, re-mouldings and 'beautifications'. But Norfolk has something fairly unusual of his – a set of rather fine church fittings, originally in Corpus Christi College Chapel, and now in Thurning Church (near Holt).

Carstone: 'Gingerbread' stone it used to be called in Norfolk. It is a soft sandstone which you can see in the cliffs at Hunstanton, not far from the old Snettisham quarries. Carstone is mostly seen in buildings in the n.w. of the county, though an ancient example of its use is in the Anglo-Saxon tower on the other side of Norfolk at Bessingham (near Cromer).

Cartouche: Sculptural representation of a curling sheet of paper, seldom contained within a formal frame. Latin: carta, paper.

Cautley, H. Munro: Suffolk architect, antiquarian, expert on heraldry, and authority on church architecture and fittings. His two books, 'Suffolk Churches and their Treasures' (1938) and 'Norfolk Churches' (1949) remain the authoritative 'bibles' for student, specialist and enthusiast.

Chalice brasses: These are small memorial brasses, surmounted by a representation of the Chalice and Host (Latin, 'hostia', victim – the bread which is The Body of Christ). It is said that there are about 40 such brasses in Norfolk, all dating from the early C16. These may all have been the work of a single craftsman working in or near

Norwich. Some good examples can be seen at Salthouse, Bintree, North Walsham and Scottow. See also *brasses* and *palimpsest brasses*.

Chantry chapels: In pre-*Reformation* times, it was the wish of every God-fearing man to have masses said for his soul after his death, especially during the month immediately following his demise. But for the rich there was the possibility of prayers and masses . . . for ever, by establishing and endowing a chantry chapel, with attendant priests, where the donor's bones could rest, sometimes with those of his family. For those who could not afford all this, there was another way – through membership of a local guild of merchants or craftsmen (see separate entry under *Guilds*). Even small parish churches might have several guild and chantry altars, with their 'lights' burning; in cathedrals there could be dozens: it is said that Lichfield had 87.

Chapling, J.C.: A Norwich sculptor in the C18. One of his monuments is to Sir Horatio Pettus, 1746, a member of an important Norwich family, which may be seen in Rackheath's remote and delightful little church.

Christopher images: St Christopher representations are almost always to be found opposite the main entrance of the church, because of the belief that no harm could come to anyone who had seen the image of the saint on the day of a journey: sensible, therefore, to place him where, on opening the door, the traveller could see him in a trice, cross himself . . . and be on his way, in safety, all in a moment. There was sometimes an inscription:

> 'The day that you see Christopher's face, that day shall you not die an evil death'.

Norfolk has many fine St Christopher representations, notable being the wall paintings at Wickhampton and Hemblington. Probably every medieval church had some representation, in painting, glass or statue – though the latter is rare, a notable exception being at Terrington St Clement. See also St Christopher's background under *Saints.*

Chrysom child: When a child was baptised, it was swaddled for the Christening service in the 'Chrysom' cloth or sheet, which often belonged to the parish. If the child died before its mother had been Churched (ie., had been to church after the birth to receive the priest's blessing and purification) it was then buried in the Chrysom cloth, thus becoming a 'Chrysom child'. In this form it was represented on tombs and brasses – as, for example, on the John Clippesby brass, 1594, at Clippesby St Peter (near Acle).

Cinquefoils: See *Foils.*

Clerestory: An upper storey, standing clear of its adjacent roofs, and pierced with windows which usually correspond in number with the number of arches, or bays, in the arcade below. Its pronunciation – 'Clear-storey' – explains the clerestory's function . . . clear glass windows letting in light on the large covered area below.

Clerk: See *Parish Clerk.*

Communion rails: The rails against which the congregation kneel to receive Communion (and no doubt taking it for granted that this is and always was their purpose) were originally installed for quite other reasons. They were to protect the altar from irreverent people and even less reverent dogs – and the balusters were to be set close enough to ensure this. Before the *Reformation,* the chancel was always closed off by a screen (*rood loft/screen*) usually fitted with doors, and the people normally never entered it. Except at great festivals, they watched through the screen as the priests celebrated Mass and themselves received the sacrament. When general participation in services and the administration of the sacrament to the people became the norm, dif-

ferent arrangements were needed. Archbishop *Laud* ordered that the altar should be railed and not moved from its n.s. position, and the rails often enclosed the altar on three sides. Whether there should be rails or no, Richard Montague, Bishop of Norwich, made his position quite clear in a Visitation question in 1638: 'Is your communion table enclosed, and ranged about with a rail of joiners and turners work, close enough to keep dogs from going in and profaning that holy place, from pissing against it or worse?' The Bishop further ordered that 'the communicants being entered into the chancel shall be disposed of orderly in their several ranks, leaving sufficient room for the priest or minister to go between them, by whom they were to be communicated one rank after another, until they had all of them received.' This was to come into conflict with the Puritan habit of demanding that communion should be received by the congregation seated in their pews. In 1643 communion rails went the way of other 'monuments of superstition and idolatry', but at the *Restoration* in 1660 old habits were resumed and the taking of communion at the sanctuary rail became accepted practice. (See also *Prayer Book Churches.*)

Comper, Sir Ninian, (1864-1960): Distinguished and highly individual architect of the Gothic Revival, who in the course of 70 years built 15 churches, restored and decorated scores, and designed vestments, windows and banners for use literally all round the globe, from America to the Far East, for both the Roman and Anglican communions. The seated Christ in Glory, with accompanying saints, on the great *reredos* of St Peter Mancroft Church in Norwich, are Sir Ninian's work (1930).

Consecration crosses: painted on or carved – indicate the points at which the walls of the church, and the altar slab (the *mensa*) were touched with Holy Oil by the Bishop at the consecration of the building. On the altar were incised five crosses – one at each corner and one in the middle – signifying the *Five Wounds of Christ*. Twelve crosses were marked on the walls, three on each of the four walls, both inside and out, at a height above the ground so that they would not be brushed by passers by. To reach them, the Bishop used a small ladder which was moved round during the service of consecration. Comparatively few survive – painted ones in various states of preservation can be seen at Bale (good), Calthorpe, Great Walsingham, Lammas and Thrigby. Alby has four carved ones – and Holt a single one placed unusually into the back of a *piscina*.

Corbels: A highly practical item which often doubles as a very decorative one. This is the support, set firmly into the wall, to carry a weight from above (see *Roofs*) and will usually be carved, either decoratively, or with heads which may be reverent or formalised, delightfully (and irreverently) portrait-like; or more fancifully (see, among others, Barney, Cley, Burlingham St Andrew, Matlask). Corbels are also freely used decoratively on the ends of *dripstones* and *hood-mouldings*.

Corinthian: A column of one of the classical (Grecian) orders, comprising a cushioned base, the shaft or pillar itself (usually fluted), and a capital (ie. the head of the pillar) enriched with acanthus leaves.

Cotman, John Sell, (1782-1842): With *John Crome*, a leading member of the *Norwich School of Painting*, and in his own right, one of the outstanding English landscape and watercolour painters. He was born in Norwich in 1782 and educated at the city's free grammar school. After a spell in London he returned to Norwich, opened a school for drawing, and joined the Norwich Society of Artists. A wealthy Yarmouth banker and antiquarian, Dawson Turner, became his patron, and it was under his influence that between 1812 and 1818 Cotman published the first series of his Norfolk etchings – the 'Architectural Antiquities of Norfolk'. Soon after came 'Engravings of Sepulchral Brasses in Norfolk' – both key works for students of the county's churches. An unusual item associated with him is the weather vane which he designed for Knapton Church.

Courses: A course is, in general terms, a horizontal layer of masonry. A *base course* will usually be at the base of the tower – a purely decorative course, a little above the ground, designed to set off the tower visually. In Norfolk, the local flint is often used to great effect here, knapped and set flush into stone panelling (thus, *flushwork*) to create a most attractive contrast, as well as a visual impression of upward, vertical thrust. A *string course* is a moulding whose purpose is to indicate the divisions of a tower into its several stages, though in some cases – Brisley in w. Norfolk is a fine example – it is carried over the tower window(s) to create an impression of lightness and uplift. Finally, a *drip course* is, as its name indicates, a raised course doing the practical job of carrying off rain from the wall surface. (See also *dripstone*.)

Cox, J. Charles: The Rev. Charles Cox was a Kent clergyman, a prolific writer on churches and their furnishings and on historical subjects in general, with a long list of books to his credit. He visited Norfolk regularly from the 1860s, but it was not until 1902 that he published, in two pocket-sized volumes, his 'County Churches: Norfolk', with second editions issued in 1910-11.

Credence/Credence shelf: This is a shelf on which the elements of the Mass or Communion are placed before consecration by the priest; usually found within the niche of the *piscina* beside the altar, or the site of a former altar. Can sometimes occupy a niche of its own.

Crockets/crocketting: This is an exuberant ornamentation of the *Decor-*

ated period, in the first half of the C14, though it was to be carried through with enthusiasm into the later *Perpendicular* style. It is a little projecting sculpture in the form of leaves, flowers etc., used in profusion on pinnacles, spires, canopies and so on, both inside and outside the building.

Crome, John (1768–1821): A leading figure with *John Sell Cotman* in the *Norwich School of Painting.* This great English landscape painter was born in Norwich, worked in the city and died there, rising from humble origins to become established and respected in his art, founder of the Norwich Society of Artists in 1803, a regular exhibitor at the Royal Academy and the British Institution, and with Cotman a master of the important English school of regional painting which the Norwich School represents. A superb collection can be seen in Norwich Castle Museum.

Cusp/cusping: These are the little projecting points on the curves of window and screen tracery, arches etc., which give a foliated, leaf-like appearance. From the Latin cuspis, a point (of a spear).

Decalogue Board: The Decalogue (a word derived from the Greek) is the Ten Commandments collectively. The Decalogue Board, it follows, is a large board upon which the Commandments are written. These became a regular part of church furnishings in the reign of Elizabeth I, when it was State policy to clear churches of the decorations and adornments which were regarded as 'Popish'. In 1560, Elizabeth ordered *Archbishop Parker* to see 'that the tables of the Commandments be comely set or hung up in the east end of the chancel.' The following year more explicit instructions were given: the boards were to be fixed to the e. wall over the communion table. Decalogues were also set up on the *tympanum* – panelling which filled the curve of the chancel arch to replace the discarded *rood loft* (See also, *Royal Arms).* In most cases

today, the Decalogue Boards have long since been moved from their position behind the altar (as at Thurning) but are usually displayed on a convenient wall of nave or aisles.

Decorated: This was the high point of ornamented Gothic architecture in the first half of the C14. (See under *Styles of Architecture.)*

Despencer, Henry le, Bishop of Norwich (1341-1406): A soldier/bishop who early in life fought in Italy for the Pope and was assigned the Bishopric of Norwich in 1370. His early reputation for arrogance rebounded on him when, in 1377, he attempted to go in procession through (King's) Lynn with the honours afforded only to their mayor: the townspeople retaliated by closing their gates on him and rained down arrows and missiles on the whole company, wounding Despencer in the process. Only intervention by the King patched up the quarrel. Despencer is most remembered however, as the man who in 1381 put down the Peasants' Revolt in Norfolk (this was a popular movement which broke out all over the country against serfdom). Despencer was at court when he heard of the Norfolk insurrection, and having raised a contingent at his manor at Burghley near Stamford, he set out for Norwich – fully armed with sword, helmet and coat of mail. Battle was finally joined near North Walsham, where the bishop himself led the assault on the rebels and joined in the fierce hand to hand fighting. Many of the peasants were killed and Despencer, acting as a judge in the King's Court, tried John Lidster the local leader of the rebels at North Walsham. He was sentenced to be hung, drawn and quartered, and then Despencer in his role as bishop took the condemned man to St Nicholas' church to hear his confession and absolve him. As Lidster was dragged at the cart-tail to the place of execution, Despencer went with him, holding up his head to spare him some of the rigours of that last Journey. A contemporary cross beside the Norwich road going in to North Walsham marks the site of the battle. The bishop's later life was punctuated by feats of arms at home and abroad, and he finally came to rest in a grave before the high Altar of Norwich Cathedral. There, in St Luke's chapel, may be seen a *reredos* which may well have been given as a thank-offering for the suppression of the rebellion in 1381.

Dogtooth decoration: An ornamental carving of the Early English period (see *Styles of Architecture*) in the C12/C13, which looks like a four-leafed flower. One suggestion is that it is based on the dog's tooth violet.

Drip course: See *courses*.

Dripstone: A projecting ledge or moulding over the heads of doorways, windows etc., serving the practical purpose of carrying off the rain. When the same architectural addition is used inside a building, as a decorative feature, it is called a *hood-mould*.

Dropped sill sedilia/window: See *sedilia*.

Dukes of Norfolk: In the church at South Walsham is an incised slab from the tomb of a C15 abbot of St Benet's Abbey, whose ruins are not far away on the banks of the Bure. After the *Reformation*, when the Abbey had fallen into ruins, that slab was appropriated – and did service as a door-step in the great Norwich palace of the Dukes of Norfolk, until it was rescued and taken home. In its day that palace, now wholly disappeared, was a vast residence, standing on the corner of Duke Street . . . where the multi-storey car parks now stand . . . and backed onto the river, still crossed by Duke's Palace Bridge. The place was partly pulled down in the first decade of the C18, on the orders of the eighth Duke, after he'd had a blazing row with the Mayor of Norwich (that worthy refused to allow His Grace's company of com-

edians to parade through the city streets with trumpets and banners). Though as the Norfolks were in financial diffi-culties at this time, it's possible that the Duke saw this as a good opportunity to rid himself of a considerable burden. There had been a palace there since the C16, but in 1602 a start was made on pulling down the old one and building a replacement – which was still only partly built when the diarist John Evelyn visited it in 1671. Nonetheless, the Howards, the Ducal family, lived there in princely state, their guests drinking from gold goblets – even the fire-irons were made of silver. In 1711, following the Duke's departure, the place had fallen to the breakers. Later still, what remained became a squalid workhouse, until 1856. Then the last vestige was used as a pub, the Duke's Palace Inn, which finally disappeared when the bulldozers moved in during the spring of 1968.

Early English: This is the style develop-ment of the mid C12 which heralded the arrival of Gothic, or pointed archi-tecture in Britain – as well as the birth of a truly native style. (See under *Styles of Architecture*.)

Easter Sepulchre: Immediately to the n. of the high altar a recess in the wall – ranging from the plain to the richly carved and canopied – housed the Easter Sepulchre (itself normally a temporary structure of wood). On Maundy Thurs-day, a Host was consecrated (Latin, 'hostia', victim – the bread which is the Body of Christ) and placed in the Easter Sepulchre, to be consumed at the fol-lowing day's Good Friday Mass. This practice still continues in the Roman Catholic and some Anglican churches today, the Host being 'borne in solemn Procession . . . to the altar of repose', to be processed back to the High Altar the following day. As in medieval times, so today 'this 'Mass' is not, strictly speak-ing, a Mass, for there is no consecration' (Little Roman Missal, p.227). Thus, on the day of Christ's death, it is not a celebration. Until the *Reformation*, the

Sepulchre would be watched over from Good Friday to Easter Day and sometimes, on Easter Morning, would be the setting for a dramatisation of the Resurrection. Most Sepulchres were disposed of during Elizabeth's reign, though in 1538, during the time of her father, Henry VIII, a list of 'superstitious lights' to be removed specifically excluded the light (ie. a constantly burning candle) before the sepulchre. Good examples in Norfolk are to be found at Northwold, Kelling and Baconsthorpe.

Emblems of the Trinity: Among the enormous variety of carvings found on medieval fonts, the Emblems of the Trinity are a regular feature. Among them: the equilateral triangle, the trefoil (three-leaf) design, three interlocking circles, all representing the idea of the three persons of the Godhead – Father, Son and Holy Spirit, three in one and one in three; also the two interlocking triangles ('Solomon's Seal', borrowed from Judaeism); a figure of God as King with Christ on the Cross and a Dove of Peace hovering over them; and lastly a shield design, linking indissolubly Pater, Filius et Spiritus Sanctus, Father, Son and Holy Spirit with, at the centre of the shield, Deus, God.

Encaustic tiles: The Victorians invented the process of burning-in different coloured clays onto tile and brick, to produce a stencil-like effect. In churches built during the C19, and in others 'restored' and 'improved' by Victoria's zealous subjects, these tiles were freely used on floor and wall, on reredos and elsewhere, to produce effects which are very much today a matter of individual taste in one's response to them.

Evangelistic symbols: On fonts and screens, in stained glass etc., the symbols of the Evangelists are represented as man, eagle, lion and ox, all winged. The biblical source is the four all-seeing, never-sleeping creatures around the throne of God, in the vision of St John the Divine:

'The first living creature was like a lion, the second was like an ox, the third had a face like a man, the fourth was like a flying eagle . . .' (Revelations 4, v. 7).

The Evangelists associated with the symbols are John, eagle; Luke, ox; Matthew, man; and Mark, lion.

Five Wounds of Christ, The: On fonts (at Blakeney, for example) and elsewhere, The Five Wounds of Christ are often represented. They are, of course, the wounds of Crucifixion – to hands, feet and side, recalling doubting Thomas's

'Except I shall . . . put my finger into the print of the nails, and thrust my hand into his side, I will not believe' (John, 20, v.25).

See also the Instruments of the Passion, which often accompany representations of the Wounds.

Flint-knapping: Flint split across the middle, with craftsmanly skill, to achieve a shell-like fracture – and a lustrous, flat surface. (See flushwork.)

Flushwork: This is the use of knapped flints, set flush into panelled patterns in brick or stone, a combination which adds visual beauty and striking impact to so many Norfolk (and Suffolk) churches.

Foils: From the C12, foils were a much used adornment in Gothic architecture. The Early English style produced the graceful trefoil, or three-leafed shape: it is said that this was intended to represent the Trinity – three in one and one in three – and that St Patrick, in C5 Ireland, so the story goes, put together three leaves of shamrock to illustrate to his converts in a visual way that profound mystery. Be that as it may, the trefoil was followed architecturally by the quatrefoil (four leaf), cinquefoil (five leaf) and multi-foil.

Four Latin Doctors: 'Doctor' here indicates one who is learned, a theologian. The Four Latin Doctors were the leading theologians of the early Christian Church in the west – Ambrose, Augustine of Hippo, Jerome and Gregory. (More about them under *Saints*.)

Galilee porches: The western porch of a church – of which examples can be seen at Little Walsingham, Cromer and Cley, among others – was often called the 'Galilee porch' because it was the final 'station' in the Sunday procession. The priest at the head of the procession symbolised Christ going before his disciples into Galilee after the Resurrection . . . In medieval times these processions were an important part of the Sunday and Feast Day services and must have made an impressive sight with the colours of robes and banners. (See also *banner-stave lockers*.)

Galleries: in churches have a fascinating pedigree. Before the *Reformation*, when every church had its *rood loft* in the chancel arch, singers might use the loft as a gallery, the singing being accompanied by a simple organ. In the couple of centuries that followed the Reformation and the destruction of the old rood lofts, galleries – usually at the w. end of the nave – became a common feature. There was housed the village orchestra (the enthusiastic, if not always entirely harmonious sounds, of clarinet, flute, bass fiddle, bassoon and hautboy – predecessor of the modern oboe). Village choirs were common, although the robed and surpliced variety were a mid-Victorian innovation. When organs again became popular they were sometimes placed in a western gallery, and there they can still occasionally be found – there is a delightful example at Hempstead (near Holt). Many more galleries were inserted in the C19 to accommodate the larger congregations of the period, but few now remain.

Gargoyles: Quite simply, a spout jutting outwards from a wall so as to throw rainwater well away from the building.

But there is much more to them than that. Almost always in ancient churches they are grotesquely carved in all manner of fanciful forms of weird beasts and dragons and devils . . . and representations of human vices like the seven deadly sins. This choice of subjects has a very positive aspect to it: if there is good in this world, there is assuredly evil; so also in the world of the spirit; so equally in the sphere of those forces 'beyond the normal' which the modern mind is again coming to examine and accept. To appreciate good and beauty, it is necessary to recognise the face of evil and ugliness – and this medieval man knew and practised. As his mixture of reverence and superstition also inclined to the view that dragons and demons were always prowling evilly round his church, what better way of keeping them at bay than putting their own kind on guard . . . on the basis, presumably, of 'it takes a devil to catch a devil'. (See also, *North Doors*).

Gesso: This is a system of coating a base, usually wood, with a thick layer of plaster of Paris, or with gypsum (one of the powdered minerals used to make up plaster of Paris). When it is hard, the artist/sculptor carves into it his chosen design, to produce an incised effect which is then painted and, in church art, almost always gilded.

Gibbons, Grinling (1648-1721): An interior decorator, wood carver and sculptor of genius, who worked for Charles II, was master carver to George I, collaborated with Sir Christopher Wren at St Paul's, and was the chosen instrument of the noblest in the land to beautify their country mansions (Petworth and Burghley, for example). He was especially known for the beauty and delicacy of his carvings of birds, flowers and foliage. One of his monuments is in Felbrigg Church, sporting, typically, large swags of flowers and fruit.

Green Man: The Green Man is a foliate

mask, often of demoniacal appearance, probably representing the spirit of fertility . . . often having living vines issuing from its mouth, and as such, an occasional device in wood and stone carving – a touch of persistent Paganism in Christian art. A green man's head peers from below the rim of the old pulpit at Guist; and at Scottow that disconcerting face looks down from a *boss* at the centre of the porch roof. An interesting diversion on the theme of the green man, indicating an east-west cross fertilisation of folk-lore, is provided by an Oriental tale told of Alexander the Great who, sad at having nowhere else to conquer, was taken by his cook (soon to become Khezr, an immortal and 'hidden prophet') to find the fountain of immortality – anyone who bathed in it would live for ever. After trials, terrors and adventures they come to a land of ebony forests and utter darkness, where they become separated. Khezr finds himself at a pool, where he decides to wash a dried fish before cooking it for his supper – but on contact with the water it comes to life and wriggles away . . . and he realises he has found the fountain of immortality. He bathes, his skin turns green . . . and wherever he goes thereafter flowers spring up in his footsteps. He is now daemon, immortal, The Green Man.

Griffin: Traditionally the guardian of treasure – but also used in church sculpture, carvings and paintings. The griffin – or gryphon – is a mythical monster with an eagle's head, wings and fore-legs; and the body, tail and hind-legs of a lion. Heraldry uses this fabulous creature too – there's a griffin on the Arms of the City of London, for example. In Oriental folklore, a couple of griffins pulled Alexander the Great in a magic chariot up to heaven . . . while he was still alive that is, just to have a look around.

Groining: This is the creation of a vaulted ceiling, divided into segments by raised, intersecting lines – these

lines, between the angled surfaces, being the actual 'groins'. Found in carved canopies, as well as in roofs – Norfolk roof examples are usually in porches, though there is a fine *Early English* example in the elegant little chancel at Blakeney. Where groined vaulting is used on the large scale, it is very grand and impressive.

Groves, William (b.1809): A sculptor who first exhibited at the Royal Academy in 1834 and subsequently for many years at Burlington House. Apart from statuary and portrait busts, he was also responsible for numerous monuments for churches. Among them is an arresting tablet memorial at Catfield to Lt. Thomas Cubitt, 1848, in which is intriguingly featured a 'peepul tree', a neatly philosophical allusion to the eastern scene of the young lieutenant's death. For this is the sacred wild fig, or bo-tree, as Buddhists of India and Ceylon called it, under which the Lord Buddha received His enlightenment. William Groves also has a monument at Shouldham, w. Norfolk, to Thomas Allen, 1841, which was exhibited at the R.A. before being transported to its present setting.

Guilds/Guild altars: In corners of churches, in the e. ends of aisles etc., may often be seen *piscinas*, and occasionally *squints* which, as is frequently repeated in the body of this book, indicate the presence of a guild or *chantry* altar in pre-*Reformation* times. Indeed, English guilds, according to one authority, 'are older than any kings of England'. They were associations of those living in the same neighbourhood who remembered that they had, as neighbours, common obligations – an obligation to put into practice the commandment to 'love thy neighbour'. Their religious commitment would often be shown by having their own altar in their parish church, served by a priest whom they maintained. There were two main divisions: craft or trade guilds, whose purpose was the protection of particular work, trade or handicraft; and religious societies or, as they are sometimes called, 'Social Guilds'. The split was one of convenience rather than a real distinction founded on fact – all had the same general characteristic, the principle of brotherly love and social charity, and none was divorced from the ordinary religious observances daily practised in pre-Reformation England. Broadly speaking, they were the benefit societies and provident associations of the Middle Ages – a helping hand as ready to help the sick or look after poor children as to lodge pilgrims cheaply. Dr. Augustus Jessop, canon of Norwich Cathedral, headmaster of Norwich School, and local historian around the turn of this century, wrote descriptively of

'. . . small associations called guilds, the members of which were bound to devote a certain portion of their time and money and their energies to keep up the special commemoration and the special worship of some Saint's chapel or shrine which was sometimes kept up in a corner of the church, and provided with an altar of its own, and served by a chaplain who was actually paid by the subscriptions or free-will offerings of the members of the guild whose servant he was'.

Nearly everyone was a member of one fraternity or another. One distinct help to the parish was the provision of additional priests for the services of the church. Beccles Guild of the Holy Ghost, for example, had a priest 'to celebrate in the church', Beccles being 'a great and populous town of 800 houseling people . . . the said priest is aiding unto the curate there, who without help is not able to discharge the said cure'. (Note: 'housel' in Old English means 'sacrifice', and was used in the English Church from St Augustine to the Reformation to mean The Eucharist; 'houseling people' – those who had received communion). (See also *chantry chapels*.)

Hammer beam roofs: A brilliant conception, architecturally and artistically, of the late gothic period, late C15-C16, in which the thrust of the roof's weight is taken on 'hammer' brackets. (See *Roofs*, figs, 6, 7, and 8)

Hatchments: Many churches display on their walls large, diamond-shaped boards, bearing a coat of arms and either the motto of the family whose 'coat' it is, or the simple word – but perhaps ultimate expression of confident faith – 'Resurgam' (I shall rise again). Dating from the second half of the C17 through to the end of the C18, these boards were carried in procession at the burial of the holder of the Arms; afterwards for some months they adorned the dead man's house, and finally were transferred to the church. The composition of the boards followed a formalised pattern – the background is black on the left hand side if the dead person was a husband, black on the right if a wife; for a bachelor, widow or widower, the whole background would be black.

Headstops: The decorative 'stops' at the ends of *dripstones* and *hood moulds* over arches, doors and windows.

Holy Water stoups: In the porches of many churches, and/or just inside the main entrance door, are basins, usually recessed into the wall. More often than not they are very plain in execution – though there are exceptions, like the very grand one at Stalham. The basins held holy water which was mixed once a week before Mass. On entering the church, worshippers dipped the ends of their fingers into the water, and crossed themselves reverently to remind themselves of their baptismal vows. For the preparation of the water, in pre-*Reformation* times, salt was first of all exorcised (the expelling of the evil spirit) and then blessed; in turn, water was exorcised and blessed. The salt was then scattered over the water 'in the sign of the cross' and another Blessing was said over the mixture.

Hood mould: See *dripstone*.

Hour-glasses/stands: There was a time when long sermons were the rule rather than the exception, particularly so after the *Reformation*, in Cromwell's Puritan period in the mid C17, and in the C18 when preachers were renowned for their long-windedness. For their own guidance preachers often had an hour glass on or near the pulpit, to indicate the passing time . . . though when the hour was up it was not unknown for sermonisers to turn the glass over and start again. Before the Reformation hour-glasses were used, though less commonly, to time private meditations etc. Numerous hour-glass stands remain today in our churches – among Norfolk examples are those at Catfield, Salhouse, Burlingham St. Edmund, and Braydeston.

IHS: The Sacred Monogram of the name of Jesus. There are two schools of thought regarding its interpretation. One says that it is the first two and last letters of the Greek alphabetic spelling of Jesus: the other that it represents the Latin 'Iesus Hominum Salvator' – Jesus the Saviour of Mankind. Either way, IHS is regularly seen carved on fonts and represented elsewhere in the adornment of our churches.

Instruments of the Passion: These are frequent among the symbols carved on medieval fonts and on the stonework of the church (for example – on an outer buttress at Blakeney). They are – Christ's Cross; the Crown of Thorns; the Spear that was thrust into His side; the cup of vinegar; and the reed and sponge by which that vinegar was offered as Christ hung on the Cross (John 19, vv 28-29). The dice which were used to cast lots for His clothing (an example can be found in the top of the e. window at Poringland), and a ladder are additional symbols.

Isolated churches: Churches far removed from their villages, or from any habitation, inevitably invite the question: 'Why?' A popular answer is that the *Black Death* (see separate entry), the terrible plague of 1349-50, was the culprit, either killing everyone in the village or removing so many that the remainder deserted the plague hole and built elsewhere. It is a fact however that there is no actual documentary evidence for this having happened. This does not mean that it did not happen. But it is a theory to be treated with caution, especially as there are some places with isolated churches which apparently suffered little or no loss at the time of the Black Death. The much more likely villain was the humble sheep! In the late C15 and early C16 century, the *Wool Trade* was big business in Britain and the Low Countries. From its profits arose some of our most magnificent churches – in Norfolk, places like Cawston, Trunch, Salle and Worstead, for example . . . indeed, from the last village came the word 'worsted', which was already in use in the C15, when a member of the *Paston family*, in the famous Paston Letters, could ask for 'two ells of worsted for doublets'. But apart from architectural glory, the Wool Trade also produced impoverishment, cruelty, misery and starvation on a terrible scale, as landowners callously demolished villages, cleared huge areas, dispossessed peasants and enclosed common pasturage . . . in order to graze yet more sheep. This period is much more likely to have created isolated churches. (It was enclosures which sparked off Kett's Rebellion in Norfolk in 1549, led by Wymondham yeoman Robert Kett . . . It ended with the rebels being slaughtered in thousands in a pitched battle just outside Norwich, and with Kett being hanged in chains from the castle). There is another consideration still. In the late C17 and early C18, when landed gentlemen were making their huge parks around their mansions, whole villages were demolished to make way. But this time there had to be reparation – which usually meant rebuilding the village (almost certainly with far better housing than before) at the park gates . . . Houghton, Gunton and Felbrigg are Norfolk examples. The 'park gates village' became quite the thing by the C18 – so one was built at Holkham, though there had been no original village to move. From all this it will be seen that the questions surrounding isolated churches are very open ones.

Jacobean: Style of architecture dating from early in the C17 with the reign, 1603-25, of James I. (See *Styles of Architecture*.)

Jamb/jamb shaft: The upright of a doorway, or the side of a window opening: the 'shaft' is a decorative shaft or slim column at the angle of the window splay with the wall, and can often be used to remarkably beautiful and delicate effect.

John of Gaunt, Duke of Lancaster (1340-99): One of the great nobles of England, second son of Edward III and father of Henry IV by the first of his three wives. But though Shakespeare would have us remember 'old Gaunt, time honoured Lancaster', he who speaks so nobly of 'this earth, this realm, this England', the truth was not so rosy – during the period when Gaunt was king in all but name during the minority of Richard II, Parliament rose in wrath against the corruption of his rule. Gaunt's vast possessions included extensive estates in Norfolk. He had a great house at Gimingham (near North Walsham) of which all trace has now disappeared; equally nothing is left of the Austin friary which he founded at Thetford in 1387. Tradition has it that he was founder of Aylsham Church: certainly in that town, in the guildhall, he held the court of his duchy of Lancaster, arriving there with great pomp. At North Walsham his arms, and those of his father, adorn the magnificent porch.

Kempe, Charles Eamer (1837-1907): In churches throughout Britain, the beautiful, richly coloured glass designed by Charles Eamer Kempe glows in innumerable windows. Guide books, reference and text books will generally say only 'Glass by Kempe' – the most assiduous search was necessary for the purposes of this note to discover his full name and dates, so that proper credit might be paid to an exceptional worker in stained glass – examples of which may be found in many Norfolk churches – and in other forms of constructional art. Langham, Glandford and Brundall are among churches having examples of his windows.

Kempe, Margery (c.1373-c.1440): A remarkable 'religious woman' with a simple faith to move mountains, the resilience of an early saint; and an unabashed fluency of tongue capable of talking the hind leg off a bishop . . . so to speak. Until the 1930s it was thought that the only writings of this (King's) Lynn woman were some brief pages of 'The Boke of Margerie Kempe of Lynn'. Then, excitingly, a manuscript came to light – an autobiography which, late in life, she had dictated (for it seems she was illiterate herself) giving an account of the many religious experiences she had undergone and pilgrimages she had made. For astonishingly, this ordinary, unlettered woman had travelled to Rome, Jerusalem and Compostella in Spain. Nearer at hand, she met that wise lady, *Mother Julian of Norwich*. Nothing daunted Margery Kempe; no-one, no matter what his rank, intimidated her (she once swapped words sharply with the Archbishop of York); and all that she saw and heard she remembered and considered. A difficult female, and a freely emotional one. Though at St Margaret's in Lynn, where she regularly worshipped, they would have forgiven her much after she had a vision in which St Margaret's was assured of being in the right in its dispute with St Nicholas' Chapel, just round the corner, for the right to baptize children . . . and collect the fees. In a disturbed and tumultuous age, Margery Kempe sought for clarity and understanding in her life and her religion.

King-posts: An upright roof beam set between horizontal cross beams; or between cross beam and roof ridge, to prevent sag and give greater stability. (See *Roofs*, fig. 3, for full description.)

Lancet: The slim, pointed window which characterises the beginnings of *Early English* architecture from about 1200. (See *Styles of Architecture.*)

Laudian: This refers to Archbishop William Laud, 1573-1644. His seven years as Archbishop of Canterbury, during which he tried to impose certain disciplines of worship on the English and Scottish churches, had far reaching effects – but for him resulted in his execution. Laud wanted to reform the English Church in a way compatible with Protestantism, yet without giving way to the sweeping changes and austerities called for by the increasingly powerful Puritans. Brought down to its simplicities, he wanted a disciplined order and form of worship which centred on the altar, placed against the e. wall of the chancel, with an enclosing rail around it; and with the communicants kneeling within the chancel to receive the sacrament. But these were matters of bitter and violent debate. From Elizabeth's I's reign, the altar often had been placed 'table-wise' – i.e. e. to w. – at the nave end of the chancel; or a temporary table was set up in the nave – the intention being in each case for the communicants to be within sight and hearing of the priest at the altar. But there were those who refused to kneel, or even to enter the chancel, and who certainly would not tolerate, in the e. end altar, what smacked to them of a Roman 'high altar', divorced from the people. The impression which comes down to us of the Archbishop is of a man of honest intent – but whose every action seemed to turn people against him. He was accused of 'popery' and of warmth towards Rome; blamed for the disastrous and ineffective moves against Scotland, both judicial and military, intended to make their churches conform with his ideas; then he

issued 'canons' (i.e. instructions) which appeared to many to enshrine the absolute rule and 'divine right' of King Charles I – whose position by now was already seriously threatened. In December 1640 Parliament impeached Laud for treason, and he was imprisoned in the Tower. But it was not until March 1644 that he was put on trial and then it was a complete mockery of justice, for the House of Lords had decided in advance that he was guilty of trying to alter the foundations of Church and State. Nonetheless they hesitated to sentence him . . . until the House of Commons threatened to set the mob on them if they didn't. On January 10th, 1644, staunchly declaring his innocence and good intent, William Laud, at the venerable age of 72, died under the axe . . . Parliament having graciously agreed that he should be excused the usual traitor's punishment of being hung, drawn and quartered. The irony is that, by the end of the century, the forms of service which developed in the 'Anglican' church were much in sympathy with the things for which Laud fought and died. (See also *Prayer Book Churches*; *Communion Rails*; and *Mensa slabs.*)

Ledger-stone: When the art and use of monumental brasses declined in the first half of the C17, sculpture in stone began to come into its own in our churches. But while those splendid, opulent examples which adorn wall or table-tomb may be the first to catch the eye, it often pays to drop one's gaze to the ground to those dark, massive slabs in pavements of chancel, nave and aisles, incised with arms, crests and epitaphs. These are our ledger stones, and a study in themselves, as many carry quite marvellous inscriptions which can so easily be overlooked – here a lusty hunting man, earthed at last 'by that subtile fox Death' (Cantley); there a touching remembrance of a parish priest 'as good perhaps as ever lived' (Little Snoring); and again, a subtly bitter-edged lament on a little seven year-old's passing . . . 'What crowds will wish their time on earth, Had been as short as thine' (Knapton). To go into a holy place with eyes cast down can be rewarding in more than one sense!

Lenten veil: It was the custom in medieval times to 'curtain off' the altar during Lent with a Lenten Veil. This was suspended from *corbels*, or hooks – of which a few examples remain in Norfolk churches – set into the chancel walls at a suitable height; one example may be seen at Horsham St Faith. Some churches continue that custom today.

Linen-fold panelling: This was an innovation in wood carving of the C16 in the *Tudor* period – an elegant and beautifully restrained representation in wood of linen laid in crisp vertical folds. Seen on a range of church furnishings.

Linton, W. of Norwich (1666-1684): A Norwich sculptor, well known in his day, whose memorial to Edmund Hobart can be seen at Holt. Another example of his work was in St Nicholas's Church, Great Yarmouth, but was destroyed in the inferno of 1942, when the church was gutted by German bombing.

Lombardic script: This is a calligraphic form of writing which developed in Italy after the Roman and Byzantine periods. A variant of it was used for Papal documents and for legal work in Rome until the early C13. From time to time it is used on tombs and memorials in English churches. Among Norfolk examples is the border inscription on an ancient coffin lid at Hickling.

Long and short work: Distinctive of *Saxon* craftsmanship, upright stones alternating with flat slabs in the quoins at the corners of buildings. (See *Styles of Architecture.*)

Low side windows: Almost as much nonsense has been written about low side windows as about 'weeping chancels'. These small, square or oblong windows were usually low down in the s. wall of the chancel, just e. of the chancel arch, and fitted with shutters so that the window could be opened. It has been suggested that these were 'leper windows' for these afflicted people to look in and thus share in the Mass – a ridiculous assertion, since not even in medieval times would lepers have been allowed to roam at leisure. The actual use of these windows, most authorities agree, was so that, at the moment of the elevation of the Host (Latin – 'hostia', victim – the bread which is The Body of Christ) during the Mass, a handbell would be rung through the opened low window, so that for a moment those in the vicinity, in village and field, might pause in their daily round, cross themselves, and thus share in the Celebration. Most low side windows are now filled in. But a complete one can be seen at Saxthorpe; at Attlebridge one is contained in the lower part of a large window and at Burlingham St Andrew there is an interesting pointed one. But perhaps the most fascinating example is at Melton Constable, which has beside it a stone book rest and a hollowed-out seat. (See also: *sanctus bell*).

Lych-gate: The word 'lych' is derived from the Anglo-Saxon 'lic' or 'lich', and from the German 'leiche', all meaning corpse. The purpose of the lych-gate is to provide a shelter and resting place for coffin bearers on the way to the church. In former times, the lych-gate would have seats and a coffin table, on which the coffin would be set. Poor people who could not afford a coffin might be placed – temporarily – in the parish coffin; but otherwise they would be wrapped in a sheet and placed straight onto the coffin table, where they would be received by the priest, who here speaks the first sentences of the burial service. During the reign of Charles II, it is worth noting, an Act of Parliament was passed which made it an offence, with a fine of £5, for anyone not to be buried without being wrapped in a woollen cloth . . . which was one way of promoting the trade in wool. Astonishingly, it was 1814 before this Act was repealed. Ancient lych-gates are rare, most being C19/C20.

Mass or scratch dials: On or near the s. porch of many old churches may be seen small patterns, usually about six to ten inches across, of radiating lines centred on a hole. In the hole was placed a metal or wooden peg known as a gnomon (Greek – indicator), whose shadow moved round with the sun . . . and each time the shadow touched one of the radiating lines, it was time for Mass. Later, largely in the C18, sun-dials became popular, providing a time-piece, sunshine permitting, for the whole day.

Mensa slabs: In pre-*Reformation* times, the high altar and altars in chantry chapels were of stone, topped with a slab or mensa – Latin, table. Each had five crosses carved upon it, one at each corner and one on the centre, representing the *Five Wounds of Christ.* After the Suppression of the Monasteries, begun in 1536 by Henry VIII, the chantries too were soon dissolved, and with them went their altars. But stone high altars remained, and in the reign of Henry's son, the boy-king Edward VI – a convinced Protestant – a movement was led by two of his bishops to have them removed and replaced by wooden tables. This was realised in 1550 when the King in Council commanded every bishop to order this change in all the churches in his diocese. Many more sweeping changes in church interiors and in forms of worship were to follow in this period, and much wanton destruction, as the demands of a new age were ruthlessly achieved. (See under *Prayer Book Churches* how these changes developed.) Locally, Hanworth had its mensa restored to its old position – it was found nearly a century ago, buried in the churchyard; Scottow has one framed as a memorial; and

Salthouse has a foot-square one set into its present altar. This last one is interesting: it is a portable mensa, which would have been used for saying Mass on unconsecrated altars. This was quite a common thing in churches in medieval times: indeed, it is recorded that, in 1367, there were 200 of them in the Archdeaconry of Norwich alone. (See also *Consecration Crosses.*)

Misericords: In the chancels of many churches remain ancient stalls with hinged seats. Underneath, the tip-up seats are carved generally with very free expression and often with exuberant irreverence and humour: anything from the wildest caricatures to cartoonish domestic scenes and upsets. All are worth examining closely, wherever they are found. On the leading edge of these seats is usually a smooth, hollowed surface on which, during long services, the elderly – or just the plain sleepy – could lean and rest. Thus the name, from the Latin 'misericordia', pity, compassion. Not to be confused with Misericord – a small room for laying out the dead which adjoined the Infirmary of monasteries in past times.

Morris, William (1834-96): Architect, painter, designer, poet, and prolific writer on artistic, literary and political matters. But best known as the man who in 1861 founded Morris & Co. and thus revolutionised British taste in furnishings, interior decoration (his wallpaper designs are still famous and in demand), ceramics, textiles and stained glass, and exercised a considerable influence on industrial design. Himself a first-rate craftsman, he was devoted to the idea of reviving craftsmanship and old handicrafts in an age already embarked on the mass production we know too well today. While at Oxford he began a life-long friendship with the painter *Edward Burne-Jones,* who made many tapestry and stained glass designs for Morris & Co. which were executed in the company's workshops. (See under *Burne-Jones* for examples in Norfolk of their stained glass collaborations.)

Mother Julian of Norwich: Julian was the C14 anchoress (religious recluse) at St Julian's Church in Norwich, who wrote the book now regarded as one of the masterpieces of spiritual literature – 'Revelations of Divine Love'. She was born in 1343 – about the same time as Chaucer – and was almost certainly educated by the nuns at nearby Carrow, a Benedictine Priory. On May 8th, 1373, during severe illness, she received a series of 'showings' from God. She became an enclosed nun, living alone beside St Julian's Church. Her name is thought to be taken from the church itself. There, during the next 20 years, she wrote her book, the first known to be written in English by a woman. Julian's cell was in use until the *Reformation*. The church survived, only to be badly damaged by bombing in the last war. Today the church and cell have been rebuilt. The cell is now a chapel where pilgrims from all over the world come to kneel in silent prayer. Mother Julian looks down on worshippers at Horstead (just n. of Norwich), from a stained glass window.

Myngs, Sir Christopher (1625-66): Admiral Myngs was born at Salthouse, on the n.e. Norfolk coast, in 1625 and baptised in the parish church on November 22nd of that year. It is said that he was the son of a shoemaker – but if that is so, a pretty prosperous one, for it seems fairly certain from extant records that the future admiral's birthplace was the manor house: later he was to acquire Salthouse Hall. He went to sea at an early age in a coastal vessel sailing out of nearby Blakeney. During the Four Days Battle, off North Foreland, when the British under George Monck, Duke of Albemarle, and the Dutch under Admiral de Ruyter, were locked in bloody combat from June 1st to 4th, Myngs was fatally wounded in the throat. Worshipped by his men, his death moved a number of them to offer themselves as a 'suicide

mission' crew of a fireship, to exact revenge upon the enemy; and also inspired a popular song. . .

> 'So here's the grave of Sir Christopher Myngs
> A great name . . . greater than my lord the King's
> He fought and bled for England
> He's lying dead for England
> And foul fall shame
> On England's name
> When Englishmen forget the name
> Of stout Sir Christopher Myngs.'

He is remembered, at least, at Salthouse, in the proud church above the shore line . . . where a copy of that song hangs on a wall. . .

Narbrough, Sir John (1640-88): One of Norfolk's several admirals, he was baptised at Cockthorpe Church on October 11th, 1640. He went early to sea, in a local vessel, possibly with *Admiral Myngs*, from nearby Salthouse. He was involved in the Battle of Solebay (the old name for Southwold Bay, Suffolk) in 1672; and the following year was promoted rear-admiral and knighted. Following distinguished Mediterranean service (mostly against pirates) he was posted to the West Indies, where he caught fever and died.

Nelson, Admiral, Viscount (1758-1805): The naval career of Norfolk's 'essential hero', Horatio Nelson, sailor for all seasons, which reached its end in death and glory at Trafalgar, is too well known to need relating here. Enough to note that he was born at Burnham Thorpe, where his father was rector of the Burnham group of parishes; that he gained a boyhood love of sea and sail off the nearby North Norfolk coast; that he brought back here to his father's home his new wife, met and married in the West Indies . . . and both nearly froze to death in their first Norfolk winter together, his lady taking to her bed for days at a time in an attempt to keep warm; that in his days of celebrity he was back in 'dear Burnham' whenever he could arrange it. In time, too, he would bring his mistress Emma, Lady Hamilton to the county. After the deaths of both of them, their illegitimate daughter Horatia (she whom Nelson, in his agonised dying breath 'tween decks on the Victory, invoked his country 'never to forget') was to come to Burnham too. She married the curate, Philip Ward, at Burnham Westgate Church, opposite the elegant Bolton House (still there) where she lived for two years. You have to go to Trunch to find a memorial to her though: and then it is merely her name, tacked onto the end of a ledger slab in the chancel floor, inscribed to Philip's parents.

Nine Men's Morris: In act II, scene II of Shakespeare's 'A Midsummer Night's Dream', Queen Titania of the Faeries says:

> 'The nine men's morris is filled up with mud;
> And the quaint mazes in the wanton green,
> For lack of tread, are indistinguishable'.

What she was talking about was an intriguing game, generally played with counters on a board set out in a frame pattern of three squares, one within the other, with diagonal intersecting lines. Titania's shepherds, as did countrymen in Elizabethan England, carved it out in the turf – thus the 'quaint maze' in the 'wanton green'. But the game is much older than Shakespeare: in the n.e. corner of Norwich Cathedral cloister you can see traces of it scratched out on a stone bench – showing that even monks could be slackers! There's a frame on a table-tomb at Hickling; and on benches in the porches at Rollesby and Braydeston. Also known as The Mill – and by various other names from Iceland to Poland – the game is for two players, each having nine counters. And the 'morris'? That probably alludes to the similarity of its moves to those in an old 'morris' dance.

Nine Orders of Angels: The theme of the Nine Orders of Angels was, interest-

ingly, only rarely employed by medieval church artists. But Norfolk has one magnificent series painted on the rood screen at Barton Turf, in the Broadland area of the county; and part of a series in stained glass in the e. window of famous Salle Church. The doctrine, and the appearance of angels, have long occupied the minds of theologians and artists. There are several Biblical references to the 'orders' of these heavenly beings: in Ephesians 1,21, and Colossians, 1,16 in the New Testament; and in Isaiah 6,2 and Ezekiel – in that wonderful first chapter – in the Old. It was around the year 500 however that a mystic and theologian, Dionysius the Areopagite (who lived in Middle Eastern desert seclusion) set out in one of his several treatises, 'The Celestial Hierarchies', an explanation of The Nine Orders of Angels and their mission as mediators between God and man. He arranged them in three hierarchies, each containing three choirs, in the following order: Seraphim (who inspire humankind towards divine love); Cherubim (who give forth endless wisdom); Thrones (flaming wheels with eyes, set about the Throne of God – again, see the first chapter of Ezekiel); Dominions (the instruments of God's all-mighty will), Virtues and Powers; and the lowest orders, Principalities, Archangels and Angels. Of these only the last two choirs have an immediate mission to men, for they are God's messengers, moving between Earth and Heaven. The word angel, in its Hebraic origin, means 'message'. But some early Christian writers saw angelic beings as ranged on two sides, some good, some bad (the Devil, after all, is a fallen angel), so that the message could be of God . . . or Satan.

Nollekens, Joseph (1737-1823): The choice of fashionable London, Joseph Nollekens occupied in the sculpture of his time the equivalent role to that of the celebrated portraitist Sir Joshua Reynolds in painting. He spent ten years in Italy studying and painting, and restoring and selling antiques, before returning to London with a reputation which preceded him. His sculpture extended to opulent chimney pieces and ceilings for great houses, as well as portrait busts for the nobility and urns and tablets and the like as memorials. But well paid and well patronised as he was – he left a fortune of £200,000 – Nollekens was renowned for his skinflint, miserly ways . . . and for a wife who was even more mean than he was. There are examples of his work at Holkham Hall, the Earl of Leicester's great *Palladian* mansion here in Norfolk; a monument at Tittleshall (south of Fakenham) and a grand one at Felbrigg (near Cromer), to William Windham, 1813.

Norman: The 'Romanesque' form of architecture, with its distinctive rounded arches and massive round pillars, introduced to England following the Norman Conquest of 1066. (See under *Styles of Architecture* for full description.)

North Doors: In the great majority of churches, the main entrance door and porch is on the s. side, with opposite, as like as not, a n. door – long since filled in in many instances. Just occasionally, the main door is on the n. side, indicating that in this direction, very probably, lay the village centre of population. One should also consider here that in medieval times the churchyard was a general gathering place for markets, sports, fairs and socialising: all this took place on the n. side; the s. side was reserved for burials. It seems most likely then that the 'secondary' n. doors were there to facilitate the processions which were such a great feature of Sundays and Feast Days before the *Reformation*, including the devotion of The Stations of the Cross, processing successively to the 14 representations in pictures or carvings depicting the closing scenes of Christ's Passion (See also *Galilee porches*.) However, there is a charming legend about these doors, which is set down here in that light only. As folk entered

the church, they dipped their fingers into the *holy water stoup* and crossed themselves – and thus, said simple superstitious belief, the Devil was expelled. But expelled where . . .? Not over your shoulder, Holy Mother forbid . . . better give him a door of his own, a Devil's Door. A quaint fiction, but worth the telling.

Norwich School of Painting: An important English regional school of landscape painting which flourished in the first half of the C19, its masters being *John Crome* and *John Sell Cotman*, with some nine principal followers. They were almost exclusively landscape painters in oils and water colour, dealing largely with Norfolk scenery. The Norwich School's importance in the world of art stands both in the eminence of its two masters, and in its influence 'in widening the expressive possibilities of water colour technique'.

Ogee arches/curves: This is a lovely, flowing 'S' shaped arch or moulding – a convex curve flowing into a concave one. Usually they are not very large because, by their very nature, they cannot carry heavy loads; but their grace lends them to the heads of canopies, to *piscina*, *sedilia* and the like; sometimes also to doorways, giving them an engaging and curiously oriental look; as well as in the tracery of windows, screens etc. Adorned with *crocketting*, ogee arches are still more attractive. They came into general use in the C14, playing an important role in the development of the sumptuous windows of the late *Decorated* period, with their flowing tracery of which the ogee curve forms an integral part (See also *Styles of Architecture*.)

Page, Robert, of Norwich (1707-1778): A prolific and important sculptor in his native Norfolk, Robert Page occupies the position of perhaps the best in his field which this county has ever produced. In his Norwich workshops he developed his skilled use of coloured marbles, and showed a facility for rococo (the C18, originally Parisian, ornate style) detail, seen in groups of cherubs' heads and in richly carved shields. Among a considerable list of his works in Norfolk churches is a fine one at Sprowston, (near Norwich), with portrait bust; and others at Gateley, Dersingham, Melton Constable, Scoulton, Colton and Catton; with a further list in Norwich itself, including his own memorial, carefully completed 'in advance' and placed where he now lies, in the recently rejuvenated St John's Timberhill.

Palimpsest brass: A memorial brass which has been turned over – and used again by re-engraving it on its plain side. This odd word, also used in relation to writing material which has been 're-used', comes from the Greek Palimpsestos – palin, again; psao, rub smooth.

Palladian: One of the foremost Renaissance architects in Italy was the Venetian, Andrea Palladio (d.1580) who took his inspiration from Imperial Rome. In the C18, there was a great movement in England, both in churches and in great country houses, to revive the Palladian ideal. Here in Norfolk is one of the finest examples in the kingdom, the Earl of Leicester's imposing mansion, Holkham Hall, built between 1734 and 1761. Occasional Palladian features and details, however, may be encountered in several churches in the county.

Parclose screen: The screens which separated chantry or side chapels, and/or aisles, from the main body of the church. (See also Rood loft/screen.)

Parish Clerk: Not the 'clerk to the parish council' of late Victorian, local government invention. But a paid office which was for centuries of central importance in church services. In short, it was the job of the clerk to lead the singing and the responses to the prayers – and to voice a healthy 'Amen' both at the end of prayers and of the sermon. Sometimes he filled the role of choirmaster; certainly he would 'give the notes' on a pitch pipe – just as unaccompanied choirs today are given on a pipe the four notes for sopranos, altos, tenors and basses. After the Reformation in the C16, the Clerk continued to exercise his role; indeed, the replanning of church interiors to meet the new Protestant requirements gave him a special seat in the Three-Decker Pulpits which appeared at this time (see Prayer Book Churches). In the C17, under James I and later Charles II, the Parish Clerks, who had the dignity of being a London Company, were given new Charters which stipulated that

> 'every person that is chosen Clerk of the Parish should first give sufficient proof of his abilities to sing at least the tunes which are used in the parish churches'.

He sang on until soon after Victoria ascended the Throne, when most of his duties were given to curates. Then came the local government acts of the late C19, which finally consigned him to history: and left only his seat at the foot of the three-deckers to remind us of a 700 year tradition.

Parish Guilds: See Guilds/Guild altars.

Parker, Matthew, Archbishop of Canterbury (1504-1575): One of the most famous sons of Norwich, Parker is remembered by an annual sermon in the cathedral and another at St Clement's Church on the same evening. He asked that a prayer be said for the souls of his parents by their tomb at St Clement's on that day – and so it is. At Cambridge University, Parker became closely associated with Protestant reformers inspired by the writings of Martin Luther – but he himself remained cautious. After serving in several parishes (including Burlingham here in Norfolk) he returned to Cambridge as Master of his old college; and soon after was elected vice-chancellor of the university. On the outbreak of Kett's Rebellion in 1549 (a popular rising led by a local yeoman, Robert Kett, against the enclosure of common land, which ended with the slaughter of the rebels and Kett's public execution at Norwich Castle), Parker visited the rebel camp on Mousehold Hill, outside the city walls. There, at great personal risk, he tried to persuade the rebels to lay down their arms. During the reign of the boy king, Edward VI, he grew in favour and was appointed to the rich deanery of Lincoln. However, his support for the ill-fated Lady Jane Grey (briefly hailed as Queen, in succession to Edward, before being deposed and executed by Mary I) meant that on the accession of Catholic Mary he had to go into hiding. Throughout Bloody Mary's reign he lived in fear of his life; but the accession of Elizabeth brought him back into favour. Briefly he returned to Cambridge. Then came a call from the Queen which he begged to refuse – but the monarch was adamant: he was her choice for Canterbury. From this time he was central in the movement which created the 'Anglican' philosophy, treading a sensible path between Puritanism and Catholicism. With courage, wisdom and steady consistency, Parker worked towards his ideal,

> 'that that most holy and godly form of discipline which was commonly used in the primitive church might be called home again'.

When Parker died, he was buried in his private chapel at Lambeth Palace, under an imposing monument. During the Civil War however, Puritan fanatics destroyed his monument, dug up his bones and reburied them under a dunghill. At the *Restoration*, his remains were reverently replaced in their original resting place. He left behind him the record of a great benefactor of education, of great scholarship and of staunch defence of his church. This then is the man who, more than four centuries on, his native city still remembers each year.

Parliament or tavern clocks: During the horse-drawn coaches era, it was necessary to have some form of public clock at the inns where the coaches stopped and put up overnight. A special wall clock, with a dial about two or even three feet across, came into use for this purpose called a 'coaching clock' or 'tavern clock', from about the beginning of the C18. In 1797 Prime Minister Pitt imposed a tax on clocks of 5s. a year, 2s.6d. on silver or metal watches and 10s. on gold watches. Poorer people gave up their timepieces and made do with the tavern clock. Inn keepers, it seems, vied with each other in having the most elaborate and accurate clocks to draw people in . . . in the hope they might also stop for a drink! The clocks thus became known as 'Act of Parliament clocks' and long kept that name, even though the ludicrous tax was abolished within twelve months. Occasionally these clocks are preserved today in churches – there is one at Wymondham Abbey, for example.

Paston, The Paston Family: For several centuries this enduring clan, who took their name from the village of Paston on the coast, dominated Norfolk. They began with one of the Conqueror's men, Wulstan, who came over soon after the Conquest of 1066 and was given a grant of land at Paston. Distinguished, warlike, resilient, educated, they weathered the years until the C16 and C17, when financial troubles increasingly dogged them. Though in 1612 they could build a fine house at Barningham, in addition to their last great house at Oxnead Hall; and 50 years later the head of the family was created first Baron Paston and Viscount Yarmouth, then Earl of Yarmouth. Like their fortunes, the title died in the first half of the C18. The family are immortally famous, however, for 'The Paston Letters', a remarkable correspondence written by and to members of the family between 1420 and 1503. This classic collection was described by the C18 historian and literary critic, Henry Hallam, as

'. . . an important testimony to the progressive condition of society, and come in as a precious link in the chain of the moral history of England, which they alone in this period supply'.

The tremendous vitality of the letters, and the picture they give of a tough and dangerous age, still make them fascinating reading. (See entries on Paston, Oxnead, North Walsham and Mautby, vol. 1).

Pediment: The low triangular gable used in classical building but often employed on classically styled monuments in churches.

Pelican: The pelican has long had a special place in religious symbolism and may often be seen as a device used in medieval carving and embellishment – a pelican crowns the summit of the great font cover at St Peter Mancroft (Norwich), for example. There is a legend that the bird tore its own breast to feed its young upon its own blood – the source of the idea, it is suggested, being that the tip of the pelican's bill, which usually rests on this ungainly bird's chest, is touched with red. In medieval art the ungainliness is replaced by a dove-like representation and the legend transmuted into a symbolism of Man's fall and Redemption through the Passion of Christ. Here we find that the parent bird was said to kill its young in a moment of irritation – then, 'on the third day', to restore them to life by tearing its breast and letting its own blood pour over them.

Perpendicular: The great age of church building, in the second half of the C14 and through the C15, in the style characterised by soaring upward lines in great windows and majestic towers. (See full description under *Styles of Architecture*.)

Pevsner, Sir Nikolaus: Author of the monumental and remarkable undertaking, 'The Buildings of England' series – 46 volumes, written between 1951 and 1974, meticulously recording the principal buildings, domestic, public and church (including the detail and furnishings of the latter) of every county in England, and masterminded throughout by Pevsner himself. His two volumes on Norfolk appeared in 1962, following a 'grand tour' round the county lasting about four months in which Dr. Pevsner – as he then was – visited every location personally.

'I found Norfolk to be the kind of county it is especially nice to do. People are proud of it, they like it, and it is a county in which one feels at home', he told an interviewer.

The University of East Anglia, Norwich honoured him with an Hon. Doctorate of Letters in 1969, the same year in which he received his knighthood.

Piscina/angle piscina/double piscina: A stone basin near an altar (its presence today indicates that there was formerly an altar there), usually set into a niche in the wall below an arch or canopy, sometimes projecting outwards on a bowl, which in turn may be supported by a small pillar. Occasionally too a piscina may be found let into a pillar. The piscina was used for cleansing the communion vessels after Mass – thus it has a drain hole in its basin, which allows the water used in the cleansing to run down into consecrated ground. It is obligatory that where water has been blessed, or has come into contact with anything consecrated, it must be returned to earth. Sometimes there is a small shelf in the piscina niche called a *credence*. The angle piscina is one built into the angle of a window or *sedilia*, and opened out on two sides, often affording the opportunity for beautiful carving and design. Double piscinas – two side by side – may occasionally be found.

Plate tracery: This is tracery in the heads of windows where the pattern is cut directly through the masonry; as distinct from *bar tracery*, which is constructed in separate pieces. (See 'Early English' under *Styles of Architecture*.)

Poppyheads: The boldly carved floral ornament which graces the ends of bench pews – said to be derived from the French 'poupée', puppet, doll or figurehead. It was during the great age of C15 church building and wood carving that poppyheads came into being and achieved their highest artistic expression. The carvers often seem to have been given a free hand, with diverse and interesting results – animals, grotesques, faces and so on; or for a noble patron, a carved crest or coat-of-arms, like that of the *Paston family* at Paston Church.

Prayer Book Churches: A phrase used to describe those churches where the furnishings and layout still embody the great shift of emphasis in church worship that came, first with the *Reformation* and then with the Puritans. The old, and strict, division of priest in chancel from people in nave was put away, and the English prayer book of 1549 required the laity to take part in all of the service – Matins and Evensong were to be conducted from the Chancel and everybody had to hear the Lessons. The altar became 'the table' for the first time in the 1552 revision. After the Civil War, Sunday services (except on infrequent Sacrament Sundays) were conducted entirely from the Reading Desk, and soon the convenient Reading Desk cum Pulpit became the rule (see *Three-Decker Pulpits*); in the C18 virtually every church in the land had its pews (often enclosed for each family – see *Box Pews*) arranged to focus on the Reading Desk. Then, in the 1830s, a 'new wave' of churchmen were inspired by Augustus Welby Pugin, followed by John Newman's 'Oxford Movement', to sweep away these things. Their vision was to have truly Gothic churches again, and C18 domestic church interiors were anathema. Today, very few of the sensible and seemly furnishings of the 'Age of Reason' are to be found, but Norfolk has some examples

– Warham St Mary and Bylaugh (excellent!), Thurning, Gunton.

Pre-Raphaelites: The Pre-Raphaelite Brotherhood was a group of Victorian artists, much reviled in its day, who sought to go back to principles before the Italian master, Raphael (d.1520) imposed his mark (one of the major figures in the world history of art, he was the painter of many celebrated works, including decorative work in the Vatican). The Brotherhood had only three members – Rossetti, Millais and Holman Hunt – and lasted only five years from its establishment in 1848. But, with its pre-occupation with biblical and literary subjects and the artists' urge for 'social realism', it had a great influence on several other artists of note, among them *Burne-Jones*. It was he who later, with *William Morris*, briefly tried to revive the brotherhood. Inevitably the Pre-Raphaelite movement left its impression on the church art of the period, as evidenced in Burne-Jones's work.

Priest's door: Most chancels have a small door, usually on the s. side, which was the priest's 'private entrance'. It fits into context when it is remembered that, in pre-*Reformation* times, the chancel was the priest's particular responsibility (only occasionally entered by the laity) while the parishioners looked after the nave. (This could also account – though it is a moot point – for the fact that the nave may often be tiled, while the chancel is thatched).

Purlin: The purlin is the main horizontal supporting beam of a roof. (See *Roofs*, fig. 4.)

Put-log holes: The holes where the horizontal members of the (timber) scaffolding slotted into the walls during construction.

Putti (singular, putto): Little naked cherub boys first seen in that form in the work of *Renaissance* artists in Italy; and regularly in the work of C18/C19

sculptors in England in the adornment of monuments and tombs. It is possible that these cherubs have their origin in the naked Eros and Mercury representations of ancient classical, pagan belief . . . one of the many examples of 'Christianising' ancient deities, places and practices.

Quatrefoils: See *Foils*.

Rawlins, Thomas, of Norwich (1747-81): Son of Thomas Rawlins the Elder, a mason and statuary in Norwich, Rawlins jr. was trained in London whence he returned to his native city and in due course was mason for the building of the porch of St Andrew's Hall, a gothic creation in full sympathy with the great *Perpendicular* hall. Among the best in his field, locally and nationally, in his time, with particular skill in the use of coloured marbles and in fine details, Rawlins has a particularly fine example of his work in St Giles' Church, Norwich, a monument to Sir Thomas Churchman, 1781; also a very elegant memorial, dated 1762, at Smallburgh. In Norfolk and Norwich there is a considerable list of Rawlins' monuments, but it is not always clear whether they are the work of 'the Elder' or 'the Younger'. Among them are examples at Mendham, Wymondham, Woodton, in several Norwich churches and in the cathedral.

Rebus: A punning representation of a name or word by the use of symbols, normally in churches referring to the name of the place or the name of a donor. Thus, at Shelton there are carvings of shells on barrels (or tuns), and at Norwich cathedral Bishop Lyhart is remembered by carvings of a deer (or hart) lying down.

Reformation: In particular terms, the great religious movement in western Europe during the C16, founded on a return to Biblical sources and their fresh interpretation, which led to the rejection of Rome and Papal authority, and the establishment of 'Protestant'

churches. In England the original motivations were more basic, being political and economic, rather than theological. Firstly, a ruthless, single minded, vastly vain and wholly autocratic monarch in Henry VIII, intent on putting away one wife and taking another by whom he could beget an heir. Secondly, his calculating eye on the wealth of the monasteries – backed by his aristocracy and gentry, who could not wait to get their hands on the spoils. Even when he had broken with Rome, however, Henry did his best to minimise the impression of any break with the tradition begun in England by St Augustine a thousand years earlier. The true religious, reforming Reformation came with his son, the boy-king Edward VI, who though young, was a fanatical Protestant (see *Prayer Book Churches*).

Renaissance: The age of 'the complete man', embodied in England in men like Elizabeth's 'perfect Renaissance gentleman', Sir Philip Sidney, courtier, poet, soldier, diplomat, scholar. Greek and Latin literature, and the inspiration of the Greek and Roman classical ages in architecture and architectural embellishment, were the visible and lasting signs. The Renaissance movement, this 'rebirth' of western culture, began in Italy in the C14 and in the C16 spread to the rest of Europe. (Refer also, under *Styles of Architecture*, to the *Jacobean/ Carolean* periods.)

Repton, Humphrey (1752-1818): One of the great landscape gardeners – the gardens of Sheringham Hall are his work, the house itself having been designed by him and his son. Born at Bury St Edmunds in Suffolk, and educated at the grammar school in Norwich (to where his parents moved when he was a boy), he lies buried outside the chancel wall at Aylsham Church with a poetic verse of his own composing as epitaph. After operating as a merchant in Norwich, he established himself near Aylsham at Sustead where he 'discharged the duties of a country gentleman'. This pleasant occupation enabled him to take up the study of botany and gardening, for which he borrowed many useful books from the library of William Windham at nearby Felbrigg Hall (now a National Trust property, with gardens not to be missed). Later he moved to Romford in Essex where he seriously embarked upon his career as a landscape gardener, and was soon to be employed by the greatest in the land.

Reredos: The screening at the back of an altar, usually richly embellished in painting or carving. Few old examples remain, many having disappeared at the Reformation and in the century following. (See also Decalogue boards.)

Restoration: The period from 1660, following the Restoration of the Monarchy after the Civil War and Cromwell's government, and the accession of Charles II.

Reticulated: A form of 'flowing' tracery in windows which was developed at the height of 'Decorated' achievement during the first half of the C14 (see Styles of Architecture, fig. 17). It is made up of circles flowing downwards to make ogee shapes. (Latin: rete, a net; reticulum, a bag of network – the link being that the tracery forms a netlike pattern.)

Rib-vaulting: This is a vaulted/arched ceiling which has diagonal, projecting ribs which form a support for the infilling of the ceiling. (See also Groining.)

Rood beam: See Rood loft.

Rood loft: In the individual accounts of churches in this book there repeatedly occur references to – rood; screen; rood screen; rood stairs; rood loft; and occasionally, to rood beam. In pre-Reformation times all churches would have been separated into two – the chancel for the clergy, the nave for the people – by a wooden, carved screen, with secure door, from pillar to pillar

under the chancel arch. Immediately above, sometimes included in the screen's construction, was the rood beam, which supported a loft or platform on which were placed a great Crucifix, with images of the Virgin and St John on either side. This loft was approached by a staircase let into the wall. At the Reformation, the rood and its images were almost universally torn down and their images destroyed in violent reaction against Rome and 'popery'. The fact that we have so many screens surviving – Norfolk is especially rich in them – is due to Queen Elizabeth, who in a Royal Order of 1561 directed that while the great rood and its figures should go, the screens themselves should remain, and be topped with a suitable crest or with the Royal Arms. Where screen as well as rood had already been destroyed, a new screen – or 'partition', as the wording had it – was to be constructed: for the Elizabethan view was quite clearly that the church should be partitioned into two distinct sections. In its heydey, the rood loft might be used by choristers, or even do service as a small organ loft; and Mass might be said there on the Feast of the Holy Cross. The issue of screens and their role was to rumble on for another century. In 1638 Richard Montague, Bishop of Norwich, was pointedly asking his clergy: 'Is your chancel divided from the nave or body of your church, with a partition of stone, boards, wainscot, grates or otherwise? Wherein is there a decent strong door to open and shut, (as occasion serveth) with lock and key, to keep out boys, girls, or irreverent men and women? and are dogs kept from coming to besoil or profane the Lord's table?' While rood stairs and screens are common in Norfolk, rood lofts are very rare – examples can be seen at Little Sheringham and Attleborough. (Refer also to Prayer Book churches; Communion rails; and Laudian period.)

Rood screen: See Rood loft.

Rood stairs: See Rood loft.

Roofs: The development, structural variety and embellishment of church roofs is a fascinating field in itself. Here is a potted guide to a richly complex subject.

Coupled rafter roofs are a simple variety, which also serve to indicate the roof components (Fig 1). The principal rafters, the feet of which are secured to a wall plate, have a collar beam to support them and prevent sagging. More support is given by the collar braces, with struts lower down giving more strength.

Another framing system is the scissor beam (Fig 2), which can exist with the cross-beams only, or with a supporting collar. As a precaution against spreading of the roof, a tie beam was often added between the wall plates (Fig 3); but as tie-beams have a tendency

to sag in the middle a central king post served to prevent this.

The arch-braced construction is where the roof is carried on a braced arch which incorporates 'in one' the strut, collar brace and collar beam (Fig 4). The function of the tie beam has already been seen in Fig 3. With a low-pitched roof, it is often used simply with struts upward to the principal rafters, and

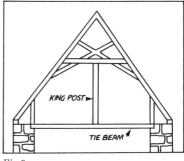

Fig 3.

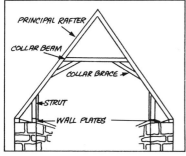

Fig 1.

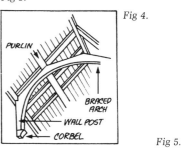

Fig 4.

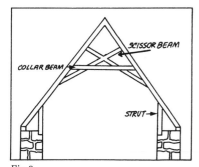

Fig 2.

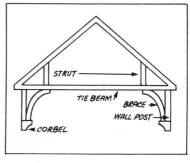

Fig 5.

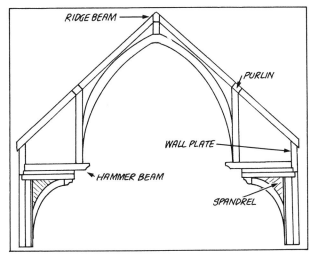

Fig 6.

downward on brace and wall post to a corbel set into the wall (Fig 5) well below the wall plates.

With the advent of the hammer beam development (Fig 6), a new splendour was added to the roof builder's art. Trunch is a superb example which comes to mind. Instead of a tie beam spanning wall to wall, there are hammer beam brackets, from which spring a vertical strut, upward to the principal rafter at its intersection with the purlin (refer again to Fig 4), the main horizontal supporting beam. Continuing upward, curved archlike braces meet either at the ridge beam; or at a collar beam, set very high (Fig 7). From there it was a natural development to the double hammer beam. Fig 8 is self explanatory – of which a glorious example may be found at Knapton. The ends of the hammer beams are often embellished with angels or decorative carvings, as Knapton wonderfully illustrates.

Fig 7.

Fig 8.

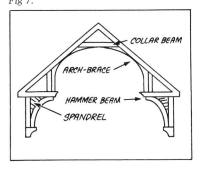

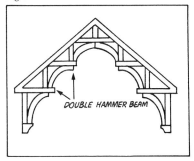

Royal Arms: Many churches display Royal coats of arms, usually square and framed, painted on wood or canvas; though they may also be found in carved wood or stone, cast in plaster, or set in stained glass. Occasionally the arms are set up and painted in a lozenge shape, like a *hatchment*, but this is unusual (Briningham, Field Dalling and Caister-on-Sea have examples). It was only during the reign of Henry VIII, when he assumed complete control of the English Church, that Royal Arms beagan to come into regular use. Catholic Queen Mary was later to order their removal, and the replacement of the old *rood lofts*. But with Elizabeth's accesssion, they began to reappear; indeed Elizabeth directed their use and indicated that the *tympanum* – the top part of the chancel arch, panelled in – was the place to display them. Inevitably many disappeared during Cromwell's Commonwealth, for in 1650 his Parliamentarians ordered 'the removal of the obnoxious Royal Arms from the churches'. In that same year, at St Margaret's, King's Lynn, the Arms were 'taken Downe & Burnt by Mr Bartholomew Wormell then Alderman', as recorded in 1660 when the local worthies met to fix a special parish rate to pay for new Arms . . . which cost £16 to carve and set up and another £10 to paint and gild. The 1660 shield is still there, though altered for subsequent reigns (something which often happened, prudent churchwardens finding it cheaper, no doubt, to change say, 'CR' to 'GR' than to pay out for new arms). The *Restoration* Parliament in 1660 made Royal Arms compulsory in all our churches – a practice continued generally until Victoria's accession – ordering that 'the Armes of the Commonwealth wherever they are standing be forthwith taken down, and the Kings Majesties armes be set up instead thereof'. Bearing this in mind there is an interesting rarity at North Walsham – on one side, the Commonwealth, on the other, Charles II.

Rye, Walter (1843-1929):

'There has never been a more prolific writer on the county of Norfolk, nor one who has expended such a vast amount of time, industry and money in tracing the minutest points of historical importance'.

So wrote the Norwich City Librarian on the death of Walter Rye. Prolific writer, athlete, historian, benefactor to his city, its last mayor in 1908-9 before the office was elevated to a lord-mayoralty, eccentric, antiquarian: Rye was all these things. And prolific too in amassing an important and invaluable collection of books and manuscripts appertaining to Norfolk – all of which are now housed in the city's central library, providing a fitting memorial to a great 'character' . . . A character who, during his mayoralty, showed his utter disregard of pomp, circumstance and title by refusing to 'dress up' for the visit to Norwich of that stickler for etiquette, King Edward VII. His Majesty, resplendent in uniform, braid and plumes, was welcomed by His Worship in tweeds and a bowler hat – thereby it is said, losing himself a knighthood.

Saints: 'For all the saints' . . . on rood screens, on fonts, in woodwork and stained glass, a panoply of saints is represented in Norfolk churches. Almost all of them have some identifying emblem – which adds yet another element of interest for the church visitor. The following is a list of those to be found in the county, with emblems, brief story background and some representative locations.

Agatha: Represented either with pincers in her hand . . . or with her severed breasts upon a dish, indicating the horrid nature of her martyrdom in C6 Sicily. She vowed her virginity to Christ, refused to yield to the lust of the local governor, who took ghastly revenge. She is invoked against fire (another of her tortures) and against diseases of the breasts. Agatha is also patron saint of bell founders.

Agnes: Her symbols are a sword, often thrust into her neck or bosom, and a lamb – Latin, agna, a pun on her name. Ancient Rome, about 300 A.D., and 13 years-old Agnes refuses to marry the prefect's son. She was publicly stripped – but her hair miraculously grew long to cover her. They tried to burn her – but the flames declined to help. So at last she was stabbed. (Cawston, Plumstead.)

Ambrose: One of the *Four Latin Doctors*: usually represented with a beehive – allusion to intriguing story of swarm of bees which settled on the baby Ambrose's cradle. Also seen wearing his bishop's robes and holding whip or scourge, recalling penance he imposed on all-powerful Roman Emperor Maximus to atone for a frightful massacre carried out at his order. Ambrose became Bishop of Milan in 374. Central figure in early church with powerful influence on the Roman Emperors.

Andrew: The saltire – X-shaped cross, Scotland's part of Union Jack – and fishing net are his symbols. One of the Twelve, he was a fisherman before he became a disciple. Legends of his later life are legion – including one that he visited Scotland – thus becoming its patron saint. Martyred by crucifixion, it is said, upon an X-shaped cross. (Stalham, Marsham, Alderford, Guestwick.)

Anne: Usually represented teaching the Virgin – a homely allusion, since Anne was the Virgin Mary's mother. Save for minimal biblical references, little is known about her. In medieval England, many parish *guilds* adopted her as their patron – as at Bury St Edmunds and King's Lynn.

Anthony of Egypt: Pigs and bells are this austere saint's peculiar symbols, and occasionally an Egyptian cross like the letter 'T'. Born about 251 in Egypt, he lived in the desert as a hermit, where he was duly and thoroughly tempted by the devil. Bestirred himself however to found a monastery, return to civilisation to refute heresies, work miracles and

write letters which are still quoted. The reliquary for his bones in Alexandria was looked after by Hospitallers who attracted alms by ringing little bells. The pigs? For reasons unknown, the Hospitallers' porkers were allowed to roam freely in the streets!

Apostles: Christ's 12 Apostles were Peter, James the Great, James the Less, Thomas, Philip, Batholomew, John, Simon, Jude, Matthew, Andrew and Judas. Matthias replaced Judas after the latter's treachery and suicide.

Appollonia: This poor saint is most often seen having her teeth forcibly removed with huge pincers – or herself holding aloft a tooth . . . representing the torture which preceded the martyrdom by fire of this aged and pious deaconess in Egypt in 249. Not surprisingly, she is invoked against jaw and tooth-ache. (Barton Turf, Ludham, Norwich St Augustine's.)

Augustine of Hippo: One of the *Four Latin Doctors* of the early church; a profound and sustaining influence through the centuries on the church's thought and teaching. Often represented (in Norfolk, on several painted screens) holding a flaming heart in his hand; or in his bishop's robes (he was Bishop of Hippo in N. Africa for 35 years to his death in 430) and carrying a pastoral staff. His saintly adulthood followed a dissolute youth, from which he was rescued by St Ambrose (Hemblington).

Barbara: A tower, and a chalice with the host (the consecrated bread) above it are her emblems. This lady, goes the story, was an early Christian convert in godless Italy, to the fury of her pagan father, who shut her up in a high tower. When she tried to escape he beat her up then handed her over to a judge who condemned her to death. She was tortured and decapitated – whereupon, very properly, both father and judge were consumed by bolts of lightning. Barbara is thus patroness of firearms, and also protectress from thunderbolts and lightning or any form of explosion. (Edingthorpe, Trunch; and elsewhere in paint and stained glass.)

Bartholomew: One of the Twelve, his emblem is the butcher's flaying knife – for thus, it is said, he was martyred somewhere along the Caspian Sea, being first flayed alive and then beheaded. More gruesomely, he is sometimes seen in medieval art carrying the skin of a man, with the face still attached to it. It follows that he is the patron saint of tanners ... (Edingthorpe, Trunch.)

Benedict: Usually seen as an abbot holding a bishop's crozier (crook) ... with which he belays howling little devils around his feet. Or he may be seen with his fingers to his lips, commanding monastic silence. Roman nobleman who became a hermit and lived in a cave. His example of piety and worldy renunciation drew others to him, enabling him at length to found his famous monastery at Monte Cassino where he devised The Benedictine Rule, the great guiding injunction of Christian monasticism in Europe. (Burlingham St Andrew).

Benet: See Benedict.

Blide or Blida: A Norfolk saint of Royal blood, usually shown crowned and/or holding a bible. Chiefly celebrated as the mother of St Walstan of Bawburgh, patron saint of farm workers. Her shrine was at Martham, near Great Yarmouth.

Botolph: No definite symbol, though he is properly represented as an abbot, occasionally holding a church in his hand. Many churches are dedicated to him, including the famous Boston Stump church in Lincolnshire ... where in the C7 he was abbot of a monastery founded by himself; though one source says that he 'dwelt in a dismal hut amidst the swamps of the fenland rivers'.

Catherine of Alexandria: The emblem of this saint is a wheel – of the devilish variety, set with spikes and knives, on which she is said to have been martyred in C4 Egypt ... and which in turn inspired the spinning firework the Catherine Wheel. The wheel, however, flew to pieces as she was spun on it, the knives etc. skewering her persecutors. Her head was then cut off ... and from the wound flowed milk, not blood. Which could explain why she is patroness of nurses. (Guestwick, Hemblington, Ludham.)

Cecilia: Patroness of music – and thus always seen with an organ or other musical instrument. Much hymned in words and music of the centuries. A Roman virgin of the C3, her colourful tale credits her with such numerous conversions that the local prefect ordered her to be suffocated in the baths. That failed to work. So a soldier was despatched to lop off her head. Three times he struck, but could not sever it. It was three days before she died ... meanwhile preaching to her hordes of converts, who came to collect her blood ... (Burlingham St Andrew, Trimingham.)

Christopher: The saint everyone recognises – a gigantic figure spanning a river, his huge staff in one hand, the Christ-Child on his shoulder, or sometimes in an outstretched hand (see also *Christopher images*). Tradition has it that he was a pagan giant who wished to give his service to the most powerful man in the world. He found a great king – but saw that he crossed himself as protection against the devil. Judging therefore that the devil must be the stronger, Christopher forsook the king and went to Satan. But then his new master carefully avoided a wayside cross – the symbol of Christ, the giant learned: here, at last, must be the mightiest of all. But how to find him? A holy hermit advised him to use his strength for Christ, by carrying travellers across a certain dangerous river. Then came the day when he carried a child, who grew heavier and heavier, taxing even his strength ... until he learned that he had 'carried the weight of the world upon his shoulders'.

Citha: See 'Zita'.

Clare: Clare's emblem is a pyx or monstrance (the receptacle in which the reserved sacrament, the consecrated bread, is contained, and suspended over the altar). This is the Clare of Assisi, spiritually beloved and influenced by St Francis, who founded the Order of Poor Clares, vowed to a life of absolute poverty. She spent her life as abbess of her convent at Assisi and never left the town. When she was old and sick, Assisi was threatened by the Saracens of the invading German emperor Barbarosa's army. Clare was carried before them, deep in prayer and carrying a pyx containing the Blessed Sacrament... whereupon the invaders fled. (Trimingham).

Clement: His emblem is an anchor – the object which was hung about his neck by the envoy of the Emperor Trajan, around 100 A.D., before he was hurled to a watery death in the Black Sea. His offence – too much efficiency in converting the local heathen, following his Black Sea exile from his bishopric of Rome. He is usually represented as a pope. (Trimingham).

Denys/Dionysius: His symbol is a severed head. Patron saint of France and first bishop of Paris – where his missionary zeal so roused the fury of the pagans that they put him to terrible tortures ... from which he emerged miraculously unharmed. So they took him to Montmartre (where the celebrated Sacré Coeur basilica now stands) and beheaded him. But 'Anon the body of St Denys raised himself up, and bare his head between his arms' ... and walked to his chosen resting place at St Denis: which is why the kings of France were traditionally buried there. He is usually represented as a bishop, holding his mitred head in his hands. Though at Hempstead (near North Walsham) he is a monk, complete with head, plus a tonsured (shaven) head in his hands.

Edmund, King & Martyr: His symbol is an arrow – or sometimes a wolf, guarding his severed head (as at Pul-ham St Mary the Virgin). King of East Anglia, defeated by the Danes in 870, he was shot with arrows, then beheaded, the head being contemptuously hurled into the undergrowth. But there it was guarded by a great grey wolf until it was found by the Faithful (its singular ability to call out 'Here, here' must have helped); whereupon the wolf followed the funeral cortege into Bury St Edmund's. (Catfield, Trimingham.)

Edward the Confessor: Usually seen in kingly crown, and holding aloft a ring. This deeply pious king of England, immediately before the Norman Conquest of 1066, built Westminster Abbey – the price for not having kept his vow to make a pilgrimage to the Holy Land. Confronted once by a beggar asking for alms, the king, having no money, slipped a ring from his finger and gave it to him. The beggar, it seems, was really St John the Evangelist, who returned the ring to English Pilgrims in Palestine ... and foretold the king's imminent death. (Burlingham St Andrew, Hemblington.)

Eligius, or Eloy: Patron saint of farriers, his symbol is a blacksmith's hammer & tongs and occasionally a severed horse's leg, as on the C15 screen at Hempstead (near North Walsham). Eligius was a charitable and devoted bishop in C6 France and Flanders, much given to good works. His most famous exploit was to lop the leg off a difficult horse which was refusing to be shod, fix the shoe to the offending limb ... then put the leg back again and make the sign of the cross ... whereupon the again-complete beast trotted happily away. (Potter Heigham).

Elizabeth: No distinguishing symbol – but usually represented at the moment of *The Visitation*, when the Virgin Mary came to tell her of the visit of the Angel to announce Christ's birth, Elizabeth already being near her time with the child who would be John the Baptist. (Houghton and St Peter Mancroft, Norwich.)

Emeria/Emerita: No special emblem and an obscure saint, who nonetheless has found her way onto the screen at Houghton St Giles. One of two virgin sisters (St Digna was the other) brought before a judge in C3 Italy for their Christian belief, probably in the persecution of Emperor Valerian. They were stretched between four stakes, cruelly beaten . . . and burned alive.

Erasmus: His symbol is a windlass. He fled from Roman persecution, about 300 A.D. to a cave, where he was cared for by a raven. But later, when he resumed his inspirational preaching, his death was ordered by the emperor Maximian . . . and he is said to have been martyred by having his bowels uncoiled and wound upon a windlass. Which explains why he was invoked against colic and stomach troubles. (Sandringham).

Etheldreda: No special emblem, but generally represented as a royally crowned abbess. Daughter of a C7 king of East Anglia, she was twice married before becoming a nun. She founded a nunnery at Ely, became its first abbess and was known for her deep devotion and piety. After death her body remained incorrupt; its miracle-working powers made Ely a great centre of pilgrimage. (Burlingham St Andrew).

Fabian: A dove fluttering down and settling on his head assured Fabian of election as Pope in C3 Rome and he became a memorable and revered pontiff. He converted the emperor Philip to Christianity but when Decius succeeded Philip, he had Fabian beheaded. Woodbastwick Church (near Wroxham) has a unique dedication jointly to St Fabian and St Sebastian.

Faith: Her symbols are a palm branch and a grid-iron . . . upon which latter object she was unpleasantly roasted to death in France about the year 287 – just a few years after St Lawrence suffered the same martyrdom in Rome, both for holding fast to their Christian beliefs. Legend has it that a thick fall of snow came down to veil her body during her suffering.

Gervasius & Protasius: This is the unique dedication of Little Plumstead Church, near Norwich. The two, twin sons of a Roman consul in the C2, were honoured as the first martyrs of Milan, during Nero's dark reign. They refused to offer pagan sacrifice before one of the emperor's military campaigns into Germany, and were put to death.

Giles: His emblems are a doe or hind at his side, sometimes an arrow piercing his hand or leg, he being dressed as a monk, or abbot with crozier (crook). He lived as a hermit in C8 France, with his doe for company. One day a king and his companions hunted the doe, which fled to the saint for protection. However, an arrow loosed off by the king by chance struck Giles. In penance the king built a monastery on that very site, Giles becoming its first abbot. About 150 churches in England are said to be dedicated to him.

Gregory (the Great): Represented as a pope, with a dove, and a roll of music in one hand. One of the *Four Latin Doctors*, he was born of noble Roman stock in 540. He became a monk and founded several monasteries, into one of which he retired. It was he who, seeing fair-haired British slaves in the Rome slave market, commented: 'Not Angles, but angels'. It is said he came briefly to Britain as a missionary but was recalled to be elected, much against his will, as Pope. It was he who sent St Augustine to these islands; and gave his name to Gregorian Chants (thus the symbolic roll of music).

Heiron/Hieron: A saint of notable obscurity who for equally obscure reasons is discovered in the C16 screen at Suffield. He was one of 33 Armenian martyrs who suffered under the Emperor Diocletian, about the year 300.

Helen (a): Represented wearing a crown and holding a cross – sometimes an Egyptian cross, like a letter 'T'. Mother of Emperor Constantine the Great, but her own parentage is mysterious. One story says she was an inn-keeper's daughter. Another (much more colourfully) says she was the daughter of King Coel of Colchester – Old King Cole of the nursery rhyme. What is certain is that she married an emperor and bore another: and that as an old lady she set off on pilgrimage for the Holy Land, where she found fragments of The True Cross and brought them to Europe. (Cawston).

Henry VI: Though modern scholarship may suggest that King Henry VI of England, 1422-61, was a bad and unjust ruler and a worse judge of character and counsel, medieval tradition saw him in a very different light – a man of piety, charity, fortitude and saintliness, and a great patron of learning. Never formally canonised, but much venerated in this part of England and the north. He appears, youthful and kingly with orb and sceptre, on the screens at Gateley and Barton Turf.

James the Great: Usually seen with a sword, or with the pilgrimage necessities of staff, wallet and *scallop-shell*. One of the apostles closest to Christ and subsequently, one of the leaders of the church, he was executed by Herod Agrippa in AD 44 (Acts 12,2). Many traditions surround him; enough churches claim relics to make up half a dozen bodies. Strongest however is the belief that his body was put into a boat, without sails or rudder, which travelled unaided out of the Mediterranean, round Spain and fetched up at Compostella, on the northern coast, where James's shrine became throughout the medieval age one of the greatest places of pilgrimage. (Alderford, Guestwick, Edingthorpe, Swafield, Trunch.)

James the Less: His emblem is a fuller's club – a curved implement like a hockey stick, used by a fuller (a 'cloth cleanser') to beat cloth – with which he was killed by a blow on the head after he had survived either being stoned (one version) or being hurled from the pinnacle of the temple in Jerusalem by the Scribes and Pharisees. This occurred after James, one of the Twelve, presided over the great Synod in Jerusalem which reached agreement on how far Gentile converts to Christianity should be made to observe Jewish rites and customs. (Marsham, Trunch, Swafield.)

Jerome: Usually seen with a cardinal's hat; sometimes with an inkhorn; and with a lion at his feet. One of the *Four Latin Doctors*, he became secretary of the Roman See, about 381, after much travel and study. (From medieval times, this office was held by a cardinal: thus Jerome's representation.) Later he travelled again, coming at last to Bethlehem, where he founded a monastery, fulfilled his ambition of translating the New Testament from Hebrew into Latin: The Vulgate of the Roman Church (thus the inkhorn). There is a charming story that a lion came to his monastery with an injured paw: the saint healed it, and the animal stayed on as his faithful companion.

Joan of Valois: No special emblem and rarely represented – though she can be seen on the screen at Upton (near Acle). She was the deformed daughter of Louis XI of France; married off at 12 to the Duke of Orleans; later, to her joy, released when he obtained a grant from the Pope to divorce her. Thereafter she devoted her life to good and pious works; founded the Order of the Annunciation for women in 1500; and five years later died aged 41.

John of Bridlington: A rarely represented figure – but he is seen on the screen at Hempstead (near Stalham), as a monk and holding a crozier (crook). A figure of renowned piety and a worker of miracles, he became prior of his own monastery at Bridlington, about 1360. Ten years after his death his shrine became a place of pilgrimage, though he was never formally canonised.

John the Divine/the Evangelist: As one of the four Evangelists (see also *Symbols of the Evangelists*) he is represented as an eagle; and also by a chalice or a cup from which a snake or devil is leaping – a reference to a story that he was given poisoned drink, but made it harmless by making the sign of the cross over it. John – 'the disciple whom Jesus loved' – was hurled into boiling oil in Rome: but he emerged unharmed. His is the last book of the New Testament, 'The Revelation'. (Swafield, Trunch, Alderford, Yarmouth.)

Jude, also known as Thaddaeus: Most often seen holding a boat, though sometimes with a club or carpenter's square. One of the Twelve, he is said to have preached in Mesopotamia, Russia and finally in Persia . . . where he was attacked and killed by pagan priests, says one tradition; another, that he was hung on a cross at Arat and pierced with javelins.

Julian: See *Mother Julian of Norwich*.

Julian the Hospitaller: His symbol is an oar – an allusion to his work in maintaining a hospice and ferry on the bank of a river, in a setting as mythical as his story. This work was penance for having killed, by horrid error, his father and mother. At length a diseased and stinking traveller came by; Julian, in pity, cared for him. Whereupon the figure was transfused with heavenly light, and revealed as a messenger sent to announce divine acceptance of Julian's penance, and of the Saint's imminent death. St Julian's Church, Norwich, is dedicated to him.

Juliana: Not often represented; but when she is, she can be seen as on the screen at Hempstead (near Stalham), with the devil haltered on a rope held in her hand. It is recorded in the 'Golden Legend' that she refused to marry the governor of her district unless he became a Christian. She was thrown into prison, where she was tempted by the devil in the form of an angel . . . but won the day through steady prayer.

Lambert: Seen as a bishop holding a sword. He was bishop of his native city of Maestricht, in Germany, from 670. There, according to the 'Golden Legend',

he 'shone by word and by example in all virtue'. But around 709 he was the victim of a revenge killing. Unknown to him, his servants killed two brothers who looted his church . . . and the relations of the two took their revenge on the bishop.

Lawrence: He shares with St Faith the emblem of a grid-iron – both were martyred by being roasted on one. He is usually shown in the vestments of a deacon, an office he held under the martyred Pope Sixtus II. During the diabolical persecutions of the Emperor Valerian in the C3, Lawrence was ordered to reveal the treasures of the church. Whereupon he disappeared into the noisome alleys of Rome to return with a retinue of cripples and beggars: 'These are the church's treasures', he declared. It was an answer which earned him an agonising death. (Hemblington, Brundall, Hempstead.)

Leonard; His symbols are chains or fetters in his hands, his robes those of an abbot. This courtier turned monk was given land near Limoges in C5 France by King Clovis, at whose court he was brought up, and there founded the monastery of Noblac, of which he became first abbot. Legend has it that the king gave him the right also to release any prisoner whom he visited – and he is thus the patron saint of prisoners. (Sandringham, Hemblington.)

Lucy: She is represented holding a sword, or with a sword driven through her neck; or with light issuing from her gashed throat; or holding aloft a plate or a book on which are two eyes . . . Martyred in Syracuse about the year 303, legend says that when she was sentenced to death nothing could move her – even oxen yoked to her could not budge her from the spot. So faggots were piled around her and lit – but the flames declined to burn her. At last she was killed by a sword thrust to the throat. The rays of light, and the eyes, are thought to stem from her name suggesting the Latin lux, light. (Guestwick).

Margaret of Antioch: Her emblem is a writhing dragon, which she transfixes with a cross. Thrown into prison in Antioch for her Christian belief, this legendary lady was tempted by the devil in the guise of a terrible dragon. Some have it that the dragon was miraculously decapitated; others that he swallowed her . . . but burst when her cross stuck in his throat; others still that she simply made the sign of the cross and he faded away. That she is guardian of women in childbirth presumably has something to do with her 'caesarian' irruption from the dragon. (Swannington, Hemblington, Norwich St Helen's.)

Mary Cleophas or Clopas: As on the screens at Ranworth and Houghton, she is generally seen with her four sons – James the Less, Joses, Simon and Jude. She was half-sister to the Virgin Mary.

Mary Salome: No special emblem – but recognised by the presence of her two sons, the apostles James the Great and John, as on the screens at Ranworth and Houghton. She is said to have been one of the women present at the crucifixion and at the taking down of Christ's body from the Cross.

Matthew: Several are the emblems of this former tax collector who became Apostle and Evangelist. His evangelistic symbol is an angel with the face of a man; but he may be represented as an old man, with the bible or his own gospel in his hand; or with a purse and a money box. But also he may have a sword or even an axe (avoid confusing him therefore with *Matthias*). (Trunch).

Matthias: Though not in the least martial, Matthias is usually depicted with some soldierly implement – axe, spear or sword. The connection is that he was beheaded in Jerusalem by the Jews. He was the disciple chosen by lot to take the place of Judas Iscariot, after the betrayer's death. (Cawston, Norwich St Julian's.)

Maurice: Represented as a knight in armour, with sword, axe or banner. A Christian commander in the army of Emperor Maximian, late in the C3. On an expedition into Gaul, the emperor ordered a sacrifice to the pagan gods of Rome. When Maurice and his fellow Christians refused to participate, Maximian ordered their execution. (Briningham).

Michael: The feathered, winged and armed angel of light who strikes down the dragon of evil; or the glorious Archangel, judging souls in his scales of justice. These are the usual representations of this most popular of dedicatory saints. Most especially, he was the protector of high places, thus the many dedications to him of churches with lofty locations.

Nicholas: Three golden balls? The pawnbroker's sign, of course. Also that of St Nicholas, for the balls represent the three bags of gold which, on three consecutive nights, this good priest tossed through a poor man's window so that his daughters might have dowries. And thus he became, via a corruption of the Russian 'Sant Niklaus' . . . Santa Claus. He is patron saint of pawnbrokers too! While he is a favourite dedicatory saint of countless churches, in Norfolk as elsewhere, he is rarely represented in art (the one at Horstead, near Norwich, is modern). But when he is, it is usually as a bishop – with three little boys in a pickling tub. In the C4, he was bishop of Myra in Asia Minor, where his miracles were legion . . . the most celebrated being his restoring to life of three boys who had been cut up by an inn-keeper and pickled in a tub!

Paul: A sword is this apostle's symbol, usually pointing down – though on the Ranworth screen it points up. With this weapon his head was struck off at the order of the Emperor Nero, about the year 66 in Rome, when his success in converting eminent people to Christianity (including one of Nero's concubines) became too much for the Emperor to tolerate. Upon his beheading, it is

said, milk flowed from the wound . . .
Paul's life-story is too well related in
the Acts of the Apostles, and in his
own Epistles, to need retelling here.
(Edingthorpe, Trunch.)

Peter:

'Thou art Peter, and upon this rock I
will build my church . . . I will give
unto thee the keys of the kingdom of
heaven'.

So Christ spoke to his beloved apostle.
And so, always, Peter's symbol is The
Keys. The gospels tell his story during
Christ's ministry on earth. But not his
ending. He was crucified – upside
down, at his request, as he did not
consider himself worthy to die in the
same way as his Master, in Rome by the
Emperor Nero, at about the same time
that Paul was beheaded there. Examples of Peter and his crossed keys are
legion.

Petronella: Legend has it that she was a
daughter of St Peter, so she is always
shown holding a key, or a key and
book. Her shadowy story says she
suffered from paralysis, from which
Peter miraculously cured her. But in
health she was so beautiful that a
Roman count desired her. To escape
this fate, she gave herself up to fasting
and prayer, praying that she might
die . . . a fulfilment which came three
days later. (Trimingham).

Philip: One of The Twelve, Philip is
seen either with a cross – for like his
Lord, he was to suffer Crucifixion, at
the hands of pagans in Asia Minor; or
with a basket of loaves and fishes,
recording his connection with the
universally known biblical story of
Christ's feeding of the 5,000. (Marsham, Alderford, Trunch, Ranworth,
Cawston.)

Roche: This saint's peculiar and unpleasant identification is plague marks,
usually displayed on his upper left
leg . . . as on the restored screen panels
at Stalham, one of the very rare representations of this saint in England.
Son of a nobleman in C14 France, who

devoted his life to the relief of poverty
and sickness, in particular of plague.
Whenever he went where the plague
was rampant, the epidemic ceased.
Eventually he did catch it himself, but
recovered – only to be hurled into
prison as a spy during his wandering
pilgrimages. There he died five years
later, in about 1355.

Sebastian: Recognisable at once, the
saint riddled with arrows – or at least
holding an arrow in his hand. This fate
befell him in early Rome, where the
saint preached and converted, and
comforted Christian prisoners – until
the vengeance of the emperor Diocletian
fell on him. There is a unique dedicaton
to St Fabian & St Sebastian at Woodbastwick, near Wroxham.

Silvester: No particular emblem where
his very rare representations are found;
but when he is, as at Houghton St Giles,
he appears robed as a pope and carrying
a double cross. Legend has it that Silvester, pope in the early C4, baptised
the Emperor Constantine . . . and cured
him of leprosy. Also, St George-like, he
is credited with having slain a terrible
dragon near Rome which daily was
killing 300 men. . .

Simon Zelotes: Simon, one of The
Twelve, is usually seen with a fish;
or with a saw, relating perhaps to one
tradition that he suffered martyrdom in
Persia by being sawn in two. He is said
to have preached in Egypt, as well as
Persia; and even, says one story, in
Britain. (Swafield, Trunch.)

Sir John Schorne: Rector of a Bucking-
hamshire parish around 1300, he is
said to have wiled the devil into a boot
and there kept him prisoner – as he is
represented here in Norfolk in Gateley,
Suffield and Cawston churches,
wearing his academic or clerical robes,
and holding a boot from which a very
displeased Satan peers. Never formally
canonised, Sir John was honoured for
his piety and for his working of miracles,
not least that of the devil-booting!

Stephen: Shown always with a heap of

stones in his hands, or on a platter or book . . . for he was stoned to death, the first Christian martyr, by the Jews of Jerusalem, when he fearlessly answered their charges of blasphemy (Acts, 6 and 7). (Hemblington, Ludham, Catfield, Hempstead.)

Swithin: No special emblem, but generally seen as a bishop – as at Bintree, for example. Everyone knows at least this much about St Swithin . . . that if it rains on his dedicatory day, July 15, then it will rain for 40 days afterwards. Bishop of Winchester in the early C9, counsellor to King Ethelwulf, and a man of piety, great charity and modesty (as a bishop he travelled anonymously by night to avoid ceremony), he was buried at length outside his cathedral. A century later it was decided to move his remains to a great shrine inside . . . a project hampered and delayed by a month and half of continuous rain.

Thaddeus: See *Jude*.

Thomas: One of the Twelve, he is represented carrying a spear – for it was with spears, it is said, that he was martyred in India. What we know of 'Doubting Thomas' – he who would not believe in the Risen Christ until he had seen Him, and touched Him with his own hands – is wholly contained in the gospel of St John (chapters 11, 14 & 20).

Thomas of Canterbury: Represented always as an archbishop, as in several Norfolk examples Burlingham St Andrew, Worstead, Stalham). Occasionally he may have a sword or an axe – reference to his famous martyrdom at the hands of four of Henry II's knights in Canterbury Cathedral at Christmas, 1170. Thomas's shrine became a place of veneration and miracles. Four centuries later, Henry VIII branded him traitor, rather than saint – which is why representations of him are often defaced with particular savagery and thoroughness (as at Burlingham St Andrew, for example).

Uncumber: A lady with a long beard, and thus not likely to be mistaken (see Worstead). Legend has it that Uncumber, also known as Wilgefortis, was the daughter of an early king of Portugal who pledged herself to a life of pious virginity. When her father insisted she marry, and produced a suitable husband, she prayed to be made ugly so the suitor would not want her. Whereupon, miraculously, she at once grew a long beard. Her father, foiled and enraged, responded by having her crucified.

Vincent: Recognisable in medieval art by the hook which accompanies him – just one of the implements with which he was horribly tortured and torn during the persecution of the Emperor Diocletian about the year 300, for his Christian faith, teaching and ministry in Spain. Legend says that his broken body was thrown into the fields, where a raven guarded it. Then it was hurled into the sea but the waves returned it to shore. At last it was rescued by Christians and buried in the church at Valencia, where it is still venerated.

Walstan of Bawburgh: Norfolk's own farmer-saint, patron saint of farm workers, usually shown crowned (denoting his royal blood) and holding a scythe (as at Ludham, Norwich St Julian's, and at Martham, site of the shrine of his mother, St Blida). The son of a prince, he chose a life of poverty, taking a job as a farm-worker at Taverham, near Norwich. After his many years of faithful labour, Walstan's master wanted to make him his heir. But Walstan declined – and asked instead for a cart and a cow in calf. She produced two fine young bulls which he trained to pull his cart. In his old age, Walstan received a divine visitation foretelling his death, which came as he worked out in the fields. His body was placed on his cart and, unguided, his bulls set out. They paused at Costessey – where a spring sprang up and continued to give water until the C18. At last they came to the saint's birthplace at Bawburgh – passing clean through the solid wall of the church, and leaving behind them yet another spring, which as St Walstan's Well was famous for centuries. His shrine here attracted many pilgrims until it was destroyed at the *Reformation*. (Martham, Ludham, Norwich St Julian's.)

Wandregisil: Bixley Church is uniquely dedicated to this C7 abbot – it used to have an image of him which attracted pilgrims. He is rarely depicted, and has no special emblems, but he is on a panel at Horsham. Though a wealthy and well married courtier to the King of the Franks, he opted for the religious life, became a wandering pilgrim, and at length a monk, establishing an abbey at Fontenelle which was a by-word for spartan discipline.

Wilgefortis: See *Uncumber*.

William of Norwich: Represented nailed to a cross, or holding a cross, hammer and nails. This pious eleven year-old peasant boy is said to have been strangled and crucified by Jews in Holy Week 1144 and his body buried on Mousehold Heath, just outside the city walls. Five years later a nun discovered the grave, guarded by a raven, and the body was incorrupt. (Loddon, Norwich St Julian's.)

Withburga: A Norfolk saint, shown as an abbess, crowned to denote her royal blood, and with two does at her feet – as at Burlingham St Andrew. Brought up at Holkham, on the coast, she later established an abbey at East Dereham and was its abbess for many years. Her community lived in poverty: during one especially hard period, it is said that two does appeared ... and their milk sustained the nuns until better times came.

Zita, also known as Citha: A devout servant girl in C13 Italy who became known for her piety ... and for the help given her by angels. She can be seen on the screen at Barton Turf and on the font at Hemblington (near Norwich).

Salvin, Anthony (1799-1881): Architect, Gothic revivalist and acknow-

ledged expert of his time on medieval military architecture. In Norfolk, he remodelled Norwich Cathedral s. transept and Norwich Castle – with more enthusiasm than sensibility; and his first essay in Victorian gothic was the Trafford mausoleum in the churchyard at Wroxham. During his working lifetime, Salvin restored and/or added to an enormous list of castles throughout the land, from Windsor and the Tower of London onwards; took in hand the restoration and improvement of dozens of halls and manor houses; built a whole list of new country seats (including one castle); provided designs for the construction of several new churches and restored a long catalogue of ancient ones; and built numerous schools and hotels.

Sanctus bell/cote: At the point in the Eucharist at which the priest elevates the Host (the bread, which is The Body of Christ – Latin, 'hostia', victim) and says: 'This is my body, which is given for you ... Do this in remembrance of me', the 'sanctus' (Latin – sacred, holy) is rung. Some churches have a little bell turret over the w. end of the chancel to house the bell, specifically reserved for this purpose. See also *low side windows*.

Saxon: The period, with its distinctive architecture, preceding the Norman Conquest of 1066 – a vital era in the general establishment of Christianity in these islands. See also *Anglo-Saxon*; and 'Saxon' under *Styles of Architecture*.

Scallop-shell: Traditionally the symbol of pilgrimage, but most closely associated with St James the Great (see under *Saints*). There is a charming legend that the boat bearing James's body to Spain at one point passed close to shore where a wedding party were riding. The bridegroom's horse bolted and plunged into the sea – but miraculously horse and rider emerged above the waves near the boat ... both covered in scallop shells. Told by the disciples in the boat that he had been saved by the agency of St James, the 'groom at once asked for baptism and became a Christian. Then, to the (understandable) amazement of his friends, he rode back over the waves. When they heard what had happened, they all asked for instant baptism too! Pilgrims to James's shrine at Compostella wore a scallop-shell in their hats; but it became a general symbol of pilgrimage, including the 'martial pilgrimage' of the Crusades, on return from which noblemen included a scallop in their coats-of-arms.

Schorne, Sir John: See 'Sir John Schorne' Under *Saints*.

Scissors-braced roofs: A roof in which the beams are crossed and interlocked diagonally in the shape of an opened pair of scissors. (See *Roofs*, figs 2 & 3).

Scott, Sir George Gilbert (1811-78): Master of Victorian gothic, foremost 'restorer' of his age (far from always with the best results) and builder of that most ornate of railway terminals, St Pancras Station. As a young man, Scott gained his most fruitful experience as the designer and builder of some 50 workhouses and orphan asylums . . . all in the 'quasi-Elizabethan' style! He is credited with having been the architect, or restorer, or the compiler of a report, on more than 700 buildings or projects – cathedrals, hospitals, churches, mansions, colleges and public buildings. In Norfolk he was responsible for a thorough-going restoration of Woodbastwick Church, among others. The pulpit of Witton Church (near Norwich) is exactly modelled on one designed by him.

Scratch dials: See *Mass dials*.

Screen: See *Rood loft*.

Sedilia: These are seats (usually made into decorative and architectural features, with miniature columns, arches and canopies, and detailed carvings) on the s. side of the chancel.

Generally there are three seats. These can be all on the same level; or 'stepped', ie. on descending levels; and/or 'graduated', ie. under separate arches but contained within a composite pattern, frieze or frame. In many cases, a simple seat is created by building a low window sill – called a *dropped sill sedilia*. The three seats were specifically for the priest, the deacon (who read the gospel), and the sub-deacon (who read the epistle). The three retired to their seats during long services while the choir sang the Kyries ('Kyrie eleison' – Lord have Mercy), the Gloria and the Creed. Though three seats are the norm, there can be just one seat (sedile, singular), two, four, five (as at Yarmouth St Nicholas); and even eight. They may be found beside subsidiary altars, as well as at the chancel high altar – as at Harpley (between Fakenham and King's Lynn) and again at Yarmouth. In places where the seats seem impractically low, it may well be, quite simply, that the chancel/chapel floor has been raised in more recent times.

Set-offs: The sloped, angled surfaces on buttresses at the points where the buttress 'sets-off' another stage further out from the wall it is supporting.

Seven Deadly Sins, The: A colourful theme for medieval artists – as at Crostwight, near North Walsham, for example, where it is represented in a fine C14 wall painting in the form of a tree. The Seven Sins are Pride, Anger, Covetousness, Lust, Gluttony and Drunkenness, Envy, Sloth.

Seven Acts/Works of Mercy: Based on Matthew 25, vv 34-39, these acts or works of mercy are: to give food to the hungry; to give drink to the thirsty; to make strangers welcome; to clothe the naked; to visit the sick; and to visit prisoners. The additional seventh is normally the burial of the dead. This was a favoured allegorical theme of medieval artists and can be seen, among others in Norfolk, at Potter

Heigham and at Wickhampton (near Great Yarmouth). The latter is an especially fine example presenting, in small square architectural panels, the succession of – receiving the stranger; giving drink to the thirsty; clothing the naked; succouring the crippled; visiting the prisoners; visiting the sick; and burying the dead.

Seven Sacrament Fonts: Among the great treasures of Norfolk's churches are its seven sacrament fonts, almost all of the C15 (a few may be slightly later); all octagonal and exquisitely carved – if often mutilated – in each of the eight panels. Seven panels contain representations of the seven holy ordinances or sacraments: Baptism; Holy Communion (Eucharist or Mass), Confirmation; Confession/penance; Ordination to Holy Orders; Marriage; and Extreme Unction (anointing of the dying, the last rites). On the eighth panel the choice of subject varies – the baptism of Christ, perhaps, as at Sloley, which has the best preserved of the 40 seven sacrament fonts to be found in the county. Great Witchingham and Bridgham (near Thetford) both have an alternative subject which is very rare, the *Assumption of the Virgin*; still others have a Crucifixion. It will be noted that those being confirmed are always shown as very young – as was the custom in medieval times.

Shovel, Sir Clowdisley (1650-1707): One of Norfolk's several Admirals, Clowdisley Shovel was baptised on Nov. 25th 1650 at the picturesque little church of Cockthorpe, near Holt. He went early to sea, at the age of 14, under the care of *Sir Chrystopher Myngs*, of nearby Salthouse – the start of what was to be a most distinguished career. After Myng's death, Shovel's career was closely associated with that of *Sir John Narbrough*, probably a relation – and also baptised at Cockthorpe. In course of time he was to marry Sir John's widow. As a dashing young lieutenant in 1676, he commanded the boats which, on the orders

of Narbrough, forced their way into Tripoli harbour and burned the ships of the piratical Bey. (An interesting sideline to this can be seen on a big table tomb below the s. transept window at Cley Church, to James Greeve 'who was assistant to Sir Clowdisley Shovel in burning ye Ships in ye Port of Tripoly in Barbary Jan 14th 1676, and for his good service perform'd was made Capt. of the Ship called the Orange Tree of Algier, in 1677 presented with a medal of Gold by King Charles ye 2nd'). This was the start of a continuing ladder of promotion for Shovel. His story, however, ends tragically. On the way home from the Med. in Oct. 1707 his fleet was hit by bad weather and driven among the rocks of the Scilly Isles. His own ship, the 'Association', foundered and broke up. Shovel was thrown ashore, still alive, but a fisherwoman found him – and for the sake of a ring on his finger murdered him as he lay helpless in the surf. Two of his four sons by his second marriage (to Narbrough's widow) were with him on the 'Association' and went down with the ship.

Solemn League and Covenant: This was an agreement between the Scots and English parliaments in 1643: the English aim was military, to get Scots support against the forces of Charles I in the Civil War; the Scots aim was religious, a 'conjunction and uniformity of religion' between the churches of the British Isles. It brought a 20,000 strong Scottish army into England – but not the wholehearted commitment to Presbyterian disciplines which the Scots were looking for on the English side. Parishioners throughout England were ordered during the Cromwellian period to consent to the Covenant by signature in their local parish registers. But at the *Restoration* the offending or embarrassing pages were nearly everywhere torn out. Copies of rare survivals are preserved at South Walsham church.

Spandrels: The triangular space between the curve of an arch or the supporting braces of a roof, the wall or upright brace, and the horizontal line above. Often filled in with rich and delicate tracery (see *Roofs*).

Squint (also called hagioscope): An opening cut obliquely in a wall or pillar to give a view of the high altar from side chapels and aisles. For priests officiating at side altars, it enabled them to elevate the Host simultaneously with the elevation at the high altar. When squints are found on the outside walls of chancels, the popular idea that they connected with an anchorite's cell (a cell occupied by a religious recluse) is only rarely true, though these cells did exist. Through the squint, the holy man or woman (like *Mother Julian* at St Julian's Church in Norwich) could receive the sacrament during Mass. Also popular lore, but having no reality at all, is that these exterior squints were for lepers to witness the Mass. Not even in medieval England did lepers wander at will – see also *low side windows*.

Stanton, William (1639-1705): A London sculptor of note, who became Master of the Masons' Company and whose skills were employed by churches and noblemen all over the country. Monuments by him in Norfolk are at Hethersett (1699), Thursford, (1666) and in Norwich Cathedral (to Dean Fairfax, 1702).

Stations of the Cross: These are a series of (usually) 14 representations in pictures or carvings, of the scenes of the Passion of Christ from Pilate's presence to the Cross outside the walls of Jerusalem: Pilate 'washes his hands' of Him; Christ takes up the Cross; His first fall under its weight; the meeting with His mother; Simon of Cyrene is taken from the crowd to carry the cross; the pious Veronica wipes His face with her veil; He falls a second time; the exhortation to the women of Jerusalem; the third fall; His clothes are stripped from Him; Christ is crucified; he dies; the body of Christ is taken down from the Cross; He is buried in the tomb provided by Joseph of Arimathea. Processions took place from station to station, with devotions at each. Note also processional details under *Galilee porches*.

Stone, Nicholas (1586-1647): Greatest sculptor of his century, he was born the son of a quarryman in Devon, but soon moved to London, then to Holland, to gain greater experience. In Holland he apprenticed himself to Hendrik de Keyser, a famous Dutch master mason. The story has it that one piece of work he carried out so delighted his master that Stone was given the hand of de Keyser's daughter in marriage. By 1614, Stone was back in London as mason and statuary; and quickly gained such a reputation that he was employed by the king on the royal palaces and on great buildings in London. Only five years after his return from Holland, he was made master-mason to James I, and in 1626 Charles I confirmed him in that appointment. In Norfolk there are a couple of the splendid Jacobean style monuments for which he is best known: Dame Katherine Paston's at Paston, 1629 (though next to hers, that to Sir Edward Paston is coldly classical, and hardly seems to be from the same hand); at Tittleshall (near Fakenham) there is the noble tomb, in contrasting marbles of black, white and grey, to Lord Chief Justice Sir Edward Coke, 1634, the man who founded the fortunes of the Leicesters of Holkham Hall; and at Oxnead, an impassive white marble bust to Lady Katherine, wife of the fourth Sir William Paston, shows Stone not at his expressive best.

Storey, George, of Norwich (1733-59): A Norwich sculptor of variable skills – and apparently of variable temper, if one can believe a contemporary letter written by the mason Andrews Jelfe to architect Matthew Brettingham, with whom he had been carrying out commissions at Holkham Hall for the Earl of Leicester: 'After I had parted with you at Norwich, I talked to George

Storey, who I don't like and will have no further dealings with'. Storey has a large and ugly monument at Scottow – work very much on an off-day; there are better things at Holt and St Peter Mancroft, Norwich.

Stoup: See *Holy Water Stoup.*

String course: See *Courses.*

Stuart: The Royal House of Stuart, who inherited the Scottish throne in 1371 and the English throne, on the accession of James I, in 1603. The 'Stuart period' is taken to be their years of English kingship: James I, Charles I, Charles II, James II, William & Mary; and finally Anne, who reigned 1702-14. After the death of Anne, George I, the non-English speaking German from Hanover, succeeded to the English Crown and the Stuart day was over, its last fling being the '45 Rebellion of Bonnie Prince Charlie, 'The Young Pretender'.

Styles of Architecture: From the days of the Saxons, before the Norman Conquest of 1066, through to the Georgians in the C18, architecture both sacred and secular has passed through many developments and details, fads and fancies, inspirations and inventions. The names we use so easily to describe those phases – Early English, Decorated etc. – interestingly were coined only in the last century, and given convenient, even precise dates. But such dating can be more than misleading. Just as fashions in costume took time to filter through from city or court to provincial outposts, so changes in architectural ideas were only gradually assimilated. In Norfolk there are plenty of examples of styles being stuck to stubbornly long after – according to those over-precise dates – they had been overtaken by new fashions. Not least, there are those instances of the lush shapes of the Decorated style still appearing after the *Black Death,* well into the 1360s and '70s – where, presumably, masons with the old skills

had survived the pestilence. For our purposes here, we shall place the emphasis on the clearest line of styles – as shown, that is, in window shapes and tracery, which are undoubtedly the most useful guide for the layman:

Saxon: From the C7 to the Conquest. Characterised by roughness of construction, crudely rounded arches and triangular-headed window openings (as in the venerable Saxon round tower at Bessingham, near Holt) – See figs 9 & 10. Equally distinctive of the period is

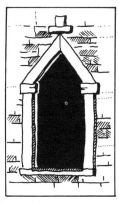

Fig 9. Saxon triangular-headed form.

Fig 10. Typical saxon round-headed window with crude arch.

their 'long and short' work at corner-angles of buildings. This is where upright stones are alternated with flat slabs, often re-using Roman tiles and other materials, salvaged from local remains. Always exciting when one finds these old quoins included in later buildings – as at Barney, near Fakenham, for example.

Norman: From the Conquest to about 1200, including the 'Transitional' phase (see below), spanning the reigns of William I & II, Henry I, Stephen, Henry

Fig 11. Norman slit window – interior view of typical deep 'arrow slit' embrasure.

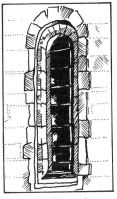

Fig 12. Norman slit window – exterior view.

II and Richard I. Massive walls and pillars are typical features, mighty rounded arches and, still, small round-headed windows, though they might be used in groups, with heavy pillar-like mullions between them. But after the Saxon crudity, here is growing crafts-manship and artistry, with rich, bold ornamentation (the fine arcade at Walsoken, in the far west of Norfolk, and in part at Binham, near Fakenham, are good examples). The small windows of the period are usually deeply splayed – see figs 11 & 12. These would origin-ally have been filled with parchment or oiled linen – glass came later.

Transitional: This is the phase of the changeover from the rounded, Roman-esque architecture of the Normans to the Gothic movement in England – the triumph of the pointed arch and, as it seemed then, a new age of learning and faith. It took three or four decades, to about 1200, for the changeover to take full effect. Massive pillars during this time became slimmer and lighter, and might sometimes bear a pointed arch, carved in Norman character, as at Walsoken. These attractive, slimmed down columns would also be used in clusters – and would continue to be so used during the full flowering of Early English.

Early English: Gothic has now fully arrived, and with it the first really native English architectural style. And lovely it is, with 'all the vigour, besides something of the coltishness of adolescence', as Charles Fox and Charles Ford enchantingly put it in their classic work, 'The Parish Churches of England' (Batsford, 1935). The style spans roughly the 100 year period from the end of the reign of Richard, through John and Henry II, and into the time of Edward II, to about 1300. The simple, elegant lancet made its appearance, first used singly (Fig 13) then in groups. As ideas developed, the space between the heads of two lancets placed to-gether was pierced with an open pattern, cut directly through the masonry: this is known as plate tracery

(Fig 16). From there it was but a step to fining down the tracery by constructing it in separate pieces – that is, *bar tracery*, of which it has been claimed that we have in Norfolk (in competition with Westminster Abbey, no less) the earliest example in England, in the great bricked-in west window of Binham Priory, which can be accurately dated between 1226 and 1244. In the Decorated style which followed, this technique reached a wonderful zenith. Intermediate, however, about the year 1300 (and a most useful dating device) came a most distinctive phase, the 'Y' traceried window – Fig 14 is self-explanatory; a development of this was the extension of the Y's through three or four lights, producing the simplest interlocking tracery with slim and graceful pointed heads. Everything at this time became finer in conception: bold buttresses, effortlessly thrusting arches, beautiful foliage carving and – most distinctive of this period – the trefoil, or three-leaf decoration (see also, *Emblems of the Trinity* and *Foils*), much used in window tracery and in decorative carving. Also popular was the dog-tooth moulding, which looks like a square, four-leafed flower, said to be based on the dog's tooth violet.

Decorated: This supreme time of architectural achievement and marvellous confidence in the use of shape and decoration, had but a half-century of full life – during the reigns of the first three Edwards – before the catastrophe of the *Black Death* struck Europe in 1349-50. Here in Norfolk and Suffolk, it has been estimated that half the population died. This was then, the high point of ornamented Gothic. Windows grew larger, tracery became progressively more flowing and adventurous: from the 'geometrical', with circles, trefoils, quatrefoils, lozenges etc. (see *Foils*) dominating the tracery, it burgeoned ultimately to the dazzling virtuosity of *reticulated* (see definition under separate entry) or net-like tracery – Fig 17 – and the creative beauty of form as seen in Fig 18. Rich ornament-

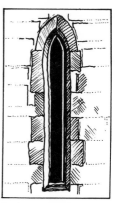

Fig 13. Early English lancet – the first arrival in England of pointed Gothic.

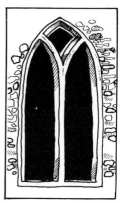

Fig 14. The typical 'Y' traceried window of around 1300.

ation and carving abounded, including the distinctive 'ball flower', a perfect little globular flower whose carved petals enclose a tiny ball; and also a sculptural explosion of pinnacles and crocketting, both inside and outside the church, from gable ends to tombs. Of many examples in Norfolk of fine Decorated work, the tracery of the e. window of the ruined s. transept at Cley may be especially mentioned – 'one of the loveliest windows imaginable', said *Munro Cautley*.

Fig 15. Early English lancets composed in a group.

Fig 17. The flowing beauty of the Decorated style's 'reticulated' form.

Fig 16. Simple geometric 'plate' tracery.

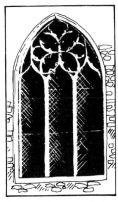

Fig 18. Decorated artistry in imaginative flow – the butterfly motif.

Perpendicular: This style takes us from the aftermath of the Black Death, through Richard II's reign, and successively those of Henry IV, V & VI, Edward IV and Richard III to the time of Henry VII, until around 1500, when the Tudor adaptation (see below) took place. The Perpendicular style was virtually created in one project by the monks of Gloucester – a story in itself which has no place here. Enough to say that the style, as its name implies, is one of soaring upward lines, drawn in great windows by vertical mullions – Fig 19; by majestic, clean-lined towers; and by meticulously panelled buttresses and parapets and the ornamented bases of walls (see also Flushwork). Rich decoration is typical, though it usually has more of the grandly formal than of purely aesthetic beauty ... Perpendicular grandly impresses; its Gothic predecessors have a beauty to touch our emotions. The important point is that, after the catastrophic plague, this magnificent, yet basically simple design was a godsend in places where all the old masons had been wiped out and only inexperienced men remained. Yet out of this grim necessity arose some glorious constructions, of which Norfolk has many splendid examples. It was also a blessing that at this time wood carving and glass painting reached a peak of achievement, with Norwich craftsmen producing stained glass of a quality to rank with any in the land. Roof building equally reached a zenith of craftsmanship – Tilney All Saints, Knapton, St Peter Mancroft in Norwich, Swaffham and Trunch are but a handful of the inspiring examples to be seen in this county.

Tudor: Here we are talking of roughly the century to 1600 spanned by Henry VIII, the boy-king Edward VI, Mary and Elizabeth. Not so much a style as an adaptation, in that the 'Tudor' mode, as far as churches are concerned, is basically the flattening of the Perpendicular arch, while otherwise retaining the same features – Fig 20. Often-seen and attractive embellishments are the lovely Tudor rose; and the heading of arches of windows and doors and open arches with elegantly used pink Tudor bricks.

Jacobean/Carolean: From the early C17 with the reign – 1603-25 – of James I (Latin, Jacobus); and continuing with the reigns of Charles I and II (Latin, Carolus). It was during James's reign that a stirring towards a *Renaissance* expression of architecture truly began in England. It was a style, and a movement, which employed the principles of the ancient Greek Classical building concepts – much 'classical' detail and ornamentation, and as in the Elizabethan period, a copious use of bricks; This stylised approach found much expression in furniture too, as will be found by many examples in Norfolk churches. During James's reign, the Renaissance movement found its resident genius in Inigo Jones (d.1652) whom James appointed Surveyor General of the Works. After Jones came

Fig 19. The classic Perpendicular window, its mullions thrusting to the head of the arch.

another genius, Sir Christopher Wren. And if his masterpiece, St Paul's Cathedral, remains one of our greatest Renaissance buildings, it was nonetheless in country houses and grand mansions that the Renaissance spirit was most evidenced. Here in Norfolk, Blickling Hall is a magnificent Jacobean example; the Marquess of Townshend's seat, Raynham Hall, an elegant product of the Inigo Jones period. In our churches, the Jacobean title applies as often as not to wood carving – pulpits, typically high bench backs etc.; and to aristocratic monuments.

Symbols of the Evangelists: See *Evangelistic symbols.*

Talbots: In heraldry, and in sculptural/ architectural adornment, talbots are dogs – they perch on the pinnacles of the C15 chancel at Rollesby, for instance.

Tester: Flat canopy above a pulpit, acting as a sounding board.

Three-Decker Pulpits: After the Civil War, the normal Sunday morning service was conducted entirely from the Reading Desk, and only on the infrequent Sacrament Sundays would

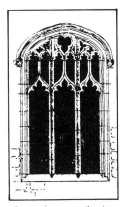

Fig 20. The Tudor contribution – a flattening of the arch over a Perpendicular window.

Minister and people move to the altar. Convenience demanded that pews be grouped round a focal point, and the C17/C18 solution was a three-decker pulpit. The service was read from the second tier, and the Minister climbed to the pulpit above to deliver his sermon (if the curate took the service, the rector would sit in the pulpit until sermon time). The Parish clerk led the responses, and conducted the singing from below. Fitted out with cushions on the book ledges, candlesticks, *hourglass*, and even a wig stand and a peg for the Minister's gown – it was the centre of congregational worship, though not the apex – that was always the altar. See also *Prayer Book Churches*.

Three Living and Three Dead: At Wickhampton, Heydon and Paston are examples, in wall paintings, of this intriguing allegorical theme, a popular subject for medieval artists, though of some 30 examples remaining nationally, only about 12 are complete enough to give an idea of its importance. Based, it is said, on a C13 French poem, the 'story in pictures' tells of three spirited young courtiers (always represented in English examples, for some reason, in royal and hunting guise, though the

poem indicates neither) who encounter three Deaths in the form of skeletons. The first young blade flees, as the first skeleton dolorously tells him that 'As I am so shall you be'. The second young courtier, though he greets the skeletons as heaven sent, is rewarded with the levelling observation that 'Rich and poor come to the same end'. Courtier number three is inspired to expound philosophically on mortality . . . confirmed by his skeleton's 'No-one escapes. . .'

Tie-beam: The wall-to-wall cross-beam or truss supporting a roof. (See *Roofs*.)

Tithe-barns: Tithes (literally tenths – Old English, 'teotha') were until relatively recent times a form of 'in kind' tax levied on landowners of all degrees in a parish to support the church and its priest – payable in corn, or fodder, for example. These commodities were stored in tithe barns, often buildings of fine dimensions and superb internal timber work, some of which remain today. In the C19 a rent charge was substituted for the 'in kind' exactions.

Transitional: Though 'transitional' can refer loosely to any change from one phase of architecture to another, it is particularly applied to the transition from the 'rounded' Norman to the 'pointed' Gothic, in the second half of the C12. (See under *Styles of Architecture*.)

Transoms: The horizontal crosspieces in window tracery, most noticeable in *Perpendicular* windows.

Trefoil: See *Foils*.

Trinity: See *Emblems of the Trinity*.

Tudor: The dynasty founded by Henry Tudor, victor of Bosworth Field against Richard III ('My kingdom for a horse . . .'). He was crowned Henry VII in 1485; Henry VIII followed, then Edward VI, Mary I (Bloody Mary); and finally Elizabeth I, who died on March

24th 1603, 'the last of the Tudors and the greatest of Queens'. For the church, it was a cataclysmic time – various aspects of this are dealt with under the headings *Communion Rails*; *Laud*; *Mensa slabs*; *Prayer Book Churches*; and *Royal Arms*. If the interiors of churches were changed beyond recognition during this era, the Tudor influence upon church architecture as such was negligible. (See under *Styles of Architecture*.)

Tudor-roses: A typical flower decoration of the period: (See 'Tudor' under *Styles of Architecture*.)

Tyler, William (d.1801): A director of the Society of Artists, and a founder-member of the Royal Academy in 1768, he was a sculptor whose work ranged from decorative interior features like marble chimney pieces, through portrait busts, to church monuments of considerable charm. Examples of his work are in Thurning (1759) and Earsham (1762) churches.

Tympanum: Space over head of door, or in head of filled in arch, plain or carved.

Visitation, The: Having been told by the Archangel Gabriel that she would bear a son, whose name would be Jesus and whose kingdom would have no end (Luke, chap. 1) the Virigin Mary hurried to tell the news to her cousin Elizabeth, already near her time with the child who would be John the Baptist. This meeting is commemorated on July 2nd as The Visitation. There is a gorgeous representation in stained glass in a panel of the e. window of St Peter Mancroft in Norwich, the Virgin robed in blue and gold, Elizabeth in yellow and dark red.

Vowess: At Witton near Norwich, is a small brass, dated about 1500, revealing in its Latin inscription that it is a memorial to a 'widow & vowess'. A vowess was a woman, especially a widow, who had taken a vow of chastity

for the remainder of her life, and would henceforward wear a habit of blue dress and white hood. She was not a nun, though 'vowess' could be used to mean one who makes a vow of devotion to a religious life, as that of a nun.

Wafer Ovens: A very few churches still have small ovens which were used to bake the wafers for the Mass. Thrigby, Overstrand and Braydeston, near Brundall have examples.

Wall-plate: See *Roofs*.

Wall-post: See *Roofs*.

Weeping chancels: Much nonsense has been written (and is still being perpetuated in some church guide books today) about chancels which incline away from the rectangle formed with the nave. The popular fallacy is that this is intended to indicate the drooping of Christ's head on the cross onto His right shoulder, as He is always shown in medieval representations of the Crucifixion. As *Munro Cautley* put it with splendid acidity, the idea is 'too absurd to be credited by any thinking person'. In any event, it should be noted that there are as many chancels which 'weep' left as right. The explanation, quite simply, is that mathematical accuracy was not the forte of medieval masons – and the chancel being 'out of true' with the nave was straightforwardly a result of ground-plan inaccuracy or expediency. Cley, Clenchwarton, Lammas and Wroxham, at scattered points of the county, are among numerous Norfolk examples.

Wherry boats: Not so long ago the Norfolk Broads, now dominated by holiday motor cruisers, were the preserve of a distinctive craft, the wherry, which plied these waters, not for pleasure, but in the way of lively local trade. A century ago there were hundreds of them; now, lovingly preserved, only two or three remain. In 1885 *Walter Rye*, in his 'A History of Norfolk', celebrated this 'local barge' in boldly descriptive words:

> 'The wherries are long low boats, built on lines much resembling Viking ships. They carry one enormous brown sail only, draw very little water and sail nearer the wind than any yacht; while for speed they can go as fast as anything. It is indeed a sight to see a 'light' (ie. unloaded) big wherry 'roaring' down over Breydon (Water) with a wind, and one that would not be forgotten easily by the owner of many a crack south-country yacht that tried to keep with her'.

Not surprisingly, the wherry has found its way into the ornamentation of several Broadland churches.

William & Mary: The 'joint' reign of William III (1688-1702) and Mary II (1688-94), he a Dutch Protestant, she the daughter of the deposed, Catholic James II. Architecturally, a period of gracious houses and fine furniture.

Willis, 'Father' Henry (1821-1901): 'Father' Henry Willis was the founder of the great London organ-building firm which still bears his name – a name synonymous, for all organists, choristers and churchmen, with fine workmanship and, as the citation put it when Willis was awarded a Gold Medal in 1885, for 'excellence of tone, ingenuity of design and perfection of execution'. Apart from installing the mighty organ in the Albert Hall, 'Father' Willis supplied or rebuilt organs in half the cathedrals of the realm and in innumerable colleges and churches. In Norfolk we have a lovely example of his small-scale work, a charming little instrument at Hanworth (near Holt), built in 1865 at a cost of just £75. Recently it has been lovingly restored so that its true Willis tone can be fully appreciated.

Woodwose: A wild man of the woods, bearded and hairy and usually carrying a club – as he can be seen in some churches in carvings on fonts (e.g. Acle), on pulpits (e.g. Felmingham), on furnishings (e.g. old *misericords* at North Walsham) and elsewhere. The woodwose appears to have some ancient fertility deity significance, closely allied with that of the *Green Man*.

Woodforde, James (1740-1803): During his time as Rector of Weston Longville, a few miles west of Norwich, from 1774 to his death, Parson Woodforde kept a diary: a detailed, observant, loving and humorous account which affords a wonderful description of English village life in the second half of the C18. The diary was unknown until the 1920s, when some 68 booklets were placed in the hands of John Beresford by Woodforde's great-great-great nephew. Beresford at once recognised it as one of the great English diaries – and in 1924 published the first volume as 'The Diary of a Country Parson'; four more volumes were to follow during the next seven years. This 'Diary' of rural delights is still available; there is an Oxford paperback of choice extracts; and a Norwich restaurant of quiet opulence perpetuates both the Parson's name and the kind of food in which, as his Diary so lovingly recalls, he took such healthy pleasure.

Wool Trade: The great C15/C16 wool boom which brought great wealth to East Anglia, and from its profits some of our finest churches. But it brought great misery too. (See under *Isolated Churches*.)

Wren, Sir Christopher (1632-1723): Greatest architect of his age, whose masterpiece was St Paul's Cathedral, one of the finest examples of English *Renaissance* architecture. His influence on architects and architecture has been profound. (See 'Jacobean/Carolean' under *Styles of Architecture*).